Between Europe and

Also by Andrew Gamble

THE FREE ECONOMY AND THE STRONG STATE: The Politics of Thatcherism

HAYEK: The Iron Cage of Liberty

POLITICS AND FATE

THE CONSERVATIVE NATION

BRITAIN IN DECLINE: Economic Policy, Political Strategy and the British State

Between Europe and America

The Future of British Politics

Andrew Gamble

First published 2003 by
PALGRAVE MACMILLAN
Houndmills, Basingstoke, Hampshire RG21 6XS and
175 Fifth Avenue, New York, N.Y. 10010
Companies and representatives throughout the world

PALGRAVE MACMILLAN is the global academic imprint of the Palgrave
Macmillan division of St. Martin's Press, LLC and of Palgrave Macmillan Ltd.
Macmillan® is a registered trademark in the United States, United Kingdom
and other countries. Palgrave is a registered trademark in the European
Union and other countries.

ISBN 13: 978-0-333-55570-5 hardback
ISBN 13: 978-0-333-55571-2 paperback

ISBN 10: 0-333-55570-8 hardback
ISBN 10: 0-333-55571-6 paperback

This book is printed on paper suitable for recycling and made from fully
managed and sustained forest sources.

A catalogue record for this book is available from the British Library.

Library of Congress Cataloging-in-Publication Data
Gamble, Andrew.
   Between Europe and America : the future of British politics/
Andrew Gamble.
      p. cm.
   Includes bibliographical references and index.
   ISBN 13: 978-0-333-55570-5 (hbk) ISBN 10: 0-333-55570-8 (hbk)
   ISBN 13: 978-0-333-55571-2 (pbk) ISBN 10: 0-333-55571-6 (pbk.)

   1. Great Britain—Politics and government—1997–2. Great Britian—
Politics and government. 3. Great Britain—Civilization—American influences.
4. Great Britain— Civilization—European influences. I. Title.
JN231.G34 2003
324'.0941—dc21   2003053613

10   9   8   7   6   5   4   3
12   11   10   09   08   07   06

Typeset by Cambrian Typesetters, Frimley, Camberley, Surrey

Printed and bound in Great Britain by
Biddles Ltd, King's Lynn, Norfolk

For my parents

Contents

Preface

This book is in part a development of earlier books I have written on British politics, particularly *The Conservative Nation*, *Britain in Decline*, and *The Free Economy and the Strong State*, but it also attempts something new. I began working on it at the time of the first Iraq war, and have finished it shortly after the beginning of the second. Many things happened in the interval to distract me from completing it, and there have been some big changes in British politics to take into account. In the course of the last decade or so it has had many different names, and has become a very different book from the one that was envisaged at the outset. Thanks are due to my publisher, Steven Kennedy, for being so patient, and supporting the project through to completion.

I have benefited greatly from discussions over the years with many friends, colleagues and students. This book would not have been possible without them.

ANDREW GAMBLE

1

English Questions

> Eighty years ago, England was a country like every other . . .
> Today it is a country like *no* other.
>
> Friedrich Engels, 1844[1]

For more than a century the great political causes in British politics were Empire, Socialism, Free Trade, Liberty and Reform. They are so no longer. If some of them still resonate, they do so in different ways. In the last twenty-five years British politics has been transformed, and a new political landscape has emerged. At the centre of this new landscape is the question of Britain's relation to Europe and to America, whether Britain can be a bridge between the two, or whether it has to choose between them. This book explores this question in relation to the historical path of development of British politics, and the imprint it has left on the British state, on British institutions, on British political parties and on British political ideologies. The relationship of Britain to Europe and America is not a matter simply of economics or of politics or of international relations: it goes to the heart of the political identity and political economy of this state formed over a very long period of development. It constantly gives rise to new defining issues in British politics, such as whether or not to join the euro, whether or not to support war against Iraq.

These dilemmas over relationships with Europe and America have moved centre stage as the historical decline of the British state proceeded and the Empire was dismantled. The post-imperial era has been marked by turbulence and trauma, as the British political class has struggled to adjust to the new position of the British state. Various political strategies were put forward, but the path which was followed has been mapped out by the governments of first Margaret Thatcher and then Tony Blair. In different ways they have been important catalysts for a set of changes which mark a watershed in British political development. The trajectory of British development has finally been broken, and a new order is struggling into being. The constitutional, territorial, ideological, political and economic forms so long established in British politics are changing.

1

A second key feature of this new landscape is the changing relationship of England to the other nations of the United Kingdom. For a long while this relationship was expressed through successive forms of the empire state, first Great Britain and then the United Kingdom, both of them primarily vehicles for English expansion. But with the ending of that expansion and the weakening and contraction of the empire state, the relationship between the British nations has begun to be renegotiated. As the empire state has gradually unravelled it has been possible to glimpse the lineaments of a new Britain and a new British politics. It is in this context that the debate about Europe and America has moved to the centre of the stage.

This book offers a series of reflections on these changing forms and relationships of British politics, and their implications for Britain as a whole. It is a book about *British* politics, but it seeks to understand the future prospects of British politics by paying particular attention to the historical meaning of *England* and the English Question in that politics. The most pressing English Question of all is how England as a nation and as a territorial space should be governed following the devolution of powers to Scotland, Wales and Northern Ireland, and how Englishness should now be understood.[2] But there is also a more fundamental 'English Question', which is how England as an empire state, formed by a particular path of development, and at the meeting point of the four circles of Union, Empire, Anglo-America, and Europe is now reforming and adjusting to new problems and new challenges.

This broader idea of England is not just England as a separate nation within these islands, but England as a world island, the name for a unique state and political economy. Although England was never in reality a true geographical island, its special path of development made it a *world* island in its own perception of itself, and in the perception of others. It was an empire of territory and an empire of trade, a system of power extending over Britain and Ireland and large parts of the world, as well as an empire of ideas, the representation of an ideal and the creator of a model, the pioneer of institutions, principles and practices which were widely imitated throughout the world. In these ways England shaped the world and was in turn decisively shaped by it, while remaining in important respects insulated from it, a world *island*, and therefore an insular world of idiosyncratic customs, practices and beliefs. This paradox has been responsible for many of the peculiarities of English and British development.[3]

One of the key foundations for this unique empire state was the Union which drew in both the other two British nations of Wales and Scotland, as well as (for a time) the Irish. As a result this state has had many names – England, Great Britain, the United Kingdom. Because of its greater size, wealth and population, England was inevitably at the heart of this state, its dominance reflected in many ways, not least in the common use of the term England as the shorthand term for the state. Its development has often been treated as so many phases in the expansion of *England*. Until quite recently histories of this state were generally entitled histories of England, even when written by Scots. Such usage derived from a particular reading of English history and the British political tradition, which is still powerful, although much weaker than it once was, a reading which emphasizes the uniqueness of England, and sees Britain as for the most part a vehicle for England. It is this idea of 'England' as an entity greater than itself, a world island, and the ways in which that has shaped and continues to shape British politics and frame its dilemmas, which this book explores.

The imperial expansion of England is now at an end, and the forms through which British politics has been conducted, and the ways in which Britain has traditionally been conceived, have begun to change. There are implications for all the British nations – the Scots, the Welsh and the Ulster Unionists – but especially for the English who for so long have not wanted to conceive of themselves as apart from the state and empire which they took the lead in creating. The unwillingness of the English to think about themselves separately from Britain, to see themselves as *a* British nation rather than *the* British nation, is at the heart of the English Question in British politics. The new forms of British politics that are developing are forcing a rethinking of the nature of England and its relationship with the rest of Britain, and raise questions about England's future now that the Empire is no more, and now that the other nations of Britain are in different ways beginning to disengage themselves and wanting to define anew the nature of Britain.[4]

The English Question in British politics is therefore the question of England's future, and Britain's status as a world island, following the end of expansion and of empire, and the fading charms of the English model. It presents a number of choices and dilemmas, which have implications not just for England but for the other British nations as well. The way in which they are resolved will help determine the future of Britain and its wider role in the world. These dilemmas may be summed up in the following way.

What should England *be* after Empire? Three centuries of expansion which built the Union within these islands and an Empire on which the sun never set gave the English many identities, and forged partnerships and links with many other nations. But the Empire has now dissolved and the Union is threatened. Should the English now accept that Britain is plural rather than singular, composed of several nations rather than one, and that its political institutions should be federal rather than unitary, based on a new partnership between the British nations of Wales, Scotland and England, and those others, from Northern Ireland to Gibraltar and the Falklands, who still define themselves as British? Or should the English gradually disengage from Britain and Britishness altogether, ultimately becoming an independent nation-state once again and recovering a separate sense of Englishness? Should they celebrate the new multicultural and multiethnic character which has become characteristic of the whole of Britain in recent decades, or should they reject it, trying to preserve as far as they can an ethnic and cultural homogeneity, based on whiteness and Protestantism? And how should these choices then connect to the great strategic questions which confront the British state? Should foreign policy be internationalist or nationalist? Should the British state remain the chief ally of the United States, and a bridge between it and Europe, or should it seek to disengage? Should it seek to be part of a wider European federation or stand outside?

What should England *do* after Empire? Successful union with the other nations of these islands helped pioneer the specific British forms of liberal capitalism, self-government, and democratic socialism, which once provided models and inspiration for many other countries, but which during the era of decline failed to adapt and came under sustained criticism and challenge. Should the Anglo-American model of a liberal capitalist economy be strengthened, or should it be radically reformed to make the British model more European? Should British democracy be improved by recovering the tradition of self-government it shares with America, or should the focus instead be on improving the effectiveness of government? Should the commitment to securing equal citizenship and reducing poverty be renewed to move Britain towards a European welfare system, or should the welfare state be dismantled to the level now reached in America?

What should England *dream* after Empire? All the British nations have had dreams, and some of them have been shared dreams. The ideal of Empire for the right and the counter ideal of socialism for the left were the great animating principles of British party politics through the twentieth century, the primary source of both emotional and intellectual commitment for the two warring camps. These were visions of two very different commonwealths and both now seem lost, in their earlier forms irretrievably, with the vanishing of England's status as a great power. The two leading parties of the state in the twentieth century, first Labour in the 1980s and then the Conservatives in the 1990s, have in turn suffered a dramatic collapse in their support and self-belief. In this altered political landscape what principles now frame the choice between the political parties in British politics? Do left and right still have meaning, or has politics now moved beyond left and right?[5] Is the real choice now between two forms of capitalism, two kinds of state, and two kinds of civil society – one European, one American?[6]

The other British nations, the Scots, the Welsh and the Ulster Unionists, are increasingly forming their own conception of what they want to be, to do and to dream. Although many individual Scots and Welsh, particularly those living outside Scotland and Wales, still identify themselves as British, and therefore with England, the achievement of a measure of self-government means that Scotland and Wales are beginning to be able to determine for themselves their own direction, and make their own choices. They are becoming aware that they no longer have to accept what England decides. They have a small but growing area of autonomy, and in the future their electorates could choose to disengage from the Union altogether. Whether that will happen depends to a large extent on what the English themselves decide on these questions. English choices will be crucial for the future direction of British politics, in helping to determine whether or not the other nations want to continue to be part of a shared British project. In this sense the future of Britain is largely in English hands.

British Politics and Decline

The supremacy of England in world affairs was built on the expansion of its power over three centuries, first through the building of a United Kingdom in the British Isles, and secondly through the expansion of the twin British empires of territory and trade. In the first half of the twentieth century this supremacy was irreversibly lost. The United Kingdom was not defeated in war or invaded, its constitution was not rewritten, and apart from the secession of Ireland from the Union, the outward forms of the British state remained the same. But the expansion of England was over, and British politics came to be dominated by the politics of decline. Drained by the effort of two world wars, British power shrank, its territorial empire was dismantled, and British military, industrial, technological, commercial, financial and cultural predominance were all lost. They were not lost all at once, and for the most part the political class persuaded itself that they were not lost at all, while gradually becoming preoccupied with managing the decline, conducting a long rearguard action in defence of what it knew and understood. There is no one date when this began, but 1931 stands out as a key moment. In that year the British Government had to admit defeat in its attempts to restore the gold standard. The direct link between the pound sterling and gold was broken, never to be restored, and hopes for a return to a unified liberal economic world order based on the gold standard were shattered. In deference to that lost order, Montagu Norman, the Governor of the Bank of England, never wore a top hat in public again.

What has perished with that lost order is a certain idea of England. The transition from Empire has been long and difficult, not just because of enforced withdrawal from so many territories which the British ruled, but also because of the gradual loss of self-confidence, the discarding of so many assumptions about the superiority of the British way of doing things. Decline coincided with the extension of democracy and the establishment of a welfare state, and the adoption of the term Britain as the preferred shorthand term for the United Kingdom, rather than England. Yet England could not be disposed of so easily. The empire state that had been constructed during the expansion of England still continued to cast a long shadow over British life and, although much weaker than before, it has continued to shape the attitudes and behaviour of the political class, which became inured to the experience of contraction rather than expansion, and to coping with its political, economic, ideological and psychological consequences.

After 1931 British politics gradually became dominated by the politics of decline and particularly so in three decades – the 1960s, 1970s and 1980s. But in the last twenty years Britain has passed through a political revolution. The pattern of decline has been decisively broken by the administering of two successive shocks – the economic reforms begun by the Thatcher Government and the constitutional reforms begun by the Blair Government. There was nothing inevitable or preordained about these reforms. British politics might have developed in radically different ways. But a new path was set in the 1980s, even if both sets of reforms have had many consequences which were unintended by their authors and are still far from complete. Both were initiated from above by different elements of the political class, and are intimately related. The first in part engendered and in part provoked the second, and together they have transformed British politics and continue to transform it.

The process of change is by no means finished, but a decisive watershed appears to have been passed, and the framework of a new political order is visible.[7] The Thatcher Government began the change, shattering the uneasy post-war social compromise between capital and labour by seeking to undo many of the reforms of the social democratic era, and to restore an Anglo-American model of capitalism and constitutional order, by calling for a return to 'market disciplines', and seeking by every possible means to discredit socialism as an alien and un-English creed, and weaken its institutions and power base in the trade unions, the public sector, and local government.[8] The Blair Government consolidated these free-market reforms, while at the same time developing a new agenda of equal citizenship which owed more to European than to American welfare models,[9] continuing the modernization of the public sector and initiating the most far-reaching reforms of the constitution since the extension of the right to vote.[10]

Many commentators, particularly on the left, regard the Thatcher Government alone as radical, the Blair Government doing little more than completing the Thatcherite agenda. Without Thatcherism it is true the programme of the Blair Government would have been unthinkable, but the Blair Government has done more than simply embed Thatcher's reforms. Despite its conservative inclinations it embarked upon a process of constitutional change which goes much wider than the Thatcherite agenda, and has produced reforms likely to prove as fundamental and lasting as anything achieved by the Thatcher Government. While the Thatcherites sought to protect the old constitutional state and breathe new life into it, the Blair Government initiated changes which have begun to alter some of its fundamental principles and structures.

The changes being introduced by this political revolution have been extremely controversial because they express fundamental judgements about the kind of society contemporary Britain is and fundamental choices about the kind of society it should become, and have consigned to the rubbish heap many things in which people on right and left used passionately to believe. Like all political revolutions there are many on both left and right who refuse to accept the changes and keep believing that what has occurred can be reversed. They hope a counter-revolution is still possible, and that their political values can again triumph.

It is sometimes said that the English do not have revolutions, only evolutions. But revolutions come in various forms, and a cursory knowledge of both English and British history reveals no shortage of them. Revolution in its original political sense means a spin of the wheel of fortune and circumstance, an instance of great change in political affairs, the creation of a new political landscape, a new order. Political revolutions are often dramatic events because government is seen to change hands, but that alone is not enough in itself to constitute a political revolution. The new government must put in place a new *régime*, a set of rules and principles which establish a new political, ideological, economic, and cultural order.

In 1688 the English termed the overthrow of James II '*The Glorious Revolution*'. After more than forty years of political upheaval and civil war which included the execution of one king, the restoration of another and the deposing of a third, as well as the establishment of a republic and the proclamation for the first time of principles of liberty, democracy and popular sovereignty, the Glorious Revolution initiated a new constitutional settlement based on the principles of the supremacy of Parliament and the Anglican religion, an undivided and unlimited sovereignty, commercial freedom and colonial expansion. The political upheaval of the last forty years has been on a more modest scale, but has contained moments of high drama such as the deposing of Margaret Thatcher in 1990 triggered by the Conservative civil war over Europe, and the Iraq crisis of 2003, triggered by the equally long-running Labour civil war over America. It has brought about the beginnings of a new constitutional settlement, based on the principles of shared sovereignty within the United Kingdom and Europe, multiculturalism and human rights, the primacy of markets, and equal citizenship. The question of the priority to be accorded Europe and America remains unresolved, and sharply divides both parties and public opinion.

The weakening of decline as an issue in British politics has come about through this political revolution; the first stage initiated by the right and the second by the left. The Thatcher Government bulldozed many of the policies and the institutions which had underpinned the post-war compromise between labour and capital in Britain, and helped to drive Labour into a damaging split and electoral collapse. For a time it appeared that Labour might cease to be an alternative governing party and become a rump party confined to its declining industrial heartlands. But the Thatcher revolution contained the seeds of its own destruction. It sought to drive socialism out of British politics by crippling the trade unions, reining back state intervention and public spending, and re-establishing the moral superiority of private over public provision. At the same time, it sought to restore national independence and the capacity of government by reaffirming the traditional doctrines of the undivided and unlimited sovereignty of the Westminster Parliament, and so attempting to breathe new life into the old imperial state. In doing so it overreached itself, weakening many traditional Conservative institutions and the base of Conservative support, and causing a deep questioning of the legitimacy of the Thatcher regime, and an outburst of new thinking on the constitution. At the same time, it provoked a huge split in its own ranks over its policy towards Europe.[11] It prepared the ground for Labour's revival in the 1990s and for the divisions and self-destruction of the Conservative party that accompanied it.

The Blair Government accepted most of the changes which the Thatcher revolution had begun; no counter-revolution on economic policy was attempted, and several of the changes were pushed further. But a new revolution was initiated, only this time it was the old constitutional state, one of the traditional bedrocks of Conservatism, which became the target. The modernization of the British Constitution, which revived many aspects of the agenda which the Liberals had been pursuing before 1914, as well as marking a more positive engagement with Europe, has begun to transform the context within which British politics is conducted.[12] In the short space of twenty-five years between 1976, the year of the IMF Loan, and 2001, the year when a Labour government won a full second term for the first time, many of the ideological and the constitutional contours of British politics had been radically changed and with them the nature of the parties and the policies of the British state.[13] This book analyses these changes and the debates around them, in order to chart the current dilemmas and the future directions of British politics. At the heart of these dilemmas is the fateful choice between Europe and America, which touches almost everything in British politics – security, political economy, civil society and identity.

Identity and Political Economy

To understand this changed landscape properly, and the choices it presents, it is necessary to explore England's understanding of itself as a world island; how the different identities of the English as well as the other British nations were shaped by England's participation in four overlapping circles – Union, Empire, Anglo-America, and Europe. The end of Empire has necessitated a fundamental reorientation of those relationships, and the posing of new questions about the identities of the English.[14] The identities which arose from Union and Empire which underpinned the expansion of England and the idea of Britishness for more than three centuries have been called into question by devolution, by decolonization, by immigration, and by European integration. As the political extensions of 'England' have crumbled, so England itself has re-emerged into the spotlight. Ireland has long defined itself as separate, but now Scotland and to a lesser extent Wales, also begin to define their interests differently from England. With the end of its Empire the English are being forced to rediscover themselves and define themselves afresh in relation to 'Britain' and the other nations of Britain. Britain is no longer simply England, even for the English. These dilemmas over identity also involve strategic choices in political economy and between them they define the key questions of contemporary British politics. It is the way these questions are answered that defines its new terrain.

Union

The first of these questions arises from the Union that gave rise to that empire and to Great Britain. As already noted, this is the current form of the English Question, but it is also the Scottish Question and the Welsh Question: how far is Britain now dissolving into its separate nationalities? As nationalisms of various kinds have grown in Scotland, Wales and Northern Ireland, there has been a gradual realization that the very heart of England's empire, the Union between the nations of the British Isles, is potentially unstable and could be dissolved.[15] The English have always tended to use the terms Britain and British as synonymous with England and English, but this depended on the other nations being content to be part of this multinational project. If they are not, Britain and British become redundant, and the way is open for an explicit English nationalism alongside Scottish, Welsh and Irish nationalism. These questions over the Union invite a range of responses. The United Kingdom has always been a multinational state, but it has also been a unitary state, in the sense of having a single centre of authority, based on London and the institutions of the earlier English state. Can it be preserved with that central authority intact, as the Conservatives hoped; can a new form of partnership between the nations be devised through devolution, allowing a new Union and a new conception of Britain to develop; or is the logical end of devolution an independent Scotland and an independent England once again?

Empire

A second question is whether Britain is any longer ethnically and culturally homogenous, or should seek to be so. Is Britain one culture or many? Abroad the last vestiges of Empire have almost gone, but the Empire is still a deep presence in British politics, and a deep influence on Scottish, Welsh and English identities. Immigration is one example. With the extensive immigration from Commonwealth countries which has occurred since 1950, the Empire has come home, and Britain has increasingly become a multicultural and multiethnic society, although one where allegiance is often to Britain rather than to England, Scotland or Wales.[16] Many individuals from ethnic groups identify themselves as British, and will call themselves Asian British or Black British but are much less likely to consider themselves English or Scottish.[17] Multiple identities have become common which means that Britain is no longer a primary identity for significant minorities of UK citizens. Will Englishness adjust to multiculturalism, or will there be a populist reaction on national lines, and the rise of

England First and Scottish First movements, of the kind that many other European countries have experienced? Can multiculturalism be incorporated as part of equal citizenship, or does it destroy the possibility of equal citizenship?

A question also arises over the foreign policy stance of the British state with the waning of Empire. Should the priority be the preservation of what remains of British imperial interests and spheres of influence? Should the British state embrace liberal internationalism, intervening to protect human rights whenever this is considered appropriate? Or should a British state that understands itself as multinational and multiethnic seek to dismantle British imperial interests and connections and move to neutralism in its foreign policy, as Ireland did long before?

Anglo-America

A third question concerns Anglo-America. How far are the nations of the United Kingdom becoming absorbed by America, both in the cultural sense but also as part of a US dominated world order? England and the other British nations of the United Kingdom, as well as Ireland, are tied very closely to the United States, once itself part of Greater Britain. With the other English-speaking nations around the world they are part of Anglo-America, a transnational space of ideological and cultural argument and exchange, of trade and investment, and security and political ties. Should the British political class, even with the Empire gone and the domestic Union fragile, continue to try and sustain the Anglo-American hegemony which under British leadership in the nineteenth century, and American leadership since the 1940s has sought to maintain a world order that is relatively open and liberal, and in the last fifty years has also sustained a strong military alliance? Or should they throw in their lot with Europe, economically, politically and militarily? In the political class opinion is divided between those who want the United Kingdom to become closer than ever to the United States, even the fifty-first state;[18] others want to maintain a special relationship while safeguarding UK independence and forging links with Europe;[19] while a third group are far more critical of the United States and of the hegemony of neo-liberal ideas, and want the UK to disengage from it.[20]

Europe

A fourth question, increasingly strongly linked to the third, is Europe. How European are the English and the other British nations? Successive

British governments have tried to avoid the choice between Anglo-America and Europe, but as European integration has gathered pace, so has there been increasing pressure to decide the priority to be given to the Atlantic Alliance and the European Union. Again opinion in the political class has been sharply divided over whether the United Kingdom should eventually be absorbed into a European federal union, with the UK being broken up into its component regions, and Wales and Scotland becoming European region-states. A small group favours an explicit federal future, a much larger number argue for continuing integration but on the basis of a looser intergovernmental federation which keeps the United Kingdom together as a unified bloc within the European Union; a significant minority argues that the UK should continue to stand outside the single currency and block further integration, being prepared if necessary to withdraw from the European Union altogether.[21]

The English Model

These questions about identities in British politics are also questions about the political economy of the United Kingdom, because they involve the unravelling of the old political economy of the UK, the organization of state and economy built up in the three hundred years of expansion. England was a world island not only because it expanded into the world, but also because it became a model which was widely imitated. It represented certain institutions and principles which many other countries strove to copy – liberal capitalism and self-government in the nineteenth century, democratic socialism in the twentieth. All of these were British rather than purely English, but they were treated by many outside observers from de Tocqueville to Marx as the hallmarks of 'England', the unique political constellation that for a time in the nineteenth century was leading the world.

Capitalism

England came for example to be widely regarded as the most important pioneer of capitalism, the first economy to industrialize, and the first to establish a commanding technological, commercial and financial dominance. Capitalism in fact like empire was a *British* not simply an English project, involving all the nations of the United Kingdom, but it became a defining characteristic of 'England'. During the long economic decline in the twentieth century, British capitalism was clearly ailing and most of the old industrial base was lost. The great firestorm of the 1980s, encouraged by the Thatcher Government, restructured British capitalism, destroying many industries that remained, and reorganizing the financial and services sector.[22] The Conservatives sought to remove obstacles to unfettered capital accumulation, and to strengthen the authority and capacity of the state. They relied increasingly on an Anglo-American model of capitalism with its emphasis on privatization, deregulation, low taxation, and shareholder value. Conservative policies succeeded to the extent that a new and more stable political economy was established, and for a time in the 1990s the British economy became one of the better performers among the leading capitalist economies. The economic decline relative to other leading economies was halted, although many doubted that the structural weaknesses of the economy had been permanently overcome, especially since productivity remained low in comparison either with other European economies or with the United States.[23] But the steady growth after 1992 and the euphoria about the Anglo-American model during the dotcom boom for a time dispelled British pessimism.

Self-government

England was one of the first countries in Europe to experience a Republic – the Commonwealth established under Oliver Cromwell in the 1650s – although it proved shortlived. England also after 1688 pioneered representative and parliamentary government, but within a constitution which retained the monarchical principle of undivided and unlimited sovereignty. This English Constitution unchanged in its essentials for three centuries became the framework for the multinational United Kingdom state, and is only now being reformed by the Blair Government, in ways which will make it more similar to constitutions in other states, ending some of its more obvious eccentricities, and through the provisions of devolution formally recognizing the multinational character of the United Kingdom. Debate continues to swirl around the reforms. Have they changed the substance or only the outward form of the constitution? Is a more balanced and less centralized political system coming into being, or has the tradition of self-government been destroyed? Is Britain passing under the control of alien powers, or is it on course to become a modern democracy and even a republic, as England briefly was once before, and as America became when it broke away from Britain?

Socialism

Ever since Engels wrote *The Condition of the English Working Class* in 1844,[24] England was renowned for having the first and largest industrial proletariat, and became a pioneer of forms of working-class organization and of socialist programmes for instituting a socialist commonwealth and welfare state. Like capitalism and empire, the working-class movement was a British not just an English phenomenon, and another of the elements which breathed real content into the Union. The long campaign of the Labour movement reached its climax in the reforms of the Attlee Government after 1945, and the emergence of a compromise between capital and labour, which gave the United Kingdom its first taste of social democracy. After this compromise broke down in the 1970s, the Thatcher Government unleashed the reforms and the economic restructuring which severely weakened Labour's power base in the trade unions and local authorities, but failed to dismantle the main structures of the welfare state, initiating instead a far-reaching modernization of the public sector, which has been carried forward by the Blair Government. A new compromise between labour and capital has emerged. The nature and stability of this compromise are controversial. Many on the left see it as preparing the way for the privatization of public services, and for the extension of the market principle into the public domain.[25] Others regard it more optimistically as providing new ways of managing the public sector to deliver what citizens want, and new strategies for remedying inequality to create a modernized but still universalist welfare state, which would be closer to European than to American models.[26]

Left and Right

In the last phase of Empire, the era of decline, the two parties which dominated British politics were Labour and the Conservatives. Each projected a starkly different ideal – for the Conservatives it was the British Empire itself, the culmination of England's expansion; for Labour it was the dream of realizing a socialist Commonwealth in Britain. The compromise between these two visions allowed the preservation of the imperial state alongside the establishment of a welfare state.

In the 1980s and 1990s this political compromise unravelled, with huge consequences for the political parties. Both in turn suffered catastrophic defeats, and a meltdown in their support. Political alignments have been recast, the two-party system no longer functions in the way it did, and a multi-party system has grown up. These changes have raised many issues. Are those rival dreams of left and right that dominated the twentieth century, of empire and socialist Commonwealth, now discredited, and no longer persuasive? If so, what do left and right currently mean in British politics? Is the Blair Government a continuation of Thatcherism by other means or a new form of progressive politics? Will the Conservatives survive as the main opposition force and alternative government in British politics? Are democracy and popular participation in politics withering, and new forms of rule emerging, with politics becoming the preserve of narrow political, corporate and media elites, as in America; or is Britain threatened with the rise of right-wing populism as in many parts of Europe?[27] Above all, are the models to which left and right subscribe increasingly European or American? Are the fault-lines between Europe and America or within them?

Plan of the Book

The book analyses the different ways in which Britain has come to be *between* Europe and America, and how this sets up a range of dilemmas which increasingly frame British politics.

Chapter 2 sets out the main argument about the historical path of England's development, analysing the roots and characteristics of English exceptionalism through a detailed exploration of the different senses in which England came to imagine itself and be seen by others as a 'world island', firstly by constructing in partnership with the other British nations of these islands a multinational Great Britain, and then a much wider Greater Britain, acquiring in the process a global reach and a global influence; secondly by becoming a model for the rest of the world; and thirdly, by remaining an insular and idiosyncratic world, with its own distinctive institutions, customs and beliefs. The next four chapters, 3, 4, 5 and 6 explore the four circles – Union, Empire, Anglo-America and Europe – and show how English exceptionalism has been defined and shaped by them, and how they frame the key dilemmas of identity and political economy in contemporary British politics. Chapter 7 analyses 'the English model', the ways in which 'England' showed to the rest of the world the image of its own future through the models of liberal capitalism, self-government, and democratic socialism it pioneered – and the fate of those models today, and how they are increasingly European or American in character. Chapters 8 and 9 examine how the rival traditions of right and left in British politics responded to decline, coped with the traumas induced by the loss of empire and the loss of socialism, and have begun to renew themselves, with the various conflicts over Britain's relationship with Europe and America often providing the main dividing lines. Chapter 10 asks whether there is life after Empire, after socialism, and after decline, and whether there is a radically different kind of England, and a new Britain, in the making, what its politics will be like, and whether its future is more likely to be American or European.

2

The World Island

This fortress built by Nature for herself
Against infection and the hand of war,
This happy breed of men, this little world,
This precious stone set in the silver sea,
Which serves it in the office of a wall,
Or as a moat defensive to a house,
Against the envy of less happier lands
This blessed plot, this earth, this realm, this England.

William Shakespeare, 1594[1]

In the preface to the first volume of *Das Kapital*, published in 1867, Karl Marx declared that England as the most advanced capitalist country of its time showed to other countries the image of their own future. To those in Germany who thought that Germany would escape an 'English' development and had little to learn from it, he cautioned them with a line from Horace: 'De te fabula narratur' (The story is told of you).[2]

By the middle of the nineteenth century, England had indeed become a model for the world, and was for a time at the centre of world affairs, a true world island, and no longer merely a nation inhabiting one part of an obscure and sparsely populated island on the periphery of the civilized world, as it had been for so many centuries. England did not do this all on its own. Through its separate Unions with Scotland, Wales and Ireland, a single state embracing all the territory in the group of islands off the north-west coast of Europe gradually emerged, a *United Kingdom*, and it was this state which acquired the world's largest ever territorial empire, which established the hegemony of Anglo-America in world affairs, which frustrated so often the territorial ambitions of other European great powers, and which was the pioneer of distinctive models of capitalism, of liberty and of socialism that were admired and imitated around the world.

17

England and Britain

In the nineteenth century when the British Union also encompassed Ireland, England was the accepted shorthand name for this state. In the nineteenth century it was common practice in Germany to refer to the United Kingdom as England, and many Scots, including historians and writers like Macaulay, did the same. 'England' included Scotland and Wales. The greater population, resources, and wealth of England made this usage normal. *The Expansion of England* by the historian Sir John Seeley became a best-selling account of the rise of this state to world pre-eminence.[3]

The relationship between Britain and England, the ways in which English identity was merged with British identity, has always been complex. The difficulty starts with the names themselves. Both England and Britain have at different times been the preferred name to describe the state whose formal name (since 1921) has been the United Kingdom of Great Britain and Northern Ireland. Until relatively recently British political history was written as though it was the history of England, and that only England really mattered. The existence of the other nations was ignored or downplayed and England was often used interchangeably with Britain. The idea of the expansion of England into first Great Britain and then Greater Britain was central to these narratives.[4] That has changed in recent years with the rise of new schools of history which have emphasized the importance of understanding British politics not as English politics with the other nations tacked on, but as a complex set of interrelationships between the four nations.[5] This four nations history of Britain and Ireland has helped transform our understanding of many familiar events such as the 'English' civil war of the seventeenth century, by treating it as a war of three kingdoms, rather than as a purely internal English affair.[6]

The recovery of the complicated multinational character of British political history has accompanied the atrophying of the project for a Greater Britain, which began with the secession of the greater part of Ireland from the Union in 1921, and continued with the pulling down of the flag in territory after territory in the old colonial Empire, and most recently has been associated with the strengthening of nationalist parties in these islands,[7] seeking separation and independence and questioning the desirability of the Union in Wales and Scotland and Northern Ireland. What all this has done is to make the identification between England and Britain suspect. In the last fifty years everyone has become so careful in public speech in talking always of Britain or the United Kingdom, and never simply of England, that England itself has tended to disappear from view, a brooding, lurking presence, seldom visible, except on special occasions when English soccer fans riot in European cities.

In the contemporary United Kingdom, sport is indeed one of the few arenas where England and Englishness as opposed to Britain and Britishness are openly acknowledged and find public expression, and even here it is limited to a few sports, such as football, because in most others, including athletics, there is a British team, selected from all parts of the UK. In other sports such as rugby there is both a British team and four separate national teams. This extraordinary diversity of the rules determining which national entity – whether the four nations, or the United Kingdom, or England and Wales, or Ireland (North and South) – is the appropriate one for determining eligibility for the national team is a microcosm of the confusing pattern of national identities in the UK which has spawned a considerable literature.[8] The English find nothing surprising in this eccentricity, although why international sporting bodies should continue to indulge it is odd.[9]

During the twentieth century, after decline set in, and expansion was replaced by contraction, the shorthand name for the United Kingdom became Britain rather than England. Use of the term England when Britain was meant was frowned upon, and politicians were heckled when they forgot. In earlier times, however, the use of the term England to refer to the whole of the British Isles and indeed to the British Empire, was uncontroversial because it was understood that 'England' carried a particular meaning – the exceptional state and society built during three centuries of expansion, which had become not only one of the world's great powers but also the world's most modern economy and society, and therefore the model others wished to emulate and surpass. It is this sense of 'England' which is used throughout this book, not to exclude the other nations of the United Kingdom, or render them invisible, but to draw attention to the way in which the British state was organized and the interests which it served. The disadvantage of using Britain as a term to describe this state, particularly in its period of expansion, is that it disguises the fact that Great Britain and then the United Kingdom were projects defined by England rather than a true partnership between equals, however important the role played by so many Scots and Welsh. Britain has often been more of an aspiration than a reality; it would be more appropriate as a shorthand term for this state if its constitutional basis became a genuine federation between its component nations and regions.

'England' is after all more than just the term for a geographical area; at a certain stage of its expansion it became also a political and economic ideal, even a state of mind.[10] It still is. Contemporary British politics cannot be understood without recognizing the nature of this 'England', and the way in which 'Great Britain' was a continuation of England and a vehicle for England. This idea of England and in particular the projects of Great Britain and of Greater Britain are all today under threat, and some think the ancient political formula of the United Kingdom is now exhausted.[11] Either Britain will break up into its separate components with England, Scotland, Wales and Northern Ireland re-emerging as independent countries once again,[12] or a new Britain will emerge, one based on different principles to the old.

The resistance to treating England any longer as synonymous with Britain reflects the understandable desire of the nations that are not English to be treated as equal partners in the United Kingdom. But this desire for a different kind of Britain should not blind us to the Britain we actually have. England remains at the centre of British politics and the UK state, and the old project of Great and Greater Britain, the vehicle for the expansion of England, still lingers. This project though is clearly not what it was. The weakening of the Union, the disappearance of Empire, and the changing relationship with America and with Europe have in turn transformed the relationship between England and Britain. But they have not changed it entirely. England took the lead in constructing the United Kingdom state in pursuit of English interests, and however significant the contribution of others and the partnership with them, the sheer size of England (currently 85 per cent of the population of the UK lives in England) makes it inevitable that it has been English interests and English choices and English votes (whether in Parliament or in the wider electorate) that have been decisive throughout the history of this state.

The dilemma now facing this state as nationalist minorities call for independence and as its power declines is most immediately a problem for *Britain*, but it is also a problem for *England*, because if *Britain* were no longer to be considered viable or legitimate, it would throw *English* identity into question. It is reasonably straightforward for nationalists in Scotland, Wales, and Northern Ireland to reassert their national identity and reposition their countries both in relation to the United Kingdom and in relation to Europe. But for England as well as for Unionist opinion in Northern Ireland, Scotland and Wales, national identity is so bound up with the British state and the history of that state, that it is very hard to disentangle the two and to say what England is apart from Britain. The English still show few signs of wanting to do so.

The English project for a Greater Britain has other problems. It produced the Union, the Empire and the hegemony of Anglo-America, but has had difficulties adjusting to the European Union. In the long imperial twilight since 1940 the many layers and attributes of this Greater Britain have fallen away. This gradual dismantling of the empire state at home and abroad has posed new strategic choices for the United Kingdom between Europe and the United States, new dilemmas on immigration, multiculturalism and devolution, and new problems of economic management, social solidarity and cultural continuity. The older narratives of English exceptionalism which nourished so many earlier generations are under attack, their foundations radically undermined.

Narratives of English exceptionalism which look most faded are those of Empire and Socialism. They dominated British politics in the twentieth century, defining its two main ideological poles and feeding off each other, pushing other ideological strands, including even liberalism for a time, to the margins.[13] Their disintegration as stable frameworks of meaning in the last fifty years has created a profound sense of loss and disorientation, inducing a deep trauma in the political class on both the right and left of British politics. The orderly process of managed decline after 1945 gave way to a much wilder and more turbulent period in the 1970s and 1980s, which saw the triumph of Thatcherism, the implosion and schism of Labour and the Labour movement and the collapse of socialist belief. Under Thatcher the Conservatives not only successfully hammered socialism, but for a short while breathed new life into their own ideological certainties, including in the aftermath of the Falklands War, the Empire itself. This triumph was however to prove shortlived, and costly. By upending the delicate balances of the post-war compromise between left and right, it unleashed new forces which led directly to the implosion and great schism of the Conservatives themselves in the 1990s.[14] With the discrediting of the ideological certainties of both left and right a major transformation of British politics was under way.

'Thatcherism' was the crucial *domestic* catalyst for the self-destruction of Labour and the self-destruction of the Conservatives, but Thatcherism has itself to be understood in the much larger context of the expansion and decline of England and its Empire. It arose at a critical moment in that decline, and helped create the conditions for resolving the question of capitalism in British politics which had dominated domestic politics for a century. It destroyed the political strength of old Labour and made new Labour possible, but at the same time it exposed the inadequacy of the old empire state. By combining radical economic reform with constitutional conservatism the Thatcher Government tried to restore the authority and the sovereignty of the old constitutional state, the state which had been at the heart of both Union and Empire, and to defend it against threats from external and internal enemies whether Argentinian generals, Scottish nationalists, Yorkshire miners, or European federalists. Some of these enemies were vanquished, but the long war of attrition on devolution and Europe only succeeded in accelerating the crisis of the old constitutional order, as well as creating deep divisions in the Conservative Party, which contributed to its electoral meltdown in 1997.

In the 1950s and 1960s the Empire Question in British politics had been focused on the timing and on the manner of granting independence to the colonies as well as coping with large-scale immigration from them. There were particular flashpoints, such as Cyprus, Aden, and Kenya, and intractable problems, such as Rhodesia and South Africa. But by the 1990s the process of withdrawal was largely complete. The Empire Question was far from finished, however: for one of the main legacies from the period of Empire was the United Kingdom itself, the British Union, and therefore the identity of England. The dismembering of Empire was also the dismembering of England, throwing into question the way in which the English had for so long understood their state and its sovereignty. It did not prove possible to lop off the wider Empire without also calling into doubt the Empire within.

The Constitutional Question

As Empire and Socialism faded as ideological forces in British politics, a new energy developed behind constitutional questions, with the emergence of the constitutional reform movement of the 1990s.[15] Constitutional reform threatened the most sacred element of English exceptionalism, the old constitutional state, the mystic thread of English history and development.[16] This explains why the Conservatives fought a long although ultimately fruitless struggle against constitutional reform. In 1997, following Labour's victory in the general election, the dam burst. A period of constitutional innovation and experiment began, with potentially far-reaching implications for how the British nations govern themselves. The merits of fundamental constitutional reform as well as the particular constitutional changes which have come thick and fast since 1997 have been hotly debated.

On the centre left of British politics, radicals, modernizers and conservatives jostle for position. Constitutional radicals advocate sweeping changes to the constitution, but are divided as to whether the cautious, piecemeal and often incoherent programme of constitutional change initiated by the Labour government elected in 1997 is likely to achieve it. They regard the constitutional reforms as a sign that the long transition from

Empire is almost over, and that radical changes are now possible which will in time create a new Britain. The Liberal agenda for constitutional reform at the beginning of the twentieth century is back. For almost one hundred years it was submerged by the argument between capitalism and socialism. Now that that argument has been resolved, the unfinished constitutional agenda has resurfaced and is making it possible for a very different kind of political system to emerge in the twenty-first century; the creation of a genuine federal system for the whole of Britain, embracing not just Scotland, Wales and Northern Ireland but the regions of England as well; the continued pooling of sovereignty in the European Union; a reformed second chamber; freedom of information; a more proportional electoral system. A more open, decentralized, democratic, even republican polity is struggling to be born.[17]

Other views on the centre left are much more cautious. The constitutional modernizers are generally uninterested in any overarching rationale or principled approach to constitutional reform. What counts is what works. They are prepared to back particular measures of reform on their own merits, without too much concern as to whether such measures are consistent. The main concern of the modernizers is with the delivery of public services, and they place less emphasis on the need for major changes to the way in which the country is governed. Nevertheless they respond pragmatically to problems, and have no special attachment to the old order, so are prepared to see further changes as and when these become necessary.[18]

A coalition of radicals and modernizers drawn mainly from the Liberal Democrats and Labour has pushed the reform programme forward since 1997. The main opposition has come from the Conservatives, but there is also a strong current of constitutional conservatism on the centre left as well, on the grounds that certain kinds of constitutional reform can reduce the prospects for introducing a socialist programme. These constitutional traditionalists on the left, such as Tony Benn, do not oppose all measures of reform, but they tend to be deeply attached to the principle of parliamentary sovereignty because they see it as the guarantor of national independence and democratic accountability, and therefore preserving their hopes for a socialist programme and a socialist Britain. Constitutional changes which weaken this sovereignty (such as proportional representation for the Westminster Parliament), or still worse threaten to undermine it altogether (such as the European Union in general and the euro in particular), are strongly opposed.[19]

On the centre right there are few radicals when it comes to constitutional reform, but instead a range of modernizers, traditionalists and nationalists. The constitutional modernizers, rather like their centre-left counterparts are

pragmatic and relatively optimistic. They refuse to believe that a fundamental break with England's past is either likely or necessary. The current
changes will turn out in time to be like many other changes which have
been absorbed and moulded to fit English traditions. These Conservatives
think the United Kingdom will survive relatively intact, its basic institutions unscathed. England will still be at its centre. The forces of cultural,
political and institutional conservatism and inertia will frustrate any
attempts at more radical change. They point out that the changes proposed
by Labour do not challenge the fundamental precepts of the constitution.
Even devolution can be accommodated without disturbing the fundamental
principles of Crown-in-Parliament, the doctrine of parliamentary sovereignty. Popular support for more fundamental constitutional change, they
argue, is weak and the need for it unproven. They endorse Thatcher's
conviction. England needs to stay constitutionally conservative if it is to
remain economically enterprising and innovative.[20]

Constitutional traditionalists among Conservatives however tend to be
pessimistic, and increasingly nostalgic. Indeed many of them have
concluded that the battle is already lost. For them the long nightmare of the
retreat from Empire seems unending. Everything they value is being
trashed. The idea of a new Britain is anathema, since its newness involves
the suppression of England as they have always understood it. Only if
substantial continuity is preserved with its imperial past and its constitutional traditions,[21] will England still be England, and that possibility is
shrinking daily. These Conservatives have become pessimistic about the
chances of saving England. They fear that the rot has already gone too far,
that England is past redemption. It has become a young country again and
lost contact with its past. All that is left is to write elegies that help preserve
its memory for other peoples in future times to discover.[22]

Constitutional nationalists on the right, however, are more combative.
They are no less pessimistic about what the end of Empire means for
preserving the Union, but they think something can be saved from the
wreck. That something is England itself. Drawing their inspiration from
Enoch Powell and Margaret Thatcher, these Conservatives redefine themselves as English nationalists, believing that England can survive, but only
if it rids itself of all entanglements and false illusions.[23] One of the chief of
these entanglements is now Britain itself. Another is the European Union.
Enoch Powell would have added the Atlantic Alliance and the
Commonwealth. These aspects of Greater Britain have now become imped-
iments to reviving a strong sense of English national purpose and identity
and to recreating the kind of single-minded English state which was so
successful in its time of expansion.

The extent to which the British political class at the beginning of the twenty-first century is gripped by constitutional debate is a sure sign that many of the formulas which sustained British politics and the British state in the era of Empire are exhausted. Conservative traditionalists and nationalists are seeing their fears come true. Since 1997 a radical experiment with all aspects of the British constitution has commenced. There has been no big bang, no constitutional convention, no declaration of principle, not even a White Paper, much to the dismay of the constitutional radicals. But there can be no doubting the potential magnitude of the changes that are taking place. Following the radical domestic policy changes of the 1980s which ended the post-war compromise between labour and capital, transformed the economic constitution of the country and changed the balance between the public and private sectors and the role of the state, radical constitutional changes have been initiated which cumulatively may shift the United Kingdom, and with it all its component nations, including England, on to a quite different trajectory of development. The deepening process of European integration is central to this. Membership of the European Union has already had major consequences for many British institutions and for the way England and the rest of the United Kingdom is governed and further change is likely, which will make the British state come to resemble other European states more closely.[24]

Much of the contemporary debate in British politics is really about whether England is changing, and finally leaving behind many of the exceptional features of state and society which have characterized it for so long, and is moving instead into an era which is not just after Empire in the sense that the old colonial empire has vanished, but also in terms of the dominant conceptions of English identity, England's place in the world, and English models of capitalism, self-government, and socialism. The relationship between Britain and England is being redefined, and the potential exists for a different kind of Britain to emerge, one no longer dominated by the old constitutional state inherited from England.

Decline

To put it another way, the constitutional changes signal that we are no longer living in the era of British decline. The great fact of twentieth-century British history was decline, or at any rate the perception of it.[25] The dominance the British state had achieved in the nineteenth century had not endured; expansion had turned into contraction. The zenith of British power had been reached in the first four decades of the twentieth century.

A long decline since then, accelerated by the impact of two world wars, had left the British state at the beginning of the twenty-first century stripped of its Empire, and its power and its role in the world eclipsed by the United States. In its tangled relations with the rest of Europe the British state has slowly if reluctantly been absorbed into the building of a new Union, the European Union, while at home its own Union has become increasingly fragile. With the traditional pillars of British identity under strain, the question of the nature of Britishness, so long avoided when the state was flourishing, has re-emerged, along with varying attempts to reassert separate identities for the Scots, the Welsh, the Irish and the English. The point of sustaining a *British* state and the idea of *Britishness* in the altered conditions of these times has come to the fore. Yet although 'England' is no longer the country which shows to the rest of the world the image of its own future, no longer the workshop of the world, no longer the ideal constitution, no longer the exemplary welfare state, it retains many of the institutions, attitudes, and conventions which were formed in its period of dominance. The idea of England as a world island, a model for the rest of the world, with a special destiny and historical importance, still resonates in countless ways in British politics. How far this is a resource for the future, and how far an impediment to reform, and to the emergence of a new idea of Britain, has become a key issue.

The withdrawal from Empire has been long and drawn-out, triggering deep-seated traumas and anxieties, and much is still unfinished. This is hardly surprising. The largely unbroken character of English institutions and the mostly uninterrupted increase in England's territorial sway and material wealth for three hundred years gave a continuity and stability to English and by extension to British experience which manifested itself in a supreme self-confidence. The decline has been gradual and in stages, at times painful, but at no point catastrophic in the way that military invasion and occupation have been for other states. Such a defining moment for the British state was close in 1940, but having survived it, the experience of resistance and ultimate victory helped to restore faith in British institutions and postponed radical reform and adjustment for several decades.[26]

The finest hour of the British Empire and Commonwealth was also in retrospect however its death knell.[27] Churchill declared defiantly after the Battle of El Alamein that he had not become the King's First Minister to preside over the liquidation of the British Empire, but that is what he did. After 1940 the great historical project of the expansion of England which had already suffered hard knocks with the secession of most of Ireland from the Union in 1921 and the collapse of the gold standard in 1931, went decisively into reverse. The price of continuing to fight against Germany and

Japan was the acceptance of first financial and then military dependence on the United States,[28] acquiescence in Russian expansion, a phased withdrawal from Empire, and a transformation of Britain's role in the world and England's understanding of itself.

Decline can in part be observed and measured as a set of objective processes, which reflected both absolute and relative changes in the position of Britain, changes which often began much earlier, some of them in the nineteenth century.[29] But it also can be viewed as a series of debates within the British political class about the present state and future of 'England' – its role in the world, its economy, its democracy, and its culture.[30] These debates involve in part the rational canvassing of alternatives, but at a deeper level they are also manifestations of the ideological traumas which the withdrawal from Empire and its aftermath created. They have therefore been about culture and morality as well as economic performance, identity as well as political economy.

Writing on decline has often had an apocalyptic tone, but the latest phase of it has been particularly gloomy in its stark warnings and in its sense of despair. A succession of books have appeared from right and left forecasting the imminent demise of Britain,[31] or of England, which for many of these writers is the same thing. For the right the rot set in a while ago, in the 1960s, that uniquely evil decade, spreading and worsening in the 1970s. But despite the Conservatives then entering on their longest spell in government in the twentieth century, the eighteen years from 1979 to 1997, under the inspirational leadership for the first eleven years of Margaret Thatcher, they apparently failed, according to right-wing critics, to restore the moral health of the nation. Communism was routed abroad and socialism at home, but for many Conservatives this was not enough. In the telling phrase of Peter Hitchens, 'The Thatcher–Major Government was unable to reverse a single part of the cultural revolution, not least because it barely tried, and did not understand it.'[32] Evelyn Waugh said much the same before him about the 1950s (the decade which Hitchens now believes was a golden age). While Waugh complained that the Conservatives never put the clock back a single second, Hitchens today despairs of the ability or the will of Conservative governments to tackle the forces which have 'abolished Britain' and with it, by implication, England.

This rage about the cultural revolution which is destroying 'England' is not new but has added force today, particularly because since the 1940s the two main issues in the decline debate were firstly the absolute decline of the position of the United Kingdom as a great power, the loss of its hegemonic role in world affairs to the United States and the granting of independence to its colonies; and secondly the relative decline of British capitalism, the apparently remorseless slide of the UK down the world rankings. In the 1990s however, with the handover of Hong Kong, the long saga of imperial withdrawal was finally over, despite a few last remaining enclaves like Gibraltar. There were strong signs too that following the Thatcher reforms of the 1980s the relative economic decline had been successfully halted.[33] The focus of the decline debate now shifted to the constitution and to culture. Several leading Conservative writers and columnists, including Simon Heffer, Peter Hitchens, John Redwood and Roger Scruton launched a series of broadsides, attacking the constitutional reform programme of the Blair Government with as much apocalyptic vehemence as the left had attacked the economic reform programme of the Thatcher Government in the 1980s.

These outbursts reflect despair at the reshaping of British politics and the burying of England, the end of centuries of tradition and continuity. The Blair Government's constitutional reforms which, as noted above, most constitutional radicals see as incoherent and timid, are regarded by these Conservatives as overturning the constitutional principles of the 1688 settlement, completing the failed revolution of the 1640s and reviving the disappointed radical hopes of the 1790s.[34] The attack on the constitution has come in the wake of the cultural changes which have swept the country since the 1960s; standards have collapsed, and the English, particularly the generations born since 1945, have lost touch with their past and with their traditions.[35]

Much of this critique from the right had been foreshadowed in Enoch Powell's earlier defence of England and Englishness.[36] Powell set out a consistent English nationalist position, uncompromising in its rigour. The imperial phase of England's history was over, he asserted, and England had to move beyond it. He argued against imperial illusions which kept the UK involved with the Commonwealth and active as the junior partner of the United States. What was needed was a sharp break with both imperialism and with Atlanticism. Nostalgia and sentiment were clouding the judgements of the British political class, particularly in its permissive attitude to immigration from Asia and the Caribbean. The other side of Powell's perspective was a resolute defence of the old constitutional order, and at its heart the English concept of sovereignty, the Crown-in-Parliament. Powell was an implacable defender of the Union, but a Union on English terms, which preserved the doctrine of a single source of authority in the state. This meant he rejected any form of devolution as inevitably leading to separation or a form of federal government that was incompatible with a single source of sovereignty. He also firmly opposed any change to the House of Lords, particularly to the hereditary principle and prescriptive right, or naturally to the status of the monarch, or to the electoral system.

But his most vehement opposition came to be reserved for the European Union, which for him represented the greatest threat of all to UK independence, and which unless the UK prised itself free in time, would end for all time the historical continuity of the unique English experience.[37]

Europe and its threat to 'England' and to the sovereignty of the British Parliament thus became the greatest post-imperial trauma of them all, and the culmination of the debate on decline. Opponents of Britain joining the Common Market in the 1960s, the European Community in the 1970s, the European Union in the 1990s, and the single currency today have always stressed the constitutional issue. This is not a simple left/right issue, since there have been many supporters on the left of the principle of national sovereignty and the need to preserve the independence of the UK from Europe, including Peter Shore and Tony Benn.

For Benn the EU is the most potent threat of all to the sovereignty of the British Parliament and to national independence. Only if there is still a free and sovereign Parliament is there a possibility of winning a democratic majority for pursuing a socialist programme. The European Union is undemocratic and unaccountable and its rules make the pursuit of socialist economic policies impossible. The dream of establishing a socialist Commonwealth in Britain had rested on public ownership of the means of production, distribution and exchange, a universal welfare state, a fiscal policy to ensure redistribution, a macroeconomic policy to deliver full employment, and employment laws to protect trade unions. Each of these principles, imperfectly but still partially realized by the Labour government in 1945, were subjected to sustained attack by almost two decades of relentless anti-socialist and anti-union legislation after 1979. The comprehensive defeat of the left and the left's alternative in these years created huge bitterness and resentment as well as bewilderment as to how the world had changed and why socialism seemed no longer relevant to it. The decline of the traditional industries which had nourished the communities of the Labour movement, the rise of consumerism and youth culture, the weakening of the independence and self-reliance of the working class in the face of modern media and mass culture, the remaking of the Labour Party in ways which broke with the party's traditions and principles. For those like Tony Benn who clung to their old socialist principles, the Labour Party was now virtually indistinguishable in its policies and attitudes from the Conservatives. It had become a second Conservative Party. Yet he still stubbornly continued to defend parliamentary sovereignty and national independence. Parliament had delivered Thatcherism, that was true, it had also delivered new Labour, but so long as it existed so did the possibility that it might in the future deliver socialism.[38]

In their rage against modern England, right and left join hands over the threat to national independence. Some of them, including Powell and Benn, were also strong critics of what they perceived to be the supine subordination of successive British Governments to the United States, but otherwise their targets are very different. Whereas the rage of the right is a lament for the lost Empire, the rage of the left is a lament for the lost socialist Commonwealth. Both express an intense fatalism about the inexorable trends which have robbed all the British nations, but the English in particular, of their identity and their hope. The despair in much of this writing is often unrelieved; on the right it regrets past golden ages, which will never return. Particular scorn is reserved for the leaderships of the Conservative Party and the Labour Party who are condemned for having betrayed, whether through ignorance or malice, the principles of the movements they were elected to serve.[39]

The Four Circles of England

At the heart of the identity which conceptions of 'England' celebrate, are four key historical relationships. Winston Churchill in a speech in 1946 used the metaphor of Britain being at the point where three circles met – the circles of the British Empire, of Anglo-America, and of Europe. Britain belonged to all three in Churchill's view but was not limited to any one of them. The notion of three circles was criticized at the time and since as a rhetorical device for avoiding a decision as to what role Britain should play in the post-war world, but as a way of thinking about *England* as a world island and its dilemmas in the post-war world, it remains suggestive and illuminating. Where England is concerned, however, there are clearly not three circles but four. Once the automatic identity of England and Britain is broken the assumption that the British state is a permanent and inviolable unity dissolves, making the British Union itself a fourth circle of England, and the first in time.

These four circles of England – the British Union, the British Empire, Anglo-America, and Europe – overlap. England, Scotland, Wales and Ireland have belonged at some time to all four, and British political history can be analysed from the different standpoints of Scotland, Wales, Ireland, or England.[40] These four circles are not just national but transnational political spaces which together have played a vital role in shaping the contours of British politics and its political economy, defining its patterns of identity, power, and order.

Identity is concerned with commitments, loyalties, duties and obligations, distinguishing us from them, friends from enemies, establishing who we are. The four circles express many different identities, sometimes over-lapping, sometimes exclusive; English, Scottish, Welsh, or Irish; British; Anglo-Saxon; and European. Power is concerned with the allocation of resources and patronage, with who gets what, when and how, with deci-sion-making, policy networks, policy communities, and political parties. A particular centre in each circle is the site where this kind of politics is prin-cipally located; Westminster and Whitehall; London; Washington; and Brussels. Order is concerned with principles, regulatory frameworks and binding rules, the modes of governance which create stability and continu-ity. Each of the four circles has supplied important political, military, ideo-logical and economic principles which have shaped British politics – for example, the doctrine of Crown-in-Parliament; the open seas naval and commercial strategy; the global liberal economic order; and the single market and the euro.

England's simultaneous involvement in all four circles provides the framework for English and British history, and points to those particular characteristics which mark its development. At the heart of each national-ist doctrine is the claim that its nation is exceptional in some way. Each nation has its own special path of development, its *Sonderweg*, which sets it apart from the history and experience of other nations, even if what makes one nation's experience 'exceptional' can only be perceived by comparing it to those others. The notion of exceptionalism implies that nations are different, but not too different, for only if they also hold many things in common is it possible for national experiences and national histo-ries to be compared and their differences highlighted. Exceptionalism can just mean an acceptance of diversity; all nations think of themselves as exceptional: that is part of being a nation. But it also has a harder edge; to claim that a nation is exceptional has often carried the additional meaning that not only is a particular nation different from all others but that it is superior to all others. Some nations proclaim that it is their manifest destiny to be the nation that leads the world, even if in the nature of things it is never easy for more than one such claim to be sustained at the same time.

Exploring how a nation defines what is exceptional about itself requires a reconstruction of its history and an identification of its own *Sonderweg*, its special path, and the defining events, ideas, institutions and turning points that constitute it and shape its identity. This is never a neutral, objec-tive, passionless exercise, which can be expressed in a single account. Rather, there are always likely to be several competing narratives, locked in fierce disagreement with one another over what is really special about the national path of development: those qualities which express the essence of the nation and should be cherished and sustained, and those which should be cast aside and forgotten. What is being argued over is the nature of national identity itself, and different kinds of political possibility. National identity is never fixed but always contested, made up of many elements, always open to reinterpretation and restatement.

Nevertheless it is not infinitely malleable, because not all the narratives which seek to pinpoint national identity have equal weight. Some are more important than others in providing the core frameworks and assumptions which set the terms of politics, giving it coherence, context and significance. England as a Protestant nation, England as an Empire, or England as a Commonwealth are examples. Each of these in its time has been a leading narrative. England's national identity as presented through them is complex, because the state which was fashioned after 1707 was not a national state but a multinational state and its politics too were multinational. There is no primary British nation to correspond to the British state in the way that there is a German nation or a French nation. Yet many of the political institutions of this state including most of the political parties are transnational – they are British not simply English, or Scottish or Welsh.

Narratives provide accounts of political history, selecting facts which are relevant and essential for the story they seek to tell. They are therefore different from myths, because although like myths they are works of the imagination, they have to be rooted in experience, in social and historical facts, to retain their credibility. This means they can be challenged. Narratives can be plausible and more or less coherent, but they cannot be objective or incontrovertible. There are of course certain undisputed 'truths' such as those contained in simple chronologies or stylized facts such as election results. Every complex narrative, however, selects and evaluates facts to construct new meanings and interpretations, and in doing so becomes open to contestation. Over time this means that every such narrative contributes to the broad general discourse on politics in its community, which will contain many layers of meaning and interpretation. No single narrative is ever finally accepted as the true and undisputed account; rather it becomes a catalyst for rival accounts and interpretations.

There is, for example, no final and agreed narrative of the British Labour Party. There is a basic account containing a large number of facts, such as when the party was founded, who its leaders were, how it has been organized, what its policies have been, how many votes it has secured in elections. Most of these are agreed and constitute fixed points for analysis. But there are then a set of more complex narratives which provide rival interpretations of the party's policies, ideology, achievements and purpose. The narratives of political parties are amongst the most complex narratives that exist, since they seek to combine and absorb elements from all other narratives in order to provide overarching accounts of the nature of British politics. One of the main ways to understand British politics and the idea of 'England' within it is therefore through the contrasting visions of the political parties, since they bear the imprint of the history of the state and are both the product of this history and shapers of the future.

In many of the dominant narratives of British politics it is 'Britain' that is construed as in some sense exceptional, but since there is no British nation, the source of this exceptionalism is actually England. It is the existence of *British* politics and the ways in which *Britishness* and *British* identity are defined which express the ways in which the English have pursued an exceptional path of development, participating in a state which incorporated other nations but did not seek to make all its citizens English. Paradoxical as it may seem, Britishness is actually at the heart of claims about English exceptionalism; what is special about England is the character of its state, the British state, and the absence of a single nation to underpin it. It has at times been claimed that the British state England established never became a modern state, in part because it did not create a new nation. But what was really exceptional about England was the specific kind of state and the specific kind of nation which developed, and the peculiar combination of nation and state at the founding of the new nation-state in 1707.[41]

The new state logically required a new nation, the British nation, to supersede the constituent nations of England, Scotland, Wales and Ireland.[42] But it did not seek to suppress the nations that already existed or to replace them. This state was organized as a union state rather than a unitary state,[43] a multinational federation rather than a nation-state. But it was never set up as a federation and never adopted a federal constitution. Yet although not a unitary state on French lines it had many unitary features; for example the central institutions at its core, Crown and Parliament, were joined together in the doctrine of parliamentary sovereignty, Crown-in-Parliament, which conferred great powers on the executive. The degree of overt centralization, however, was mitigated by the existence of governing codes which tolerated and even encouraged considerable local diversity and autonomy and the practice of self-government, and not only resisted direct control from the centre but insisted on the idea that the centre was not absolute but subject to the rule of law.[44] This combination of centralization with self-government made it an oddity in the eighteenth century, and it remains an oddity today.

The narrative of the history of this Union came to constitute one essential part of Britishness. But it was also defined not just through the expansion of this state within the territorial space of the British Isles, but also through its expansion beyond them. Over the course of three centuries England became an Empire; an empire of ideas as well as of territory, of capital as well as of sea-power, of liberty as well as of order. England, a small island kingdom, a minor player in the European Middle Ages, embarked on a remarkable career of expansion from the sixteenth century onwards which saw it established by the nineteenth century not only as a great power, but as the leading world power. A nation with a relativly small geographical base in population and resources had become the richest nation in the world, and the possessor of the largest world empire. It was no longer just an island, but a world island, a key player in shaping the rules and institutions of world order.

England as a World Island

As explained in the first chapter England is a world island in several ways, depending on whether the emphasis is on world or on island. It is both insular world and world exemplar, a model for development. What England is not is a geographical island. It is part of the archipelago situated off the north-west corner of the continental land-mass of Europe, occupying the largest part of the island of Britain, which is also the largest island in the group. The actual name to be given to this group of islands has always been contested.[45] The islands were for a time ruled from a single centre and considered one imperium, but they have never been the preserve of one nation. England has therefore strictly never been an island, because it shares the island of Britain with Wales and Scotland. This has not prevented the English thinking of themselves as an island people, and their territory as an island territory. The famous speech of John of Gaunt in *Richard II* celebrating England's island character, part of which heads this chapter, subsequently became a key text of *British* nationalism, but was written by Shakespeare in the 1590s before there was even a Union of the Crowns of England and Scotland, and is even more anachronistic for the England of the fourteenth century, the period when the action of the play is set.[46] England was far from enjoying jurisdiction over the whole territory of the island of Britain. It is texts like Shakespeare's which confirm to the Scots and the Welsh that they are invisible to the English and that Britain is no more than England writ large.

The achievement of unified rule over the whole archipelago, following the union with Scotland in the seventeenth and eighteenth centuries, made the uniting of England with Britain come to seem part of the natural order of things, even though separate nations and separate national traditions continued, most obviously in Ireland and Scotland. Attempts were made to create a new national identity of Britishness to cement the union, and to strengthen the state, but this was in addition to existing identities rather than a replacement for them. This made British nationalism a highly political kind of nationalism, just as the English church was a highly political church, created to serve the purposes of the state. One of the most important features of British political experience has been the extent to which alongside the formal institutions of the state though which Britishness was sustained and promoted, such as Crown and Parliament, there existed many other established public institutions which were primarily important for the governing of England; their writ did not run in Scotland and they often had little legitimacy in Ireland. Examples include the Church of England, the English legal system, the English Constitution and the Bank of England.

The combining of the separate islands under the rule of a single state helped emphasize the new state's island status as well as enabling it to face outwards, and see itself as a distinct entity in relation to its neighbours. From this arose different meanings of England as a world island; an insular world and a world exemplar. England's success as a state encouraged both insularity and openness. The sense of insularity was developed by defining first England and then Britain in opposition to Europe, while the sense of openness was achieved by conceiving England as the centre of a global empire and a global hegemony.

Awareness of England as an island separated by a small but significant physical distance from the rest of Europe helped make England *Little England*, an insular world, a world of its own, idiosyncratic in its institutions and customs and conventions, and resistant to outside influences; 'this little world', as Shakespeare called it. The eccentricity of the inhabitants of England became a commonplace, both ridiculed and celebrated in equal measure.[47] England's path of development diverged in significant ways from that of other European countries, and the close cultural and institutional ties which had characterized the relationship in earlier centuries were substantially weakened, although never broken. This isolation of England from Europe which began when England embraced Protestantism in the sixteenth century became still more marked subsequently. Scotland followed a different path.[48] Although it too adopted Protestantism it remained closer in some respects to France and other European countries even after the Union with England, and many of its institutions, particularly its legal system, its church, its schools and universities, developed along more mainstream European lines. England was more idiosyncratic, clinging to institutions and procedures which grew ever more peculiar and insular. Some, as a consequence, now see England and the state it created as a case of arrested development, a regime stuck in pre-modern times which never managed to cross the threshold into the modern world.[49] But at the same time, this state has a strong claim to be considered the most success-ful state of the modern era, preserving institutional continuity since the seventeenth century.[50]

The most important meaning of England as a world island is the way in which over three hundred years the state formed from its successful Union with the other British nations became a pioneer, an exemplar, a model for the world, and an object of imitation. For three hundred and fifty years it has been a state and society with a global reach, in terms of its power, its products and its ideas, and a number of attributes came to be associated with it.

The British became renowned as innovators and pioneers: the voyages of exploration from the sixteenth to the nineteenth century which helped bring the whole world into the European orbit through colonies and trade; the political revolutions which took place in England and Scotland limiting the powers of the Crown and creating one of the first balanced constitu-tions, and establishing the principles of representative government, the rights of citizens and the rule of law; the industrial revolutions of the eigh-teenth and nineteenth centuries with their drastic changes to the structure of occupations and the balance between city and country; the establishment in the nineteenth and twentieth centuries of one of the first and most durable models of parliamentary democracy; the creation of the welfare state and institutions to regulate and civilize capitalism; and the creativity in scien-tific discoveries, in new technologies, and in culture. In this way the British nations in the form of 'England' are depicted as having been for several centuries at the forefront of many of the key developments in politics, economics, and culture which have defined modernity.

A second attribute of Britishness was a capacity for leadership, derived from the British state's prolonged exercise of leadership in the global econ-omy and the international state system despite its relatively modest base of population and resources. This period of leadership reached its zenith in the nineteenth century but cast its shadow long into the twentieth, and shaped many British institutions and attitudes, from the civil service and the armed forces to universities and companies. British dominance was not only economic, political and military but also cultural. The expectation of British superiority and the idea that 'England' had something to teach the rest of the world, based upon its exceptional national experience, became deeply ingrained.

A third attribute was a preference for political stability and institutional continuity. The survival of the state established in 1689 for three hundred years without internal overthrow or external invasion, although not entirely without parallel, is in marked contrast to the fate of most other states in Europe and is responsible for many particular and idiosyncratic features of British institutions such as the uncodified constitution, the survival for so long of an unelected second chamber based on heredity right and patronage, and the doctrine of parliamentary sovereignty. The degree of continuity has often been questioned, since the preservation of outward institutional forms can often mask deeper changes of substance. England was no stranger to shocks and discontinuities. It went through major periods of upheaval – the 1790s, the 1820s, the 1840s, and the period between 1880 and 1930.[51] This state lost its American colonies, it lost Ireland, and after the Second World War it lost all its other major colonies. But it never experienced the abrupt and comprehensive modernization of institutions and replacement of its political class which many other countries have had to undergo. This state was a world island which for a time became the centre of the world, based upon its dual empire of territory and of commerce, an island open to the whole world, and yet still retained its own self-enclosed and self-contained world. This contrast and this tension between insularity and openness is one which recurs many times through this book, and is a key to understanding the character of British politics.

England after 1532 and particularly after 1689 became a world island, in the two senses already outlined, even if it could not strictly claim to be a geographical island until the Treaty of Union in 1707 established a single jurisdiction over the whole island of Britain. This was an island, or more accurately a group of islands, which reached out to the whole world and became for a time the centre of that world, and the arbiter of its fate. But it also remained a distinctive, idiosyncratic and insular world, often isolated from and resistant to external influence, confident in its own superiority, its own institutions and ways of doing things. These attitudes were acquired in the historical experience of this state, which having consolidated its control throughout the territory of its archipelago, proceeded to extend its formal rule to a quarter of the world, and its informal rule to much more. It enjoyed extraordinary success over a long period, whether measured by the continuity of its institutions, the liberty and welfare of its citizens, the extent of its possessions, or the wealth of its economy. By the middle of the nineteenth century 'England' had attained a remarkable position of economic and political leadership both in the system of states and in the world economy. From being minor and peripheral medieval kingdoms constantly at war with one another, England and Scotland emerged in the early modern period as significant independent polities, whose union formally created a new state, Great Britain, which was to become the administrative and military centre of a world empire and the economic and ideological centre of a world economy. It was the undisputed hegemonic power, and the world was increasingly made in its image.

The success of Great Britain made it for a time in certain respects the quintessential modern state and modern society, which represented a model for others, either to emulate or to avoid or to resist. But England's relationship to modernity has never been straightforward. The successful expansion helped disguise, as we have seen, the extent to which the state never became a fully modern state. Its premodern origins were still highly visible throughout the twentieth century in the survival of so many antiquated rituals and institutions, such as the House of Lords and the Monarchy, and which led to England coming to be regarded as the last *ancien régime* in Europe. The British state was not created by revolution, and at the end of the eighteenth century shunned the new republican forms of government and conceptions of citizenship associated with the United States and with France. It fought wars against both of them in defence of the principles of monarchy and aristocracy. It seemed to have more in common with some of the monarchical and aristocratic regimes elsewhere in Europe, and often made common cause with them. In the nineteenth century in a world of autocracy and empires the British state did not look out of place. But the wars and revolutions of the twentieth century redrew the political map of Europe, and made many aspects of the British state appear increasingly anachronistic.

If England had remained rich and powerful, if it had remained an Empire in all or even some of the four dimensions – ideological, economic, military, and territorial – in which it had projected its hegemony in the nineteenth century this might not have mattered. But in the second half of the twentieth century it surrendered its pretensions to hegemony across all four dimensions, and as a result the nation-state, which had been at the heart of this Empire, and the pillars of British identity which it had sustained came under challenge, both internal and external. These pillars included the Union on which the state was founded, the idea of a Greater Britain spreading throughout the world, the superiority of British industry, commerce and finance over all competitors, and the liberties, rights and welfare of British citizens.

In recent times all these aspects of British identity have been questioned, bringing into sharp relief the wider English Question, the role of England in British politics. How do the English wish in future to govern themselves and what if anything do they wish to salvage from the wreck of Greater Britain? In the decades after Empire, England has been transformed from being one of the undisputed great powers in the international state system and the leading imperial power to just one of many European powers once more. Reminders of the former importance of this state remain – such as the its permanent seat on the Security Council of the UN and its membership of the G8. But the adjustment to a reduced status has not been easy and is still incomplete. The former position of Great Britain in the world, and the idea of the British Empire, shaped many English as well as British institutions and attitudes; it shapes them still. So powerful has been the hold of empire on the English political imagination that it has continued to dominate the thinking of much of the English media and many British politicians as well as resonating in popular culture, and provides the framework in which many contemporary issues, particularly the relationship of the United Kingdom to Europe, are still discussed.

This narrative was fashioned when the British Empire was at its height at the end of the nineteenth century, the time when the idea of empire first really took root. In this narrative, English exceptionalism was built upon the commercial and military exploits of England. The Empire which had resulted was a territorial empire, a commercial and financial empire, an industrial empire, and an empire of ideas. It had been built upon internal union, external expansion, industrial revolution, and political stability. From these foundations the major institutions of the state arose, created through the actions and struggles of many generations, which continue to constrain and enable political action in the present. The empire narrative accurately captured some important features of what made England exceptional, but like all narratives it tended to freeze these so that in time they were converted into myths. The challenges to this narrative and the freeing of England from these myths has taken both practical and intellectual forms. Even when the different parts of Empire began to fall apart, many of the habits of thinking, many of the institutions, many of the symbols remained unchanged.

Finding new identities is painful and slow. The old narrative continues to cast a long shadow over political debates, but gradually new issues and new directions have emerged. The debates on devolution, on Britishness, on Europe, on economic decline, on multiculturalism, and on constitutional reform are evidence of that; all in different ways reflect legacies of Empire and different conceptions of English exceptionalism, as well as proposing ways of moving beyond it. It is to these debates that we now turn, through first an exploration of each of the four circles and the way they shape contemporary British politics.

3

The State of the Union

> This realm of England is an Empire, and so hath been accepted
> in the world, governed by one Supreme Head and King having
> the dignity and royal estate of the imperial Crown of the same,
> unto whom a body politic, compact of all sorts and degrees of
> people divided in terms and by names of Spirituality and
> Temporality, be bounden and owe next to God a natural and
> humble obedience.

> *Preamble to the Act of Appeals*, 1533

> If England is leaving the English, where will they be?

> Neal Ascherson, 1988[1]

England could not have become a world island without the first of the four
circles – the Union between the four nations of the British Isles, England,
Ireland, Scotland and Wales. Union created a state which was independent of
the rest of Europe, just as its American colonies were to become independent
of it. The choice between Europe and America which now confronts the
British state only exists because of the success of the Union, and the Empire
it made possible. But the urgency of this choice has itself been a factor in the
serious questioning of the Union which has emerged in British politics.

Despite long political and military labours over several centuries, the
incorporation of all four nations into one United Kingdom with one
Parliament was not finally completed until 1801. It was England's first
Empire, and the one that made possible subsequent expansion. But however
much the Union owed to the strategy and calculations of the English political class, it was always more than England writ large. It made possible the
emergence of a British state and a British political class, through particular
institutional forms such as the Monarchy and Parliament, the British Army
and the Royal Navy, while preserving special arrangements for its different
nations and regions. The Union is the first circle within which England

stands, the first of the transnational spaces which has shaped British history and politics, and has defined Britishness.

Strong claims of exceptionalism are often linked to the history of particular states and most often arise in those nations in which the history of the nation and the history of the state are closely intertwined, and in which the state has played a major role in nation-building. This is true of the United States[2] and it is also true of the United Kingdom.[3] The idea of an overarching British 'nation' and therefore a separate British identity was fostered by the government of this new state after the Act or Treaty of Union between England and Scotland in 1707, just as an overarching American nation and American identity were fostered by the federal government after the American Civil War. Governments have not been slow to understand the powerful legitimation that nations provide for states in the modern era. Where a state has lacked an appropriate nation to underpin it the natural impulse of its governing class has been to encourage one to form.[4] Even where nations already existed as cultural and ethnic entities, they often had to be reconstructed if they were to perform the role which states required. This explains why states have at times been so keen to crush national and ethnic groups which do not fit into their plans or which they judge to be incapable of assimilation. The nation-states of the last three hundred years are political constructions rather than natural phenomena. Nations have often been remodelled by states, and sometimes they have been called into existence by states.[5]

A major problem therefore arises when the national identity on which the legitimacy of the state has been founded starts to crumble. Many think such a fate is beginning to overtake the United Kingdom. Norman Davies has put it particularly bluntly. The English have never joined anyone, and now everyone is leaving them.[6] But this breakup, if that is what it turns out to be, has been quite unlike the dramatic breakups of other great multinational states, Austria–Hungary in 1918, or the Soviet Union in 1991. The first to leave the United Kingdom were the Irish, and that was eighty years ago. The secession of the 26 counties, four fifths of Ireland, in 1921 severely damaged the original conception of the Union, but the United Kingdom somehow survived it. Since the late 1960s, however, the Union has come under new threats, and has had to cope with the rise of nationalist movements in Scotland and Wales, renewed conflict in Northern Ireland, and growing pressure for devolution of powers from Westminster to Scotland, Wales, Northern Ireland and even to some of the regions of England, culminating in the reforms after 1997.

These political challenges have also brought questioning of the traditional notion that the Union created a unitary state and a unified British nation. Several historians have argued that the British Isles has always been a multinational space, and that the British nation was an artificial creation which served the interests primarily of England.[7] The separate histories and experiences of the four nations have been overlaid by too much emphasis upon England, as though only English history mattered, and that the histories of the other nations were just sub-themes within it. Recovering these different national pasts is seen as essential for disentangling England and Britain, and for perceiving clearly the alternative futures for the Union; the renegotiation of the terms of the partnership to create a true federation between the different nations, or the breakup of the Union into separate nation-states.

The possibility that the Union might be dissolved has begun to undermine the unthinking English identification of English with British, and has therefore put in question the survival of Britishness. The notion of 'Britain' and a British nation has come under sustained attack from nationalists, who have claimed that the idea of a British nation is now unravelling before our eyes, and with it the foundations of the British state.[8] The superstructure of the British State has become top-heavy, it is said, and is visibly tottering; as its supports are eroded it may collapse altogether. Britain is about to 'break up'.

If there never was a British 'nation', however, we are left with a puzzle. What then was and is the nature of Britishness which has endured for such a long time? Can an identity which was once so strong really be about to disappear?

The Construction of Britishness

One very odd aspect of Britishness is the confusion that reigns about how to use such terms as the United Kingdom, Great Britain, Britain, and England,[9] what Bernard Crick has called 'the minefield of nomenclature'.[10] As he puts it, 'I am a citizen of a country with no agreed colloquial name.'[11] Strictly speaking there is no entity that can be called Britain (the old name for the Roman province). The name was revived in the reign of Elizabeth I as another name for England, and was revived again in the twentieth century as a shorthand term for the UK. The state officially has always had other names; before 1707 there was a separate kingdom of England which also ruled over Wales and Ireland, and a separate kingdom of Scotland. The Crowns of the two Kingdoms were united in 1603, but the two kingdoms did not become one state until the Union of the Parliaments in 1707. This new state was a 'composite' monarchy; composite because it was made up of several kingdoms.[12] The name – Kingdom of Great Britain – was promoted by some Scots to make the loss of their own Parliament more acceptable, and adopted willingly enough by the English to placate them. It could not disguise the fact that the Union was arranged largely on English terms. In 1801 this state became the United Kingdom of Great Britain and Ireland, following the incorporation of the Irish Parliament into the Westminster Parliament, and in 1921 it became the United Kingdom of Great Britain and Northern Ireland, following the secession of the rest of Ireland from the Union and the recognition of the Irish Free State.

Britain is currently the shorthand term applied to this Union, and reflects the fact that the name for this state has always been a matter of political convenience. The frequent changes of name conceal the fact that the state itself has not really changed. Its core was always the English state, which adopted a different nomenclature in order to incorporate other nations, and which on occasion made concessions to them, but which was never willing to share power with them in a federal constitution. The idea of a British state and a British nation was fostered to encourage these other nations to identify with England and give their loyalty to it. In the case of Scotland and Wales this policy proved generally successful, and a real commitment to Britain and Britishness developed, reflected in the strength of Unionist politics in both countries. The greatest failure was in Ireland. Even in Ireland, however, there were strong pockets of Unionism, most notably the Irish Protestants concentrated in Ulster. Ever since William of Orange broke the resistance of the Irish Catholics who had rallied in support of the deposed Catholic King James II at the Battle of the Boyne in 1690, the Ulster Protestants have been vociferous in their loyalty to the Crown and in parading their British identity.[13]

Occasional attempts were made to win over the rest of the Irish to the new British identity, but the divorce between the Protestant landowners and the Catholic peasantry made it very difficult, since Protestantism, which was already one of the central features of Englishness and Scottishness, became during the eighteenth century one of the defining aspects of Britishness.[14] The Irish were excluded and viewed with suspicion. Yet moderate nationalist opinion in Ireland was at one stage not averse to the idea. After the abolition of the separate Irish Parliament in 1800 and the proclamation of the new United Kingdom, Daniel O'Connell even toyed with the idea of the Irish becoming West Britons, just as the Scots were North Britons. But the idea never took hold, and West Briton later became a term of derision in nationalist circles. By the end of the nineteenth century, Irish nationalists had decisively rejected the notion that Ireland should adopt a British identity or that its history was part of British history.[15] They set out to construct the idea of an Irish nation and to demand for this nation its own state. As a result Britain and British were not neutral terms for the Irish. They did not denote a transnational space or a joint project in which different nationalities could be partners. Instead it signified the English state and a national identity which excluded them. In their struggle for national self-determination the Irish sought to purge their culture of its strong British tradition by conflating Britain and England.

The British state was an odd creation, principally because it was so unlike the nation-states which were later to be formed across Europe after the French Revolution and which expressed the principle of national self-determination. What is puzzling from the modern experience of nation-building is how unsystematic and careless the English were in constructing the British state and the British nation. At all times England predominated, both in size and population (even in 1800, 60 per cent of the population was in England; by 2000 it was close to 85 per cent). Yet despite their dominance in numbers, and their greater wealth, the English were never able or willing either fully to incorporate the three other nationalities or to suppress them. Calling this state in 1801 by the clumsy and long-winded name of 'The United Kingdom of Great Britain and Ireland' implicitly conceded that it was not a nation-state, and that a British identity was not the primary identity of its citizens. Instead it acknowledged that the United Kingdom is and always has been a multinational state, comprising at least four ethnic national identities in addition to the British national identity, which was at first essentially a political identity, depending on allegiance to the new British state.

This multinational state created several centuries ago as the result of a series of accidents has persisted through the modern era, and is now widely perceived as one of the most important manifestations of English exceptionalism, its special path of development. It was not always so. Traditional accounts of the British state have treated it simply as a unified nation-state, played down any mention of the separate nations submerged within it and sometimes obliterated them entirely.[16] The history of the other nations was absorbed without hesitation into English history. It is as if the other nations were not really considered to have had any history worth speaking of until the moment that they were fortunate enough to become part of English history.[17] English politicians even today sometimes speak of 'Britain' in Tudor times, or even further back. The British state was presented as a unified and coherent entity, with a settled policy and settled system of government. England and Britain were used interchangeably, so that events in the two hundred years before the formal founding of the British state in 1707 with the Union of the Parliaments of England and Scotland, were treated as if they were part of the subsequent history of this state. There is no easy way around this since, although Wales and Ireland had already been annexed by the English Crown, Scotland never was. The word British is therefore strictly always an anachronism when used about the state before 1707. But since there was so much continuity between the English state before 1707 and the British state thereafter, it is hard to draw a sharp line between them. The English Parliament regarded the new Parliament created by the Act of Union as the continuation of itself in a new form. The Scots insisted that this Act was a Treaty, by which they had agreed to suspend their Parliament, and accept representation in the Westminster Parliament.[18] And as noted in the previous chapter, in the nineteenth century it was common for 'England' to be the term used to describe the British state both within the UK and outside it. 'England' was preferred to either 'Great Britain' or the still more cumbersome 'United Kingdom of Great Britain and Ireland'.

The Union of 1707 created a British state, but raised questions about the purpose of this state and what bound it together. What did being British as opposed to being Scottish or being English mean? What was the Union for? The English political class which negotiated the Union was not much troubled by these questions. The purpose of the Union was to serve the interests of England. Great Britain was a more promising vehicle for doing this than England alone, mainly because of the opportunity it provided to secure England's borders. The broader question was settled by the success of this new British state. The state which resulted from the Union embarked on a career of expansion abroad and industrialization at home which brought unparalleled prosperity and power to its citizens. The meaning of Britishness became tied inexorably to the expansion of this state, its military triumphs and its industrial productivity. It offered opportunities to all the nationalities within it which they could not have secured on their own, and these opportunities were often gratefully seized, with the Scots in particular to the fore, so that it was not long before individual Scots had acquired a prominent part in the running of the state and the Empire.[19]

Even after the Union with Scotland the British state remained a relatively loose body, to such an extent that some observers have questioned whether it ever really became a state at all on the pattern of the rest of Europe.[20] This state in contrast with the state in many other polities, was not conceived as a separate legal entity standing above society but as one closely integrated with it. The borders between the British state and the public institutions of British civil society have never been sharply defined, and this has contributed to the cohesion of the British political class.[21] One of the consequences, as reformers have never ceased to complain, is that it has often proved difficult to modernize British institutions piecemeal because they have always been so interlocked through the good offices of the ubiquitous British Establishment, making them resistant to comprehensive reform,[22] and instituting a form of 'club government'.[23] This unique complex of institutions and traditions gave rise to a distinctive British political identity and conception of statehood, which has been particularly evident in the doctrine of Crown-in-Parliament, and the territorial code by which this state has managed relationships between the centre and the periphery, maintaining the autonomy of the centre while tolerating the diversity of the periphery.[24]

The doctrine of Crown-in-Parliament is explored further in Chapter 7. What is important to note here is how this doctrine brought together the two key institutions which bound the new state together. The upheavals of the seventeenth century had ended with the retention of the monarchy, but a monarchy forced (at first reluctantly) to acknowledge that it depended on the consent of Parliament. The executive power, the undivided and unlimited English sovereignty, came to be exercised not by the Crown alone, nor by Parliament, but by Crown-in-Parliament. The prerogative powers of the Crown, and therefore the principle of a strong executive, remained, but the consent of Parliament to taxation and to fundamental issues such as the maintenance of an established religion and the details of the royal succession were henceforth unchallenged. It opened the way for the King's ministers gradually to exercise executive power on behalf of the King.[25]

The Crown became the symbol of the new British state, the focus for allegiance, but Parliament became its essential representative forum and clearing house, the guarantee of self-government and participation in shaping political decisions. The right to representation in Parliament was based principally on the ownership of land and on gender,[26] which made the political class a tiny fraction of the population, but also provided a set of common interests which united the political class across all parts of the Union. It helped that in Ireland the Catholic landowners had been dispossessed and a Protestant landowning class installed in their place.[27]

The importance attached to Parliament as a binding agent in the new state was shown by the provisions that were made for representation of the other nations in the Westminster Parliament. It began a tradition of over-representation of Scotland, Wales and Ireland in the British Parliament which has continued to this day.[28] This agein was not thought to be peculiar, since the idea of representation in the English Constitution was not based on any notion of strict proportionality or mathematical exactitude. The anomalies of the Constitution were legion, but what mattered was whether they served to promote a greater purpose. The dominance of

England meant that a greater representation than the other nations were strictly entitled to was justified if it helped to ensure their loyalty and commitment. Giving the landowners of each nation a significant voice in this sovereign Parliament was an important step in ensuring their commitment to building the new state. The English political class was ready to make concessions and to tolerate diversity throughout the King's dominions, so long as the fundamental principle of sovereignty was not challenged. It got into difficulties whenever it failed to follow this policy, as happened both with the American colonists and the Irish, and did not make concessions in time, and then compounded the error by interpreting the resistance it encountered as a challenge to its sovereignty.[29] Conservative governments made the same mistake in relation to Scotland in the 1980s and 1990s, with the result that in the 1997 election the party failed to win a single Scottish seat.

London and the Parliament at Westminster became the new centre of this state. The growth of London, already considerable, now became unstoppable. The doctrine of the unlimited sovereignty of Crown-in-Parliament contributed to the centralization of power in the United Kingdom and the focusing of all the key political, financial, administrative, and cultural networks on London. No other country in Europe, not even France, acquired so dominant a capital as London.[30] As the British Empire and British world role expanded, and as communications improved and the capacities of the state were extended, this dominance increased still further. London had no serious competitor within the United Kingdom; there were other important regional centres – Manchester, Birmingham, Glasgow, and Edinburgh among them – but they could not match London, although in the nineteenth century they did develop thriving civic cultures. But these were undermined in the course of the twentieth century by the pull of London, so that the contrast between centre and periphery became ever greater. There remained a great deal of regional diversity in the periphery, much of which the centre tolerated, but without real political independence the consequence tended to be regional stagnation. The dominance of London tended to inhibit the growth of a strong civic culture in the regions, or to weaken it where it did exist. While the energies of the state were being channelled outwards, the excessive centralism and dominance of London did not seem to matter. Later during the decline, when the state was turning inwards, it became a liability. The constitutional reformers of the 1980s saw the excessive centralism as one of the main causes of the lack of dynamism and the poor quality of British government.[31]

This dominance of the centre affected the way in which centre–periphery relations developed. The British state was from the start a centralized state, but not excessively so. There was little formal constitutional devolution of powers, but in practice there was a great deal, and the metropolitan centre managed the peripheral regions over which it ruled by striking deals with the local landowning elites, later with local Labour elites.[32] In principle the British state was centralized and unitary, but in practice it was more of a union state, in which substantial local differences in administration and law were tolerated and even encouraged by the centre, so long as they did not encroach upon the policy areas with which it was most concerned.

This solution to the problem of territorial management in the United Kingdom meant that there was no concerted attempt to suppress the different nationalities or ethnic groups in the British Isles, not even in Ireland. This had not always been so. English rule in Wales had been marked for a time by a drive to eliminate the Welsh language, and forcing all Welsh people to adopt English names. But the use of state power to impose national unity and suppress diversity was rare under the British state. An exception were the Scottish Highlanders who after the 1745 Jacobite rebellion in support of the exiled Stuarts were perceived to be a threat to the security of the state: they were driven off the land and their way of life destroyed. More common was the encouragement given to the different nationalities and regions to retain some independence, to think of themselves as joint owners of the state, and to identify with what had become by default its central project and mission, the expansion and defence of the British Empire. People could retain particular identities so long as they also accepted the British identity alongside their own, and were willing to acknowledge its claims to their loyalty in matters relating to the state. Once the Highlands had been pacified and depopulated, the symbols of Highland life such as the bagpipes and the kilt were reintroduced to promote a new Scottish identity.[33] This revival of Welsh and Scottish identities in the nineteenth century however was considered safe because they were not political; they did not threaten the way power was concentrated in the British state.

Empire and Socialism

Crown and Parliament were binding agents for the new state, and London provided the site where deals were struck, decisions taken, and resources and offices allocated. But broader popular allegiance also depended on the development of projects with which the people could identify. Two such projects have been crucial for the British Union – the British Empire from the eighteenth century onwards, and British socialism in the nineteenth and twentieth centuries. It is not an accident that these were associated with the two leading British political parties in the twentieth century, Conservatives and Labour. British socialism was a relative latecomer, growing up with the extension of the franchise, the rise of the Labour movement, and the pressures of mass democracy. But the British Empire was one of the original rationales for the Union. England had been expansionist for some time already, and many Scots were keen to join in. Scotland's accession helped accelerate the process.[34]

The importance of the building of a *British* Empire to the success of the British state was enormous. It allowed the development of a particular genre of British histories in the nineteenth and early twentieth centuries which treated 'England' as a nation-state with its own special path of development. A favourite analogy was that between England and Israel, two peoples chosen by God for his special purposes. The same identification was later to be made even more strongly by Protestant Fundamentalists in the United States.[35] According to this religious interpretation of England's destiny, divine providence meant that the English (and by implication the Scots, Irish and Welsh who had joined with them) had been singled out to be rulers, leaders and pioneers. For a long time this seemed no more than commonsense to the British themselves. They received daily confirmations of it, in the evidence of the extraordinary prowess and inventiveness of British industries, the extent of the map of the world that was coloured pink, and the financial and political stability of England, and all in such marked contrast to the other countries of Europe.

The nature of the British Empire and its emergence as the second circle of England are considered in the next chapter. What needs emphasizing is the importance of the Empire for the Union, since it was a project that bound all parts of the Union together. It was their common project, and as such it gave Britishness a focus, a cause, and an identity. The British became settlers, traders, soldiers and sailors in this Empire. The Royal Navy from the beginning and later the British Army (although it took longer) became key *British* institutions, even if the British Army retained separate national regiments. The contrast with other institutions, like the Church or the City or the Universities or the Law, was marked. They remained fundamentally English – there was to be no attempt to create a Church of Britain or a Bank of Britain.

The ability of the Empire to give some substance to Britishness was assisted by the use in the eighteenth century of the idea of the British as a Protestant people defending their liberties against absolutism and popery. It reinforced the idea of the British as the new Children of Israel, isolated, defiant, beset by enemies, but also singled out and protected by God.[36]

Britishness became associated with insularity and hostility to foreigners, particularly the French.[37] The string of victories in the eighteenth century against the French became cause for popular rejoicing and a feeling of British invincibility. Defiant and triumphal ballads like *Rule Britannia* captured the mood.

Some historians indeed think that war and empire did weld the British together into a nation, a process which reached its culmination in the two world wars of the twentieth century. They argue against the emphasis which the school of new British history places on the multinational character of the British state. The predominance of England in the Union, and the willingness of the Scots and the Welsh as well as many of the Irish, to be involved in the project of empire meant that so long as the Empire existed there was a tangible meaning to Britishness. In the colonies Britons did not divide up into Scots, English, Welsh and Irish – they were seen simply as British, the citizens and agents of a single state and sharing a single nationality.[38] The cohesion displayed by the British in the wars of the twentieth century was much higher than in other multinational unions, such as the Austro-Hapsburg Empire. The British political identity commanded loyalty in a way that the Austro-Hapsburg identity did not.

All this suggests that whatever they may have been in the beginning, the British state and the British nation became much more than expedient political constructions. They put down popular roots, and in the twentieth century in particular, the experience of two world wars and the establishment of a welfare state led to a high point of Britishness in the 1940s and 1950s.[39] In the twenty-first century there may be doubt and uncertainty now about what the United Kingdom is for and what British identity actually is, but the projects of empire and socialism for a long time gave it substance. If Britishness is in trouble it is because both projects have faltered, and neither the Conservatives nor Labour are any longer very good advocates of them.

The other project, that of British socialism, was associated particularly with British Labour, but aspects of it, particularly collectivist welfare, also became linked to empire, many imperialists arguing that minimum standards of security and welfare for all the citizens of the imperial heartland were essential both to ensure its efficiency and its legitimacy.[40] The model of Germany was important here, as was the example of the collectivist turn in German policy in the 1880s engineered by Bismarck, which tied German military and social policies closely together.[41] But welfare and security also became the defining project of British socialism and of the Labour movement, seeking to redistribute wealth and opportunities, and committed to using the machinery of the centralized British state to create universal welfare programmes, so defining citizenship in social as well as political and civil terms.[42] With the retreat from Empire in the second half of the twentieth century, the welfare state assumed new importance as the decisive bond of Britishness, a common citizenship and shared stake in a centralized system of welfare.

British socialism, however, was severely weakened by Labour's inability to meet the challenges and dislocations of the 1970s, or to find an alternative. It then had to suffer the onslaught of the policies of the Thatcher Government. The welfare state was not dismantled,[43] but it was substantially remodelled, and resources no longer rose in line with needs. By the 1990s it had ceased to be any kind of leading model either for Europe or the rest of the world, and was firmly bracketed with the other liberal, Anglo-American welfare states.[44] After the return of a Labour government in 1997, there was a renewed commitment to universal welfare, but at the same time the constitutional reform programme, and specifically the proposals for devolution, threatened to undermine *British* socialism still further, by making most public services the responsibility of the new devolved governments rather than of the Westminster government. The existence of separate welfare states with varying standards of provision and care became an eventual possibility, even if the divergence at first was expected to be small.[45]

In the last forty years of the twentieth century, the precarious nature of Britishness, and the idea of a British nation came to be recognized. The end of the British Empire and the challenges to British socialism, as well as the pessimism inherent in the interminable debates on decline and what role the UK should play in the world economy, raised the issue of whether Britishness still has a secure meaning. If there is no longer a British project what is the United Kingdom for? Why should its separate nationalities continue to be loyal to the United Kingdom, rather than to a state of their own? During the expansion, the zenith, and even the decline of the British Empire, the advantages which the nationalities obtained from it appeared so great that the multinational character of the British state was regarded as a secondary feature. When the British state was founded it meant that after many centuries the once numerous political jurisdictions in the British Isles had given way to a single state. To the protagonists of Union, convinced of the grandeur of the British project, it seemed incomprehensible that there could be a reversion to separate jurisdictions again.

This however is the prospect which now faces the British state. When it was created four distinct national communities continued to exist. The attempt to weld these into a single new national identity, a British identity, was an essential project of the new state, and the success of the new state breathed life into Britishness. But Britishness has not replaced the older identities, and it is they now that are being reasserted, most obviously in Scotland, as the basis for a different kind of future, some of them outside the old Union. Britishness by contrast has lost much of its old rationale.

Ireland

This process of disengagement from the Union is not new. The secession of Ireland was the first great dent in the Union, the first major contraction of the transnational space which England had created, and which had formed the basis of its long and successful expansion. Defending the Empire against its enemies and maintaining the Union became touchstones of Britishness at the height of British power, and explain the bitterness with which the campaign by the Irish to secede from the Union was fought. The protagonists of the Union believed that only full integration of all parts of the realm into the British state could maintain the integrity of the idea of a United Kingdom and of Britishness. Gladstone proposed Home Rule for Ireland in the 1880s after he came to the conclusion that it offered the only hope of preserving the Union, but the opponents of Home Rule regarded it as the first step towards destroying the Union. If the Irish or anyone else were allowed to define themselves apart from the Westminster Parliament they would seek further self-determination. For the Unionists there could be no compromise. The United Kingdom was defined by the central institutions of the British state, and to be British meant accepting those institutions.[46]

These arguments were to resurface in the debates on devolution to Scotland and Wales in the 1970s and 1990s. The opponents of devolution again urged that to give the Welsh and Scottish nations political self-determination, even in the rather limited forms which were being proposed, would lead to the breakup of the United Kingdom and the end of 'Britain'. Yet Unionists too could support Home Rule under certain circumstances. The refusal of the Sinn Fein MPs elected in 1918 to take their seats in the Westminster Parliament followed by the outbreak of armed rebellion led to the 1920 Government of Ireland Act which made provision for Home Rule Parliaments in the North and South. Republicans boycotted the Parliament in the South, but the Parliament in the North was seized on by the Unionists, because it guaranteed they would not have to join a Dublin Parliament where they would be a minority. The negotiations, which ended military hostilities in 1922 and set up the Irish Free State inside the British Empire, also activated the Government of Ireland Act and established the Parliament in Belfast which became Stormont.[47]

Despite the implacable opposition by Unionism to Home Rule over the previous forty years, the six counties retained under British jurisdiction were therefore given their own version of Home Rule, instead of being integrated fully into the United Kingdom. The Westminster Parliament abandoned the Southern Unionists. The Irish Free State was given Dominion status within the British Empire, which signalled that it was still subordinate to the British Crown; the British retained military and naval bases in Ireland; and the Irish had to accept partition of the country. These conditions meant the Treaty was unacceptable to a large section of Sinn Fein and led to civil war. But it was still de facto independence, which was quickly to become full independence. As such it represented a huge defeat for Unionism and for the idea of the British Empire, and for the continuing expansion of England. It presaged the end of British power and British independence.

The supporters of the Union had always used two key arguments against making any concession to the Irish. The first was a security argument. If Ireland was given any measure of independence it might at some point be used by an enemy as a military base against the UK. In any future war in which the Empire was involved, the UK might have to start by conquering Ireland in order to ensure its security. The second argument was even more important. Giving up Ireland, a key component of the home base of the Empire, meant giving up the idea of empire itself. If England could not hold Ireland, what other part of its Empire could it hold? And what would it mean for the very idea of Britishness? Would it not hasten the day when the United Kingdom would break up, and when even Scotland would leave the Union? As Leo Amery, leading Unionist and imperialist, and later Colonial Secretary, wrote in his diary in January 1913:[48]

> The only thing I regret is that not a soul throughout these debates ever says anything to suggest that he feels that the United Kingdom really is a nation and that Irish nationalism in any shape or form means the end of United Kingdom nationalism. If only a single name could have been invented in 1800 for the United Kingdom and the Vice-Royalty abolished, I don't believe that Home Rule would ever have been considered.

For the Unionists even to consider abandoning Ireland was to consider the end of the Union and the end of the Empire, and the means to preserve England's independence. They took the same view that the Northern States in America had taken of the southern secession in 1861. It had to be contested by force. The Union had to be preserved at all costs if the United States was to survive as a nation and as a state. In 1914 the Conservatives and Unionists were prepared to act unconstitutionally and defy the elected Westminster government by encouraging the Armed Forces to disobey its orders in order to preserve the integrity of the Empire, and the Union of the nations of the British Isles which was its core, by keeping them British.[49] By 1920, however, after world war and the Easter Rising in 1916, the will of the Unionists was weaker. Enough were prepared to accept the compromise of partition, to safeguard the Unionist people of Ulster with a redrawing of the borders to guarantee a permanent Unionist majority, to keep one part of Ireland forever British and part of the Union. The rest of Ireland was allowed to disengage, and subsequently to move outside the Empire and outside the United Kingdom altogether.[50]

The Conservative Unionists could not understand how any of the grievances which the Irish claimed to have could not be solved within the framework of the United Kingdom. What they could not acknowledge was that the majority of the Irish had come to feel no identity with the United Kingdom, and therefore no loyalty to the Empire and the institutions of the British state. The Irish did not accept that they were a British nation, and that the British state was their state. Unionists clung to the idea that the nationalists were only a minority of agitators, not truly representative of the people. Another view, based on what had happened in South Africa, was that in time even the fiercest opponents of the British Empire could be brought to accept its authority, once they had gained concessions for their people within it. It was this that encouraged the hardliners in Unionism to argue that absolutely no concessions should be made even to constitutional nationalists and certainly not to armed rebels. They would have used maximum coercion to hold on to Ireland, in the belief that eventually the rebellion would be crushed, and nationalism rendered harmless, and the Irish reincorporated as full members of the British Empire.[51] Even in 1922 this was not unrealistic. Michael Collins, the first leader of the IRA, believed that the rebellion was on its last legs and would have collapsed if the British had kept up military pressure. But ultimately the moral and political cost of coercion was too great for the British. The political class was not ultimately prepared to be ruthless enough, and did not care enough. It did not give priority to preserving the Empire at any cost. The surrender of Ireland was the first of the long line of surrenders and withdrawals in the twentieth century, punctuated by periods of defiance and resistance, as in Cyprus, Aden, Kenya, and the Falklands, but still proceeding irresistibly towards the final divestiture of all the appurtenances of Empire, culminating in the handover of Hong Kong to China in 1997. A few unreconstructed Unionists and imperialists were still muttering about that even then. They saw absolutely no need to hand British citizens over to China.[52] It was the same state of mind as the young Enoch Powell's when he rushed into Churchill's office in 1947 to tell him how many divisions he would need to reconquer India after it had been granted independence.[53]

In Ireland the experiment with Home Rule in the North lasted fifty years. The public disorder and resumption of the IRA's military campaign in the North after the civil rights marches of the late 1960s led to the suspension of Wtormont in 1972, and, after the collapse of power-sharing between the communities, twenty-seven years of direct rule, until the establishment of a new Northern Ireland Assembly and the formation of a new power-sharing executive in 1999. Throughout the years of direct rule the Westminster government tried repeatedly to devise a political formula which would reconcile nationalists and Unionists and allow Ulster to govern itself. But a significant section of Unionist opinion both in Northern Ireland and in the rest of the UK was always opposed to power-sharing and advocated either the restoration of the Unionist ascendancy, or argued against devolution and power-sharing altogether, on the grounds that they were means by which Northern Ireland would be eased out of the United Kingdom and lose its British connection. They were regarded as signalling that the British government was losing the will to rule, just as the earlier Home Rule proposals had proved in the case of the rest of Ireland. On this robust view, a state like the British state, a political project from its inception, could only be sustained if the political will to rule did not falter. The right of secession could not be conceded without damaging, perhaps irreparably, the right of the state to exist. Since there is no ethnic British nation in the way in which there is a Scottish, or Welsh, or Irish nation, anything which encourages the separate nationalities to think that they no longer need the British state to achieve their central political objectives will undermine it. Irish secession in the 1920s was the first step in a fundamental transformation of the British state which is far from finished.

The British desire to disengage from Ireland altogether if a way could be found, became painfully apparent after the re-emergence of armed conflict. The Stormont Parliament had been left to its own devices for fifty years between 1922 and 1972; Westminster had simply turned a blind eye to the systematic discrimination which was practised against the Catholics by the majority community.[54] Once Westminster was forced to send back troops and then impose direct rule, it was plain that there could be no going back to the old Unionist ascendancy. A solution involving power-sharing between the communities and the involvement of the Irish Government became essential. The British came to recognize that the problem was one of two nations inhabiting the same territory, and that there was no solution other than finding ways in which they could begin to live together in relative peace.[55]

This policy was condemned as surrender by hardline Unionists, who demanded the return of Stormont as a reward for their loyalty to the British Crown. Other more far-sighted Unionists argued that the Unionists' acceptance of Home Rule in 1922 had been a terrible mistake. It had preserved Ulster as a place apart from the rest of the United Kingdom, an isolated province, always vulnerable to renewed nationalist agitation. Enoch Powell argued that the only solution was for Ulster to accept full integration into the United Kingdom, so that Ulster was governed in exactly the same way as Wolverhampton.[56] This might have been achieved at an earlier date, but by the time Powell proposed it as MP for South Down after 1974, it was too late. The Unionists did not want it, and there was no chance the British government would concede it, since it was unacceptable to the nationalist community and to the Irish government. The strategy that was pursued instead culminated in the Anglo-Irish Agreement of 1985 and the Downing Street Declaration. With their customary realism Conservative governments proved ready to talk secretly to the IRA and to establish a framework which admitted openly the possibility of an eventual British withdrawal from Northern Ireland. The most revealing sentence in the Downing Street Declaration spoke of the United Kingdom having no selfish or strategic interest in Northern Ireland. Nicholas Budgen, Enoch Powell's successor in his Wolverhampton seat, asked in Parliament whether the government would ever declare that it had no selfish or strategic interest in Wolverhampton. The British government insisted that the constitutional status of Northern Ireland could only be changed with the consent of a majority of its people, but it accepted that if a majority ever wished to leave the United Kingdom it would not prevent it. Conservative Unionism had conceded defeat. The Union was contingent rather than necessary.[57] The endgame had begun.

Devolution and Self-government

The campaign in the 1970s for measures of self-rule to be given to Scotland and Wales and to be returned to Northern Ireland highlighted the enduring multinational character of the British state. It had never exactly been denied during the long years of Empire, but it had certainly been played down, and only limited concessions, such as the establishment of the Scottish Office in 1885, had been made. What infuriated Unionist opinion within the Conservative Party was that as the devolution campaign developed, the same pattern was present as with Irish Home Rule before 1914. The cause of the nationalist enemies of the Union and of the UK was embraced by a section of opinion within the British political class, which became persuaded that concessions needed to be made to them.

But by the 1990s this debate had encouraged the separate national identities to affirm their separateness rather than their sense of connection. If the United Kingdom is to survive as a single state, it will have to do so as a multinational state rather than as a nation-state. But what makes this difficult is the size and dominance of England relative to Scotland, Wales and Northern Ireland. While the English still tend to use English and British interchangeably and to see themselves as both English and British, growing numbers in Scotland in particular now identify themselves only as Scottish. The reassertion by the Scots of their own identity and national history, has been accompanied by increasing demands that the Scots should reclaim the independent statehood which they gave up three hundred years ago.[58] The argument for breaking away draws fuel from the evident disarray of the projects around the various meanings of Empire which in the past defined what the UK meant and which made it exceptional. The strongest and most vociferous defenders of Britishness tend to be the beleaguered inhabitants of small imperial enclaves like Gibraltar and the Falklands, leftovers from England's imperial past, embarrassments to governments in London, who seek to offload them, but meet passionate resistance. In 1981 the Thatcher Government was negotiating with Argentina to give up sovereignty over the Falklands, and in 2002 the Blair Government put forward proposals to share sovereignty over Gibraltar with Spain. Passionate resistance was encountered in both cases.

The campaign for devolution to Scotland and Wales was however quite unlike the earlier campaign for Irish independence. It was clear from an early stage that England would not resist by force the settled will of the Scottish people if at some stage they chose independence rather than remaining in the Union. The British political class, including the many Scots in its ranks, was very divided as to how to deal with the rise of nationalism in the 1970s. The success of the Scottish nationalists (they achieved 30.4 per cent of the Scottish vote in October 1974, higher than at any time since) encouraged both the Conservatives and Labour to consider devolution, but this was to be mainly administrative devolution, rather than the concession of full home rule and an independent parliament. When Margaret Thatcher became Opposition Leader in 1975 Conservative policy was reversed, and the party led the opposition to the devolution legislation, aided by a significant contingent of Labour rebels.

The key issue for the opponents of devolution was that it threatened to break up the Union, and to destroy the partnership between the nations of the United Kingdom, by making transparent what was best kept mysterious.

Each part of the United Kingdom was already governed in a distinct way; a unitary state on European lines had never been imposed. Unionists were content to live with the anomalies, in the belief that the arrangements were flexible enough to ensure that everyone got a good deal out of the Union, and grievances could be handled. The unity of the whole Kingdom and the confirmation of a *British* citizenship was guaranteed by having a single Parliament whose members were members of the UK Parliament, and therefore able to discuss and vote on all UK matters.[59]

Once that principle was countermanded by the principle of devolving powers and competences to subordinate bodies, the unity of the Kingdom would be lost, and numerous anomalies would arise, such as the 'West Lothian question', first raised by Tom Dalyell, then MP for West Lothian. He asked whether after devolution Scottish MPs at Westminster would have any right to vote on matters that affected only England. What it ignored was that Scotland, Wales and Northern Ireland were already being treated differently by the Westminster Parliament.[60] What devolution did was to expose the asymmetrical relationships between the different parts of the United Kingdom by making them more visible and in this way made them more likely to be contested.

One way to resolve this would have been to propose an explicit federal arrangement between the different parts of the United Kingdom, a new constitutional arrangement embracing England and the English regions as well as the other three nations. In the long run this may become the only way in which the Union can be preserved and Britain sustained. But in the short run the Blair Government has chosen to proceed in a piecemeal and pragmatic fashion, in the long-established tradition of the British state, pursuing a statecraft that recognizes diversity in the territories over which it rules, the better to preserve its autonomy and authority.[61]

Devolution, however, is much more than just a patched up Union. It challenges the principles on which the British state has been based for three hundred years. The most significant development in this respect has been the changes in the way Scotland is governed. The initial proposals brought forward by the Callaghan Government were defeated because although a majority in Scotland voted in favour, the threshold of 40 per cent of the electorate in favour, which anti-devolution MPs had succeeded in including in the bill, was not reached. Shortly afterwards, the Callaghan Government was defeated in the 1979 general election, and this ended any immediate prospect for devolution because the Thatcher Government believed that the best way of preserving the Union was to rule out all talk of devolution. The difficulty with this strategy was that to work it needed the Conservatives to regain the kind of support they had enjoyed in

Scotland in the 1950s. Instead Conservative support continued to fall, and this contributed to the widespread perception in Scotland that the Thatcher Government was an English government for which the Scots had not voted. This led directly to further erosion of the Conservative vote in Scotland, and to a new surge in support for devolution. The catalyst proved to be the Scottish Convention established in 1989 which brought together all elements of non-Conservative opinion in Scotland, including for a time the Scottish Nationalists. The issuing by the Convention of a Claim of Right asserted that the Scots were ready to re-establish their Parliament which had been suspended by the Treaty of Union in 1707. The Convention made a claim of sovereignty for the Scottish people ('We the People') which had never been relinquished and which it now proposed to take back.[62] Like all other modern constitutions, the Claim of Right asserted that sovereignty rested directly in the people rather than in Parliament, something which had never been conceded in England.

The Liberal Democrats were united behind the demands for the restoration of the Scottish Parliament, but the Scottish Labour Party was divided. In the end, however, opinion moved decisively to embrace it, in part because of the unchallenged supremacy of the Conservatives at Westminster. Scotland with its fifty Labour MPs (almost 25 per cent of the parliamentary Labour Party in 1983) became Labour's main stronghold during the Thatcher years. The commitment to devolution became a central plank of Labour's new programme, first under Neil Kinnock and then under John Smith. By the time that Tony Blair became Labour leader in 1994, he could not have changed the policy even had he wished. The legacy of John Smith to the Labour Party was the strong commitment to constitutional reform, and to this was now added the attempt to forge an anti-Conservative alliance between Labour and the Liberal Democrats, and to reunite the centre left of British politics.[63]

The new agreement about the need for constitutional reform forged in the Scottish Convention and advanced by campaigning groups such as Charter 88 and by think-tanks such as the Institute for Public Policy Research (IPPR)[64] was the background for the establishment of a joint Committee by Labour and the Liberal Democrats before the 1997 election to discuss constitutional reform. Most of the proposals of this committee found their way into the Labour Party Manifesto, and the proposals to hold referendums on establishing a Scottish Parliament and a Welsh Assembly were high on the list of priorities.

For many of the people involved in this programme it represented the re-emergence of the Liberal agenda for constitutional reform at the end of the nineteenth century, unfinished business of an earlier radicalism. The reforms proposed in the Labour Manifesto were considered by many of the constitutional reformers only a first step.[65] After all, Gladstone had wanted Home Rule all round, and although Scotland was to be given a Parliament, Wales had to be content with an Assembly, while England was to receive nothing at all. Nevertheless, the changes introduced were a significant step towards the long-standing Liberal hope of a federal Britain. The Scottish referendum delivered a clear mandate for change, 75 per cent vote in favour on a 60 per cent turnout. In Wales the referendum vote was much tighter, and in the end only a bare majority was secured. But the results meant that legislation was passed to establish the new devolved institutions.

Nobody supposed, however, that the reforms would rest there, especially since so many anomalies were created by the legislation. There was for a start the difference in powers between the Welsh Assembly and the Scottish Parliament, the lack of any powers for the English regions, and the question of the representation of Wales and Scotland at Westminster, now that so many powers were devolved. Many wondered also about the point of retaining a Scottish Secretary and a Welsh Secretary in the Cabinet, now that there was a Scottish First Minister and a Welsh First Minister. It was also unclear what should be the precise demarcation of powers between Westminster and the devolved bodies and who should adjudicate in the event of any disputes. Most sensitive of all was the Treasury rule known as the Barnett formula first devised in the 1970s to determine how resources should be distributed between the different parts of the UK, and which by the 1990s meant that Scotland was receiving on average 20 per cent more per capita public spending than English regions, some of which had lower per capita income.[66]

All these questions raised important constitutional issues and the ways in which they are resolved will be important for the future of British politics. In their early years the devolved institutions encountered many problems and considerable media mockery, but they gradually became established. Polls showed Scottish voters were dissatisfied and disillusioned with their Parliament in the early years, and turnout at the second Scottish Parliament Election, held in 2003, fell but only a very small minority wanted it abolished.[67] In the future it seemed inevitable that pressure would build for greater powers to be given to the Parliament rather than less, and that the example set by Scotland would be copied by Wales and the English regions. The White Paper on regionalism in 2002 opened the possibility for referendums in those English regions which wished them, to test support for the creation of regional assemblies. In this piecemeal and evolutionary manner the United Kingdom appeared to be edging towards a new federal constitution, in which powers were formally decentralized, and the preservation of the old constitutional principle of undivided sovereignty was being laid to rest.

4

The Empire Within

> Under a condition of universal free trade, the dream of the
> sixties of the last century, industrial life and empire might be
> dissociated, but when competing countries seek to monopolise
> markets by means of customs tariffs, even democracies are
> compelled to annex empires. In the last two generations . . . the
> object of vast British annexations has been to support a trade
> open to all the world.
>
> Halford Mackinder, 1902[1]

The second circle of England is *Greater* Britain, and in particular the
British Empire, the vast overseas territories which were acquired over the
course of three centuries and then surrendered within the space of three
decades. This is the circle which appears least visible today, but whose
legacies still throw a long shadow across British politics. It is the weakening of Empire that has undermined the Union as well as throwing into stark
relief the choice between Europe and America for the future of British politics.

The rulers of England had long thought of their realm as an empire, an
imperium. But this empire has passed through several distinct phases. The
first was the Empire which the Norman and Plantagenet kings established
through conquest and dynastic alliance across England and France after
1066 and which finally fell apart irretrievably in the Hundred Years War in
the fourteenth and fifteenth centuries. The second was the British Union
itself for which the Norman Kings established the foundations, by annex-
ing Wales and most of Ireland. They failed to consummate it, however,
because of their inability to conquer Scotland, and success was only finally
achieved much later, following the union of Crowns in 1603 and the union
of Parliaments in 1707. The third phase of Empire was based on the
colonies on the eastern seaboard of North America, but this Empire
foundered when the colonies rose in rebellion and seceded from Great
Britain and from the British Crown at the end of the War of Independence

in 1783. The focus of British attention then moved to India and to Africa, which became the heart of the fourth phase of Empire through the nineteenth and twentieth centuries. This empire, the British Empire, was dubbed the expansion of England, but it was also an expansion of the multinational British Isles.[2] At its greatest extent in the 1920s and 1930s it spread over one-quarter of the earth's land surface and contained one-fifth of its population.[3] By the end of the twentieth century little was left.[4] A loose association of former colonies in the Commonwealth and a miscellaneous collection of territories, some with no resident population, were all that remained of four hundred years of expansion; Anguilla, Bermuda, the British Antarctic Territory, the British Indian Ocean Territory, the British Virgin Islands, the Cayman Islands, the Falkland Islands, Gibraltar, Montserrat, Pitcairn Island, St Helena, South Georgia, the Turks and Caicos Islands. These thirteen territories had a combined population in 2000 of less than two hundred thousand people, enough to fill two medium-sized English towns.

If the circle of Empire has shrunk so much in the last fifty years, does the Empire matter any more in British politics? The answer is that it still seems to matter a great deal. The late nineteenth century view of Empire may have lasted a relatively short period of time, but during that time it was extraordinarily intense, unlike earlier ideas of Empire which were much more narrowly focused and which excited much less passion. The Victorian conception of Empire by contrast touched every aspect of Bvitish life, and many English and British institutions and traditions were remodelled or invented to fit in with it.[5] Empire for more than a century was the most important transnational space inhabited by the British and it had a profound impact on British politics, particularly on the way British people thought about race, and about the role of the British state in the world.

Race and Empire

One of the most important legacies of Empire was that it redefined ideas of Englishness and Britishness by giving them explicit racial associations. The superiority of Anglo-Saxon racial stock over other Europeans, but particularly over all the different racial groups in the Empire became a central motif of imperialist writing and propaganda, and was reproduced endlessly in popular culture, through music-hall songs, novels, poems, newspapers, comics, and later, films. The Atlantic trade in African slaves (twenty million were transported from Africa to the Americas of whom it is estimated two million died in transit)[6] and the extermination of other races, such as the Native Americans in North America, were often justified on the grounds that these peoples belonged to inferior racial stock. Popularizations of eugenics and evolutionary theory contributed to an obsession with racial stereotypes, and to the belief that the English (and therefore the British) belonged to a superior race, the bearers of a higher civilization and therefore entitled to rule over lesser species.

These racial conceptions of identity at the popular level were combined for the governing class with the doctrine of the white man's burden and the idea of trusteeship.[7] The particular genius claimed for the English was the capacity to rule over less favoured races, a gift bestowed on them by God. The English (which included all the British nationalities) were a people endowed like the Romans with a genius for government, and their imperial policy was motivated by the desire to spread the arts of self-government throughout the world.[8] The British political class, steeped in Latin and Greek, liked nothing better than to imagine themselves as modern Romans, shouldering the burdens of government, keeping the flame of civilization lit, and the barbarians from the gates. Other races could be gradually led towards civilization and eventually would be ready for self-government. But that was envisaged as a very long way into the future, and in the meantime the subordinate status of other races daily reminded the English of their superior status.

This strong racial component to English and therefore to British identity is not solely a product of Empire, but the experience of Empire did a great deal to reinforce it, and to entrench racial attitudes in the United Kingdom. The expansion of the European Empires to cover the whole globe was presented as a struggle between races.[9] Racial theorists proclaimed that the Teutonic race and in particular its Anglo-Saxon offshoot was the highest racial group yet to have evolved, and that in the struggle with other races it was only natural that weaker races should go under; only the socially efficient races would survive and would deserve to survive. Once all other races had been subjugated, the white races themselves would fight it out for supremacy. The conviction of innate racial superiority meant that at the end of the nineteenth century Englishmen regarded themselves as belonging to a more excellent type than other men, and possessing an unchallengeable right to rule.[10]

But another legacy of the Empire has provided the means for these racial attitudes to be challenged, and for a rethinking of the notion of Britishness itself. There has been a long radical British tradition of opposition to racism, drawing on Christian beliefs in fundamental human equality, and exemplified in the nineteenth century by the successful campaign against the slave trade and support for the anti-slavery side in the American Civil

War, as well as support for anti-colonial movements and struggles. But this opposition to racism and to empire tended to be exercised at a distance. The problems of racism came nearer home with the immigration of large numbers of Black and Asian people into the UK from the 1950s onwards, a development which has had profound effects on the racial composition of many British cities, and has forced the issue of a multicultural society on to the political agenda.[11] The Empire was always something far away, something which the British imposed on less favoured races far from British shores. But with the arrival of the immigrants the Empire came home.

The United Kingdom had had waves of immigrants before, particularly Protestants from Europe such as the French Huguenots, and Jews from Eastern Europe,[12] as well as large numbers of Irish needed to build the railways and the towns of the Victorian era.[13] The Union meant that many Scots and Welsh as well as Irish also moved to England. The nationalities remained distinct, however, and this was particularly true of the Irish. Although after 1801 they were full members of the United Kingdom, it was a sign of the problems to come that they were not seen as British, full members of a 'British' nation, with equal rights of citizenship, but as aliens, with an inferior status.

Apart from the Irish, most other groups, including the Scots and the Welsh, were successfully assimilated. The immigrants from the Caribbean and from India and Pakistan were different, partly because of their colour, partly because of their culture, and partly because they came from countries which the United Kingdom had recently ruled or in some cases was still ruling. Having exported their fellow-citizens for so many centuries to the far corners of the globe, the British now found the tables reversed.

It is still one of the great puzzles of British politics in the last fifty years why this was allowed to happen. The United Kingdom was a relatively homogenous and a very white society. There were large differences between the rural shires (the traditional heartland of England) and the industrial cities where the bulk of the population now lived. But within the urban areas there was a remarkably uniform and solid working-class culture and community. It was destroyed within the space of a few decades.[14] The arrival of black immigrants was not the only cause, but it was a major one, and moreover it was one which was in the power of the state to prevent.

The reason it was not prevented was partly economic. In common with other European economies growing rapidly in the 1950s and 1960s the British economy needed to increase the supply of labour, and bringing in young, enterprising, and able black people was the easiest and most efficient way to plug the gaps.[15] But the other reason was political. The vision of Empire which had taken such a hold on the British imagination meant that many in the political class were swayed by the idea that the Empire should provide a new form of international citizenship. Just as the Romans had extended citizenship in their Empire allowing many of their subjects to declare that they were Roman citizens, *civis Romanus sum*, with appropriate rights and duties, so the British political class was taken with the idea of a universal British citizenship, so that its subjects too could declare *civis Britannicus sum*.

If all citizens of the Empire enjoyed British citizenship under the Crown, however, did they not have the right to move freely around the Empire and to enter the United Kingdom? One of the main benefits of citizenship had to be free movement, so that when serious immigration from the Caribbean and from India and Pakistan began in the 1950s, it was at first unrestricted. Immigrants that came either from the existing colonies or the former colonies automatically received British citizenship.[16]

As numbers increased a new question of identity came to be posed. Were Englishness and Britishness synonymous with Whiteness? Was Englishness one culture or could it embrace many cultures? Concern about immigration grew rapidly in the areas that were most affected, mainly working-class inner-city areas, and right-wing politicians were soon raising the alarm. Concerted pressure in the Conservative Party led to the first major legislation to control the flow of immigrants, the Commonwealth Immigrants Act of 1962.[17] Despite denials, the aim of this act was to control black and Asian immigration from the New Commonwealth. The white Commonwealth of the old Dominions and the last outposts of white civilization in Africa were 'kith and kin' and largely exempt from the new measures. This position could not be sustained, however, and as political pressure for more drastic restrictions mounted, so the 1962 Act was followed at regular intervals by further and each time more draconian measures to define British nationality ever more tightly, culminating in the British Nationality Act of 1981.[18] By this time all special protection for kith and kin had disappeared, and one of the aims of the Act was to remove any entitlement to residence in the United Kingdom from the citizens of Hong Kong, anticipating the time (sixteen years in the future) when the British concession on Hong Kong would expire and Hong Kong would revert to Chinese sovereignty. To achieve this the Bill was drafted in a way which put the final nail in the ideal of an imperial citizenship, by denying citizenship rights to the residents of all remaining dependencies, including the Falkland Islands. This was to prove embarrassing the following year when Argentina invaded the islands in pursuit of its sovereignty claim and the British state went to war on behalf of 1800 Falkland Islanders whom until then it had not been willing to make full citizens of the United Kingdom. The position had to be changed after the war.

The tightening of British immigration rules and the new definition of nationality brought the UK into line with most other countries, although curious anomalies remained, such as the right of Irish citizens living in the UK to register and vote in UK elections. Even after the Irish had broken all formal ties this right was still not rescinded. The English only very reluctantly gave up the idea of Greater Britain and the wider citizenship which it was intended to promote. Against these imperial dreams of a loose association of peoples under the British Crown and the Westminster Parliament a new breed of hardheaded nationalists emerged, of whom Enoch Powell was the most charismatic and outspoken.[19] Powell had formerly been a passionate imperialist and in love with Empire, but once the spell was broken with the granting of independence to India and Pakistan and their subsequent decision to become Republics, Powell emerged as an unsentimental English nationalist who argued that nationality should be tightly drawn and that too much cultural diversity undermined national identity and with it the legitimacy of a state.

Powell saw himself as a cultural nationalist, not a racist (the same could not be said for many of his followers). In his most famous political intervention in 1968 he argued strongly against the policy of allowing black and Asian immigration: 'Those whom the gods wish to destroy they first make mad: We must be mad, literally mad, as a nation to be permitting the annual inflow of some 50 000 dependants, who are for the most part the material of the future growth of the immigrant-descended population. It is like watching a nation busily engaged in heaping up its own funeral pyre.'[20] Numbers he argued were the heart of the problem, and quoted the views of a constituent: 'In this country in fifteen or twenty years time the black man will have the whip hand over the white man'.[21] Powell advocated a complete halt to any further black or Asian immigration and schemes of voluntary repatriation with cash payments to persuade immigrants already here to return to their countries of origin. If this were not done, he warned, there would be deepening racial conflict and racial disturbances on the scale of the United States: 'As I look ahead I am filled with foreboding. Like the Roman I seem to see "the river Tiber foaming with much blood".'[22] A multicultural UK was not only undesirable but a recipe for division and conflict. Immigrants would never be *English*: 'The West Indian or Asian does not, by being born in England, become an Englishman. In law he becomes a United Kingdom citizen by birth; in fact he is a West Indian or Asian still. ... With the lapse of a generation or so we shall at last have succeeded – to the benefit of nobody – in reproducing in "England's green and pleasant land" the haunting tragedy of the United States.'[23] The homogeneity of the British and the British identity would be lost forever, and with it one of the crucial bulwarks of the British state.

The agitation which Powell helped to fan succeeded for a time in slowing new immigration from any quarter to a trickle, including from some of the most loyal British communities in the world. But his other policy, of voluntary repatriation was only taken up by the far right. The ethnic communities grew steadily and by the end of the twentieth century had become an established and permanent feature of Britain, comprising ten per cent of the population and making Britain a multicultural and multiethnic society. This was one of the least anticipated but most far-reaching legacies of Empire.

There were those in all parties who continued to oppose it as best they could. Legislation to outlaw racial discrimination and the establishment of the Race Relations Commission were mocked in the right-wing press as establishing a 'race relations industry' and later as 'politically correct', but gradually a framework of rights and rules was put in place, which suppressed the cruder kinds of racism in British public life, and began to expose more deep-rooted forms of institutional racism, in a range of institutions from political parties to the police. The need to establish policies to promote ethnic diversity through employment practices, school curricula, and celebration of different cultures began to be recognized, although there have been lively debates about how far tolerance of different cultures should go, if tolerance means condoning practices that infringe universal rights of British citizenship.[24] Aspects of the treatment of women in Islamic communities and the curriculum of faith schools have been particular concerns.

The overcoming of the centuries-long tradition of racial and imperial attitudes was always likely to be slow, and was subject to periodic setbacks, as well as occasional outbursts from politicians such as Norman Tebbit who proposed an assimilation test for the ethnic communities – did they support the *English* cricket team or the team from their country of origin? For politicians like Tebbit only those prepared to define themselves as English deserved citizenship (it was difficult to know where ethnic minorities in Scotland, let alone the Scots themselves fitted in Tebbit's map – were Scots required to support the English cricket team too?). This attitude to nation-building was of course commonplace elsewhere – but rarely so in England. It was another sign of the confusion about what being British meant, and what steps the state should take to ensure that every citizen was brought up to be British. The obvious problem was that so much of British identity as it had been taught to the English was associated with Empire, wars, conquest, slavery, and the supremacy of Europe, Christianity and the white race. Finding different narratives of Britishness, and still more of Englishness, which did not exclude those who identify themselves as black British, has been no easy matter. Gradually however they are beginning to emerge, with sport, fashion and music as the leading catalysts.[25]

The Expansion of England

England was already an Empire and an expansionist power before the Act of Union with Scotland, but the securing of these islands against foreign penetration and anti-English alliances gave a great boost to the single-minded pursuit of expansion. This expansion was at first more about over-seas estates and commerce rather than about political rule. Nevertheless the profit which came from it and the success of the British in engaging in it was so great that it could not be ignored, and the political dimensions and consequences of England's increasingly extensive possessions soon emerged.

In the nineteenth century this expansion became the story of the British Empire because the Empire was the most obvious expression of the success of the British Union. When John Seeley wrote his famous book on Empire, he called it *The Expansion of England*.[26] England here included Scotland, Wales, and even Ireland. It was the expansion of the United Kingdom that Seeley was concerned with, his term for which was England. This kind of history made much of the insignificance and remoteness of England before the sixteenth century, compared with its greatness and expanding power since.

Seeley and the thousands of others who painstakingly constructed the narrative of Empire in the nineteenth and first half of the twentieth century, wanted above all to demonstrate that what made England an exceptional state and a great state was precisely its ability first to secure, then to hold its Empire. This history was one of military conquests followed by the creation of new systems of administration and government for the new territories. Empire brought great wealth and power to England, but it also brought great responsibilities. The imperial doctrine emphasized that it was the duty of the British political class to discharge those responsibilities.

The 'expansion of England' is marked by a roll-call of great battles and victories, and therefore also of great heroes. Like the textbooks of other nations British imperial textbooks ignored defeats, particularly those inflicted by France, and concentrated on victories (the one defeat always included is the Battle of Hastings). The more adventurous (and less scrupulous) histories were prepared to find 'English' patriots as far back as Queen Boadicea, King Arthur, and King Alfred. The code here was not hard to decipher. Anyone who resisted the imposition of external power and who was in some way 'rooted' in native soil was fit for inclusion in the Pantheon. Opponents of the Norman invaders like King Harold and Hereward the Wake were also suitable. But all this somehow assumed that Boadicea and Arthur represented the same unchanging *Volk* as Harold and Hereward. The difficulty in all such nationalist accounts was that at some point they had to make the leap to embracing the Normans as English, even though the Norman Kings and their court went on speaking French until the fifteenth century.[27] Even those kings later woven into the national myth like Henry II, Edward I, Edward III, the Black Prince, and Henry V were 'Norman' rather than 'English' in their primary identity and allegiances. As has been pointed out, William the Conqueror should really appear in English history books under his Norman and less flattering name of 'Gillaume le Bâtard'.[28] Many of the Plantagenet Kings spent more of their reigns in France than they did in England, and their French possessions and their position in the French feudal order often mattered more to them than their English possessions. That has not prevented some of the battles in which the English were victorious becoming celebrated as great national victories – Crécy, Poitiers, Agincourt. The defeats were seldom mentioned; indeed it would be hard to know from reading English history school textbooks of a certain vintage that England lost the Hundred Years War, and that it was this event in the fifteenth century which finally broke the connection between the English and French landowning classes, and made possible the development of an independent kingdom under the Tudors.

Seeley himself does not dissent from this. For him the crucial period of nation-building emerges after two key turning points in English history: the end of the Hundred Years Wars over the French succession, and the internal bloodletting of the Wars of the Roses. The emergence of the Tudor dynasty which ruled England through the sixteenth century is a key building block making possible England's later success. The two defining moments in that century are 1532 and 1588, the English Reformation and the Defeat of the Spanish Armada. By turning England into a Protestant state and resisting (somewhat fortunately) invasion from Catholic Spain, the leading military power in Europe in the sixteenth century, the real foundations of the later national myth were laid.

All this of course predated any union between England and Scotland. During England's long embroilment in French dynastic and territorial quarrels, Scotland was able to preserve its independence. The victory at Bannockburn in 1314 proved decisive for Scotland. The incorporation of all other land in these islands under the English Crown was achieved, the Welsh and Irish defeated and subjugated. But Scotland managed to resist. The consequence was that alone of the different national groups within these islands the Scots were able to negotiate the terms of their union with England. The union was formed in two stages, the Union of the Crowns in 1603, followed by the Union of the Parliaments in 1707. From the perspective of Empire the most important feature of the Union was the increased security which it eventually brought, but for a long time it was also a source of disunity and conflict, as a result of the constant struggles to establish a single source of authority in the three kingdoms, a single legitimate dynasty, and a single religion. The Stuart Kings were kings of England, Scotland and Ireland, and this composite monarchy was beset throughout the seventeenth century by conflicts within and between the three kingdoms.[29]

In England the seventeenth century was also dominated by the battle between Crown and Parliament for political supremacy. The issue was intertwined with religion and the Protestant ascendancy. The settlement of 1689 decided both, the first in favour of Parliament, the second in favour of the established Anglican Church. The preoccupation with internal conflicts however did not prevent the steady development of England through the seventeenth century. The military prowess of Cromwell, the successful implantation of English colonies in North America, wars against the Dutch and the French, as well as the quickening pace of intellectual discovery and experimentation were all signs of growing English power. Many historians have seen the reorganization of the state under Cromwell, particularly the transformation of the navy, as particularly significant for later developments.[30]

After 1689 the expansion of England begins in earnest. The Act of Settlement in 1701 settled the succession on the Electors of Hanover and therefore confirmed both the Protestant ascendancy and the subordination of the Monarch to Parliament. The choice of who was to sit on the throne was too important to be left to a genetic lottery. George I was fifty-eighth in line to the throne,[31] but he fitted the job description well enough. Meanwhile the conclusion of the Union with Scotland in 1707 which protected England's northern frontier, opened the way for the Scots to become full participants end collaborators in the expansion of England through the British Empire.[32] The pace of British trade and colonization now quickened and in the wars with France in the middle of the eighteenth century Great Britain emerged victorious, acquiring a dominant position in both India and Canada.

The unbroken ascent of the new British state was checked by the rebellion of the North American colonies, and their departure from British rule in 1783. But these events were soon to be overshadowed by the struggle with revolutionary and Napoleonic France, from which Great Britain ultimately emerged victorious. Two of its military victories, Trafalgar in 1805 and Waterloo in 1815, loomed large ever afterwards in the British political imagination, and provided Britain's two leading military heroes for the modern era, Nelson and Wellington. Victory against Napoleon ensured for the United Kingdom after 1815 a dominant position in the international state system, through the extent of its colonial possessions, the strength of its navy, and the vigour of its commerce. This was to be transformed into a still more powerful position by the impact of the new industries on British wealth. By the middle of the nineteenth century the British economy had a technological lead over other nations which gave it industrial and financial supremacy within the world system.[33]

It was this position of dominance and leadership maintained throughout the nineteenth century which gave rise to the interpretation of British history as the smooth and largely uninterrupted growth in the powers and capacities of the state which the internal Union and external Empire had created – the United Kingdom. This successful 'national' history came to form one of the main strands of Britishness, emphasizing the military and colonial prowess of the British state and celebrating a political class which was small and aristocratic (the Upper Ten Thousand)[34] rooted in landownership, and closely connected with the land and with the established institutions of the state such as the Church, the Law, the Army and the Navy. The idea of Empire, along with the Union, became closely associated at this time with the Conservative Party, appealing as it did both to ideals and to interest. Maintaining and strengthening the Empire was regarded as not just the best protection of British prosperity and British security, but also the best way to promote British values and to civilize the world.[35]

The Imperial Idea was not confined to Conservatives. By the end of the nineteenth century it had invaded all parties. The civilizing mission of the British in the world appealed to many Liberals and some Socialists, conscious of the huge responsibilities as well as opportunities of governing one-quarter of the world's land area. Empire could not be wished away, and although the older expedient attitude to the colonies, which saw them as foreign estates intended to contribute to national wealth, never entirely disappeared, it was now supplemented by high-flown notions of imperial service and the white man's burden.

The need to organize the Empire and defend it against its enemies put the emphasis on efficiency and order, and gave rise to the doctrines of social imperialism. For social imperialists the interests of the state had to come before the individual; they were strongly opposed to laissez-faire and free trade, and in their attitude to welfare and state intervention had much in common with the new and more statist forms of liberalism and socialism which were emerging at the beginning of the twentieth century.[36] The veneration which was given to the idea of public service by the existence of the Empire was an important factor in encouraging the rise of collectivist attitudes towards the state in the twentieth century, which many Liberals and Socialists were only too happy to endorse. The model for many British public services in the twentieth century, including the early nationalized industries, was military and imperial, emphasizing hierarchy, discipline, and precision.[37]

In the twentieth century the story of Empire was further embellished, and the ideology of Empire reached a new intensity with the annual commemorations of the war dead and the institution of such events as Empire Day. The two world wars saw the Empire united in a common cause and common sacrifice as never before, but because the wars drained British financial strength they undermined British power and exposed the problems of sustaining the Empire.[38] It also led directly to the rise of the United States. The First World War was judged harshly in retrospect for its enormous human cost, and the pointlessness of the slaughter. But at the time it was enthusiastically supported by imperialist opinion, as a struggle to the end to defend the British Empire, for which no sacrifice was too great. Imperialists welcomed the contribution of so many countries of the Empire to the imperial war effort as binding the Empire together in ways they had always wanted, just as they welcomed the collective organization which had to be imposed to win the war as ending laissez-faire and the liberal cosmopolitanism of earlier times. War strengthened Britishness, and reaffirmed that it was military conflict which was its essential core, by making the idea of a British nation and an imperial Commonwealth of nations more tangible.[39]

But although the First World War in one sense consolidated the idea of Empire, helping to freeze British life into patterns from which it only began to break free in the last third of the twentieth century, its legacy was also ambivalent for the imperial cause. The great battles of the First World War, although dwarfing in scale anything in which the British had been involved before, could not be woven into the imperial story as easily as earlier battles had been. There were no decisive victories, only vast and indeterminate engagements like the Battle of the Somme, whose costs in terms of the number of lives lost and the dissipation of British strength seemed to outweigh by a considerable margin the benefits of emerging victorious.[40] The war was won, but it exposed the limits of the Empire on which the sun never set. And there were consequences too which could not be disguised; the secession of Ireland was the first great crack in the imperial structure since the loss of the American colonies; and these American colonies were now in the ascendancy. Naval superiority, on which the expansion of England had depended, would never be restored. The United States now insisted on parity with the Empire. More serious still were the threats to the Empire's financial and industrial supremacy, both of which were now passing inexorably to the United States.[41]

The Second World War completed the undermining. It was the last great war England was to fight as an Empire, and although once more the Empire emerged victorious, and Britain itself was spared invasion, it was again at a very high cost – the Empire was gravely weakened, parts of it overrun, and the legitimacy of British rule brought into question. At the same time British financial resources were exhausted. The outcome of the war also signalled the emergence of the United States as the leading power in the international state system, and it was immediately clear that the United States was not prepared to support indefinitely the continuance of the British Empire. Without its Empire the future of the British state would be uncertain, and the need for reassessment of its relationships with both Europe and America pressing. Britain's place in the world would be very different from what it had been.

Much of this was obvious, but was also ignored by many in the British political class, partly because the Second World War had an extremely conservative effect on the British state. It appeared to vindicate the stories of Empire and its expansion which the British had for so long been telling themselves. Unlike the First World War, the Second World War provided a potent addition to the national story, because it helped reinforce some of its dominant motifs. 'England' with its back to the wall and facing Germany alone had survived, and continued to fight, in time orchestrating an alliance which had destroyed Hitler. It quickly came to rank with the defeat of the Armada and the defeat of Napoleon in the national myth, even if like them there was some selective retelling of the story.[42] The problem, which imperialists had painfully to acknowledge, was that it was also the end of Empire. The withdrawal was orderly and spread over twenty-five years, but by 1970 almost everything had gone. Churchill declared in 1940 that even if the British Empire lasted a thousand years, men would still say, this was their finest hour.[43] But the British Empire had only a few hours left. Even Churchill could not have imagined how few.

Patriotism and Empire

Empire made London the imperial capital, the nerve centre of the far-flung colonial network, and the principal site within the Empire for its administration and coordination, and the distribution of patronage and resources. Large numbers had to be recruited for the imperial service, as soldiers, sailors, administrators, and many more were encouraged to emigrate and become settlers in the new Dominions. Direct experience of the Empire in some form became a factor in the lives of a large proportion of the British people, and indirect experience became that of everyone. If they did not have direct experience of the Empire themselves, there was likely to be a family member who did have such experience, and many families came to have members who were living or travelling in different parts of the Empire.

London was transformed by degrees from a national capital to an imperial capital; its Parliament became an imperial Parliament and Queen Victoria added the title of Empress of India to her many titles. Three of her successors were crowned Emperor as well as King, the last being George VI in 1936. To the medieval honours of English chivalry and the titles of the landed aristocracy were added new honours – the Order of the British Empire, with its various grades – OBE, CBE, MBE. It is a mark of how slowly Britain changes that these honours are still awarded with ritual solemnity every year, even though the Empire to which it refers no longer exists.

The physical layout of the capital was consciously remodelled to reflect the experience of Empire: the two great processional routes from Buckingham Palace through the Mall and Horseguards Parade to Whitehall and Westminster Abbey, and from Buckingham Palace through the Mall, Admiralty Arch, Trafalgar Square, the Strand, Fleet Street, Ludgate Circus to St Paul's and the City of London for grand state occasions, the renaming of squares, the numerous statues of long-forgotten generals and admirals, the Commissions and Embassies of the white Dominions clustered around Trafalgar Square, the memorials in St Paul's Cathedral to British seapower, the great Victorian government offices, grandest of all the Foreign Office, the Cenotaph in Whitehall, scene of the annual Remembrance parade, and the Palace of Westminster itself, built in its modern form in the nineteenth century.

Apart from this physical remodelling of London as an imperial capital, Empire also had an important effect on the alignments of British party politics. It helped redefine the meaning of patriotism, and divided political opinion into supporters and critics of the Empire. At first it was often the party of the smaller landowners, the Tory squires, who were most opposed to endless imperial adventures because of their cost, whereas the great Whig grandees, the party of commerce and colonization, pressed for further explorations and acquisitions to be undertaken. As late as 1852 Benjamin

Disraeli was expressing in a private letter sentiments widely shared in his party that these 'wretched' colonies were 'a millstone round our necks'.[44] But with the defeat of protectionism and the onset of competition between the European empires, the Conservatives transformed themselves into the party of Empire, of annexation, of imperial grandeur and derided their opponents in the Liberal Party as radicals, pacifists, cosmopolitans, and Little Englanders.[45] Retrospectively they identified the Empire with British naval prowess and the long history of expansion. Many Liberals by contrast came to see the Empire as an engine for military conquest, the enemy of free trade, and the creature of the aristocratic and military classes who used it to drain the state of resources and were forever embarking on unnecessary and costly wars.[46]

By the twentieth century the British state had become one with the British Empire as far as Conservatives were concerned, and the imperial idea the most important idea in British politics, marking a clear dividing line between Conservatives and Liberals, and still more between Conservatives and Socialists. But what the Empire also did, as will be explored in Chapter 8, was to shift the Conservatives for a long period towards collectivism and an enthusiasm for state intervention. This was partly in reaction to the laissez-faire doctrines of nineteenth century liberalism, but it was also in recognition of the need for a much more interventionist state to improve the health, education and well-being of the working class, and because of the appeal of the ethos of public service and the public good to the imperial mind.[47] Such policies were needed to try and counter the appeal of socialism to the masses, and also because an unhealthy and ill-educated working class gravely damaged the ability of the Empire to defend itself and compete with other empires. Social imperialists supported both economic protection and social reform and believed that only by combining the two might the threat of socialism be averted.[48]

Given the strength of the agitation for democracy, the narrow basis of the old parliamentary franchise could no longer be defended, yet to many Conservatives the authority of the state over the masses seemed precarious. Their response was to stress the need to rally patriotic opinion around the defence of King and Empire, and to protect the rights of property while sanctioning an expansion of the state to fund welfare programmes to provide reasonable security for the working class. At the climax of Empire the Conservatives succeeded in fusing the British Empire and the established order of the state into a single ideological and institutional matrix, which they intended to defend against the gathering armies of the proletariat outside it, but also hoped to divide the proletariat and enrol a large part of it in defence of the Empire.[49] But what was clear to all imperialists was that the Liberal era was over, and the future of England would be decided by a fight to the finish between imperialists and socialists.[50]

What the Liberal opponents of Empire most decried in the imperial creed was its militarism and the way in which the Empire helped diffuse militaristic values throughout society. One prominent leading Liberal writer, John Hobson, called 'Pax Britannica' an impudent falsehood; it had bred almost constant imperial wars and an arms race with the other European empires; and it was associated with oligarchy, racism, nationalism, protectionism, bureaucracy, and monopoly. But what he most disliked about Empire was the way it had changed British politics by filling up the South of England with a rentier class: 'The South of England is full of men of local influence in politics and society whose character has been formed in our despotic empire, and whose incomes are chiefly derived from the maintenance and furtherance of this despotic rule'.[51] In this he echoed Cobden and a long line of English radicals. But even within the Liberal Party this point of view was far from universal. Many Liberals supported the Empire, and the notion of its civilizing mission, the Liberal Prime Minister, Rosebery, calling it 'the greatest secular agency for good the world has ever seen'.[52]

The State and the Empire

The significance of the Empire in British politics can also be observed through the lineaments of the state which it did so much to create. The Empire reinforced many of the traits of the existing state, particularly its centralized character and the absolute and unlimited nature of its sovereignty, but also its pragmatism and willingness to set up ad hoc arrangements to cope with particular circumstances so long as the integrity of the sovereign power was not infringed.[53] On the whole this worked as well for the Empire as it did for the Union. The British political class developed a strong sense of when it was appropriate to make concessions, and indeed how to make concessions without conceding matters of real substance. It did not always work out like this. There were a number of disasters, the loss of the American colonies and Ireland being the two most conspicuous. But in general the model of a strong centre and a diverse periphery managed to sustain British rule.

Problems often arose whenever territories on the periphery began to seek more autonomy. The reaction of many imperialists was to search for ways to bind them more tightly into the centre, but they were invariably frustrated by the unyielding quality of English sovereignty, which ruled out any attempt to create a federation by dividing powers. Yet without serious division of powers there was no incentive for territories to stay under British rule once they had reached a certain stage of development. Once they began to demand self-determination there was little the British political class could do to satisfy them, other than to yield gracefully and prepare to grant independence. There were sustained attempts by the Empire to suppress movements for independence from India through to Cyprus and Aden, but ultimately these were all in vain. The tactic of direct rule was also not tried. While the French government directly incorporated some of its colonies into the sovereign territory of France, the British always kept their distance from the territories they ruled, and this meant that the project of Greater Britain was only going to be possible if other territories agreed to be forever subordinate to a British sovereignty, in which they could have no share.

The Political Economy of Empire

The transnational space of Empire may have dwindled in importance today but its legacies are still enormously powerful, both for national identity and for the way in which the British are governed. The iconography of the state was refashioned at the height of Empire and much of it still lingers. But beyond that the organization of the state as an imperial state brought a new and obsessive emphasis on national security, which began to be conceived in a much broader way than external defence, extending to the protection of the British way of life and the preservation of order, authority and moral health throughout society, including key institutions such as the schools and the family.[54]

As a result of this reordering of the state, the Empire in the twentieth century became not contingent to the nature of the British state but fundamental to it, and the order that was created imparted a structural bias to the organization and activities of the state which is still immensely important. The state was organized to facilitate expansion, and it pursued a consistent commercial and military strategy to achieve it. The state was conceived as a military organization, an apparatus of force and coercion, and particular stress was therefore laid on the importance of the industrial/military complex which sustained it, particularly the naval shipyards from the seventeenth century onwards, and more recently the aerospace industry.[55] A certain kind of industry has been very important to this state, and the technological dynamism associated with it. In the Whig interpretation of British history much emphasis is placed on the absence of a large standing army in England in peacetime unlike other European monarchies, a principle which was upheld until the twentieth century. In the imperial interpretation of British history, by contrast, it is the military prowess of the state that is continually stressed, traditionally the navy, but increasingly the army, and more recently the airforce. England is regarded as a significant military power, and its people as a warrior people.[56]

This history of expansion and conquest was not only crucial in defining national identity in the ways that have been described but also in defining the public interest. As noted above, it permitted a much larger space for a public realm than the liberal doctrines of laissez-faire seemed to allow. Partly as a result of Empire, for example, a strong ethic of public service has pervaded the armed services, the colonial service, and the civil service. It has been both embodied and reinforced by the Crown, and expressed through the oath of allegiance taken to it. In its support for many organizations in the state and in civil society, the Monarchy has long been one of the main upholders of a public realm in British politics.[57]

The sense of a strong national public purpose which the Empire supplied was also important in generating wide support for public ownership of essential national public services from the Post Office to airlines, the Fire Brigade to the BBC. It was taken as axiomatic that like the armed forces and the colonial administration there was a role for public services which were altruistic, above politics and the marketplace, serving the public good, and meeting high standards. Many of these services as a result came to be organized on military lines, with strong hierarchies and strict internal discipline, as well as an ethos that placed serving the public good above all other aims.[58] The public good was seen as coterminous with the strength and well-being of the Empire. In this way the Empire helped to sanctify the public service, and create a particular kind of public ethos, which made some extensions of the state appear legitimate, as well as creating a distinctive form of public institution, a mould which was to be cracked open by Margaret Thatcher.

The imperial nature of the British state has always been controversial, its supporters arguing that it expressed the character of the British people and guaranteed their security and prosperity, as well as benefiting subject nations, while its critics have seen it as responsible for many of the least desirable features of British life, such as jingoism, sexism and racism, as well as for inflicting great harm on those ruled. This idea of the Empire as a burden, a drain on the energies and resources of the British people has been a constant refrain up to the present. In the debates on British decline one of the most influential interpretations of the United Kingdom's loss of its status as a great power in the twentieth century has been 'imperial overstretch', the inability of the British state to maintain and defend such a far-flung empire with such inadequate resources.[59] The trade-offs between domestic investment, domestic consumption, and military expenditure were resolved in ways that held back domestic investment. In choosing between growth and grandeur, the British state frequently opted for the latter.[60] Many Liberals and Socialists regarded the Empire as helping to preserve all that was backward, anti-democratic, and anti-libertarian in the British state.[61] Other critics have argued that the Empire promoted a 'gentlemanly' capitalism,[62] and encouraged a set of attitudes which put less store on the vigorous virtues of competitive capitalism,[63] and fostered an ethos in education and towards technology which was inimical to the conditions for a successful industrial state.[64]

The supporters of Empire by contrast regarded it not as a burden but as providing an enlarged sphere of action for British citizens. It coloured the map red and made England pre-eminent in many parts of the world. It provided opportunities for soldiers, administrators, entrepreneurs and settlers. It established new ways of conceiving British national identity, by creating the idea of a Greater Britain, a wider citizenship, and a British mission in the world, to provide good government, to extend civilization, and to preserve the international liberal order.[65]

As an imperial state, England reached its zenith in the second half of the nineteenth century and the first part of the twentieth. But before this, it had established a position of moral leadership and economic and naval supremacy which made it for a brief period hegemonic, a model for the world. This hegemonic role is the subject of Chapter 5 on Anglo-America, and Chapter 7 on the English model. Anglo-America is the third transnational circle of England, and needs to be distinguished from the circle of Empire. Although the existence of the territorial empire in the shape of the colonies and dominions with direct ties to the metropolitan centre was an important prop to the status of the British state as a great power, it rested for the most part on the direct control and administration of particular territories. Hegemony was different. It arose from a cosmopolitan rather than from a territorial conception of order, and was concerned with the governance of the global order, with patterns of trade and investment, the movement of peoples, goods and capital.

The territorial empire established an economic sphere dominated by British companies, and a currency sphere in which the pound sterling was the accepted master currency.[66] But of even greater importance for the wider hegemony established by England was its other empire, the empire of trade which the British ruled not in any direct administrative sense but through the superiority of British commerce, the penetration of British investment, and the acceptance of the pound as the undisputed international currency. The British helped spread the ideas and institutions which supported a liberal economic order – free movement of goods, capital, and people – and provided many of the financial and commercial services which such an order required. There were no formal international institutions, but an informal set of rules and understandings developed for the conduct of the affairs of the global economy as well as the operations of British national institutions such as the Bank of England and the the City of London, which helped sustain a long period of stability.[67]

The experience of hegemony and Empire created the view that England could only be England if it was at the centre of a wider network of economic and political relationships, and exercised leadership. What form this leadership should take, however, and which was the appropriate network, was always controversial. In the past the choice was between Empire and Anglo-America, and then between Empire and Europe; now it is between Anglo-America and Europe. During the period of Empire itself there was a long conflict between free-trade imperialists and social imperialists, the former favouring the empire of trade which would include the territorial empire but go much wider, and would be based on maintaining a liberal world order; the second favouring consolidating the territorial empire, through the imposition of tariffs, abandoning laissez-faire, and pursuing collectivist policies to increase security. Military strength was seen as depending on domestic policies and institutions which promoted economic efficiency and social solidarity.[68]

The loss of the territorial empire after 1945 might seem to destroy the basis of perceiving England any longer as an imperial state. But many of the structures and attitudes of this state are still in place, and fierce political debate still surrounds the position of the United Kingdom in the global economy. What has happened however is that support for the social imperialist position has dwindled; serious advocacy of protection, even as a policy for the EU, has become a rare position in British politics. Instead the free-trade imperialist position has become split between those who put priority on the Atlantic link, and those who put priority on the European Union, as the best way of safeguarding British interests and British prosperity. Both of these views inherit something from the idea of England as an Empire. For Atlanticists the role of hegemon in a liberal world order was taken over by the United States from England, and in acknowledging this fact they offered full support to the United States in its economic and its military roles in the post-war order. Atlanticists believe that maintaining a liberal world order and maximum openness for trade and finance, and military support for the United States in policing this world order, should be the top priority for British policy. The Europeanists by contrast place great emphasis on involving the United Kingdom more fully in the process of European integration, in the belief that this experiment in an open and democratic regionalism offers the best framework for prosperity, and for maintaining significant influence for British governments in world politics.[69]

This argument between Atlanticists and Europeanists cuts across an older argument about foreign policy, between national imperialists, liberal imperialists and anti-imperialists. National imperialists from Salisbury to Thatcher see England's interests as best served when the focus is on securing immediate national interests, and safeguarding the spheres of influence which it has established around the world. This national imperialist position was revived by the Thatcher Government, but allied to a strong commitment to Atlanticism. It sought to support those areas of the world such as the Middle East linked directly to Britain through arms sales and other business connections, but to limit involvement elsewhere, especially where no direct British interest is at stake. Where such an interest is at stake, as in the 1982 Falklands conflict or the 1991 Gulf War, intervention is sanctioned.

Liberal imperialists from Gladstone to Tony Blair, by contrast, while still safeguarding spheres of influence consolidated through the arms dealings and military links of the imperial state, also embrace wider concerns where no particular national interests may be at stake. The British intervention in Kosovo in 1999 is a striking example, but so too was the British intervention in Sierra Leone in 2000, both criticized by the Conservative Opposition. This liberal imperialism or liberal interventionism is often driven by a concern with human rights and a wider agenda for securing the conditions for world order.

Anti-imperialists from John Hobson to Tony Benn have always criticized both positions, arguing that England should disarm and follow a neutralist foreign policy as Ireland or Sweden have done. Any military intervention from this perspective is damaging both to the state that suffers from it and the state that perpetrates it. Only the dismantling of the military state will end the constant temptation to use force to settle international disputes.

In the present period of transition from Empire to a deeper involvement in Anglo-America and in Europe, Britain is far from being neutralist. The dominant stance of British policy for a hundred years since the Boer War through appeasement in the 1930s to the phased withdrawal from the territorial empire had been national imperialist. The Thatcher Government reinforced this, and in some ways strengthened it in a doomed attempt to rescue this part at least of the old imperial state. It is one of the more intriguing and less remarked features of the Blair Government that it broke with this long tradition of British foreign policy, embracing liberal imperialism and liberal internationalism, with strong commitments on a variety of international problems such as Third World poverty and climate change, as well as readiness to intervene militarily – in Kosovo, Sierra Leone, Afghanistan, and Iraq in support of human rights and democracy. This represents a significant shift. But in other respects the Blair Government faced the same dilemma as its predecessors, choosing between Anglo-America and Europe, while in its case denying that such a choice needed to be made. The source of this dilemma is the subject of the next two chapters.

5
Anglo-America

The Anglo-Saxon race is infallibly destined to be the predominant force in the history and civilisation of the world.

Joseph Chamberlain, 1900[1]

The British Empire and the United States will have to be somewhat mixed up together in some of their affairs for mutual and general advantage.

Winston Churchill, 1940[2]

Anglo-America is the third circle of England. Originally within the Empire it has grown in importance as the circle of Empire contracted. Anglo-America includes not just the United States but those other colonies of settlers, especially Australia, Canada, and New Zealand, where English is the first language. These former imperial possessions once shaped by England now shape 'England' in return, none more so than the United States. Modern America both attracts and repels in equal measure, leaving most people ambivalent in their feelings towards it. For many Britons America represents the things they most value as well as the things they most detest.

In contemporary British politics America has become a central preoccupation. Cultural Conservatives fear the British are becoming American, and rail against the swamping of British culture through the flood of American media, films, music, and consumer goods which are transforming British life, generally for the worse.[3] The common English language makes such Americanization of culture particularly hard to resist. But the ubiquity of American culture is only one part of the much bigger phenomenon of the global hegemony which the United States has come to exercise since 1945. Attitudes in British politics towards this new hegemony have always been ambivalent, on both right and left. Many have criticized the close military, economic and ideological ties which have bound the United Kingdom and the United States together in the last sixty years, captured in the common jibe that the UK is no more than a satellite of the United States, the 51st state, and the British Prime Minister, in Nelson Mandela's comment during the Iraq crisis, no more than the foreign minister of the United States. In many polls conducted at that time a majority of respondents thought that Tony Blair was acting as George Bush's poodle. Similar less extreme views had been expressed about the earlier relationships between Ronald Reagan and Margaret Thatcher and between Bush Senior and John Major. But such opinions raise the question why British governments would choose to get so out of step with their public opinion and with some of their key European allies?

Anglo-America is perhaps most often thought of as a *special relationship* between two states, the United Kingdom and the United States, each with its own distinctive foreign policy and internal domestic politics. But it is also much more than this. Throughout the modern period British politics has been conducted in a much larger frame than the nation-state, reflecting the different worlds of Empire, Europe, and Anglo-America in which England and then Britain became involved through its career and self-image as a world island. As explained in the last chapter, Empire was from the start closely bound to the expansion of first England and then Great and Greater Britain, a territorial conception of empire, in which British power was projected outwards, carving out its own exclusive sphere. This sphere was consciously imagined as an alternative to Europe, a sphere which the British state could not dominate or easily expand into, but against which it needed to protect itself. The expansion of the Empire came to be seen as the best safeguard for maintaining British separateness and independence from Europe.

While Europe was constructed in this way as a potential enemy and threat, Anglo-America had a very different role in the narratives of English power and identity. At first the American colonies had been the most important symbol of England's overseas Empire, the greatest success of England's expansion overseas in the seventeenth century. The colonies were bound to England through the Navigation Acts, so that all their trade had to be carried in English ships, and they were regarded as vast overseas estates which were to be developed and exploited for the benefit of England itself.[4] The rebellion against the British Crown broke apart this first territorial empire, but one of its consequences was that it helped persuade part of the British political class, encouraged by the arguments of Adam Smith, that free trade rather than mercantilism was the best policy to increase the wealth of the nation, and that the pursuit of territorial empire could be an obstacle to prosperity rather than an aid.

The end of British rule over the American colonies did not end the Anglo-American relationship; rather it transformed it in ways which allowed it eventually to emerge as one of the most important circles of England, shaping its national identity and political economy. In the British imperial imagination Anglo-America at times has often played the role of a lost empire – the Anglo-Saxon federation, the Greater Britain which was never consummated.[5] But it also represents more than this. The severance of the two states in the 1780s was crucial in allowing an alternative idea of empire to emerge, the liberal idea of a cosmopolitan trading and financial order transcending territorial empire. From the beginning Anglo-America was the heart of this fledgling cosmopolitan order with the Atlantic trade crucial to the development of the global economy in the nineteenth century. This cosmopolitan empire of trade and investment extended far beyond the British territorial empire, and required the evolution and design of new institutions and rules to govern it and organize it, beyond great powers with their armies and fleets. The beginnings of a new conception of hegemonic order appropriate to the emerging global economy were apparent. England was hegemon in its commercial empire in a manner that was different from the way it was hegemon within its territorial empire; in the former, England ruled mainly through consent rather than coercion; in the latter, coercion was more overt. Yet it was the territorial empire which became predominant in the conception of 'England', both in the conception the British had of themselves as well as the way in which they were perceived by others, especially after British power was threatened at the end of the nineteenth century.

But in the long run the territorial empire proved impossible to sustain,[6] and by the end of the twentieth century had withered away. The cosmopolitan order had also proved impossible for the British state to uphold on its own, but a new support appeared in the shape of the United States. In this way Anglo-America as a global hegemony continued to thrive and on a much grander scale and with much more explicit purpose and intent. British supremacy within this order was replaced by American. After 1945 both Anglo-America and Europe came to play a much larger part in British politics as territorial empire dwindled; they began to be seen as representing alternative identities and alternative futures for the British state, and so became the cause of major dividing lines within parties and between them. The question of priority between Anglo-America and Europe became a central issue in British politics, not yet resolved, but crucial for determining its future course, as the war on terrorism launched by the United States after 9/11 was to demonstrate.

The Meaning of Anglo-America

Anglo-America is a political space constituted by wider economic, political, ideological and cultural relationships, and is as a consequence many-sided. It is a military alliance, a model of capitalism, a form of government, a global ideology, and a popular culture. Anglo-America is all these things, a complex set of inter-linked narratives and institutions which together has created a global hegemony in the last two hundred years, which has passed through several stages and has most recently been the site of the discourses and projects of globalization and of the new world order.

The *special relationship*[7] between the United Kingdom and the United States has been an important part of this global hegemony since 1945. Its origin was the military alliance in the Second World War which was relaunched after the war as NATO and extended into many other fields of cooperation. At first this appeared a real partnership, but the widening disparity in power between the UK and the US made many question whether the relationship between the two was at all 'special' at least as far as the United States was concerned. The UK was only one of many special relationships which the US entertained. This view became stronger during the second phase of the special relationship, which began after the Americans refused to support the British and French invasion of Suez in 1956. It received further confirmation when Harold Wilson refused to commit British troops to Vietnam in the 1960s, and the UK committed itself to join the European Community, appearing to confirm that the UK no longer saw itself as a global power. The United States also appeared to have more important allies – Germany and Japan – and the UK was increasingly irrelevant. But after 1980 with the election of Ronald Reagan and Margaret Thatcher a third phase of the special relationship commenced. The context was the new Cold War and US awareness of its geopolitical and economic vulnerablility following its defeat in Vietnam and the new weakness of global capitalism. The United Kingdom became valued again as a chief ally, at first through the shared ideological project of the Thatcher and Reagan Governments[8] to roll back socialism at home and abroad, and to confront the Soviet Union through a major arms build-up. Military cooperation was renewed, at first in the Falklands conflict and continuing through the bombing of Libya. The new world order that George Bush Senior proclaimed following the collapse of communism in Europe intensified the new special relationship, first in the Gulf War in 1990/91 and then in a series of military interventions – Kosovo, Afghanistan, and Iraq. At the beginning of the twenty-first century when Tony Blair was feted in Washington and invited to address Congress following 9/11 the special relationship appeared a major force in British politics once again.

But there is more to Anglo-America than the special relationship, however much the media like to focus on it and speculate on its health, especially when there is a change of president or prime minister. Like the other circles Anglo-America is a political space, an 'imagined community',[9] and its boundaries do not coincide with any one state, nor is there any likelihood of there ever being a single state in Anglo-America, although apostles of Anglo-Saxondom often dreamt that there might be.[10] Its two main poles are the states of the United Kingdom and the United States, but there are several other states too within its ambit, including Canada, Australia and New Zealand. It has no single centre. What characterizes it as a political space therefore is that it is transnational rather than national, which means it cannot be an exclusive space for the states within it, all of which belong to other political spaces as well. For the UK the main transnational spaces which shaped its politics for so long were its own territorial Empire, (particularly Africa, India, and Arabia), and Europe, with Europe most often playing the part of the hostile other, confirming England as separate and apart.

Transnational political spaces then are imagined communities which have always overlapped with national political spaces. In the modern world the basis on which such spaces have been constructed has often been a common language. It facilitates the expression of a community of interests and a community of ideals, as well as the identification of who belongs to that community. Other examples of such transnational political spaces include Germany's concept of Mitteleuropa, and similar political spaces have formed around France and Spain in the past and will form around China in the future. Every transnational political space of this kind has its own special characteristics, rooted in specific economic, political, military, ideological and cultural relationships. These give rise to common feelings, common interests, points of contact and shared activities, which nations use to imagine their place in the world.

The main significance of Anglo-America for the future of British politics lies in its continuing existence as a global hegemony. It has been carried forward at different times by particular political projects over the years, from Greater Britain in the nineteenth century to Atlantic Union in the 1940s, to the Washington consensus and the new Cold War in the 1980s, to the new World Order in the 1990s and the war against terrorism after 9/11. It has different aspects – military, economic, political and cultural. In the twentieth century the most visible aspect of this global hegemony was the military alliance, originally created in response to the attempt by

Germany and Japan to found new exclusive territorial empires in Europe and East Asia, and was continued through the period of the Cold War, aimed at preventing the expansion of the territorial empire of the Soviet Union. A second aspect has been the elaboration and promulgation of a particular model of capitalism, the Anglo-American model, which furnished the ideal of a liberal world order and the norms for its governance, as well as specific institutional arrangements for the internal ordering of capitalism, in relation to the state, capital and labour. A third aspect has been advocacy of a model of democracy and government, centred around the ideal of self-government, although taking different institutional forms, and with different notions of rights and how they are to be protected. Finally, there is culture, the English language itself, and Protestantism and individualism, and their manifestations in particular styles of community and of consumerism. Global hegemony is how Anglo-America appears to those outside it, as a hegemonic order fashioned over two hundred years, in which the differences between its various states are less important than what they have in common, and their allegiance to a common project. The ability of Anglo-America to renew itself has often struck observers, most recently in the dissemination of the idea of globalization with its far-reaching implications for global governance.[11]

This global hegemony can often seem more monolithic than it is, particularly in the current era of overwhelming American military power. For those outside Anglo-America, it appears as a system of power which excludes others and seeks to impose its solutions and its conceptions of order on them. But one of the reasons for the vitality of Anglo-America and its capacity for renewal is that it is also a diverse ideological community, in which fierce ideological debates about the true values of Anglo-America are carried on. There has never been a single view. Such debates reach back to the founding of the colonies in North America, the Protestant tradition of dissent, the struggle for American independence, the debates between republicans and monarchists, the American Civil War, Irish independence, monopoly capitalism, the Empire, the New Deal and the welfare state, the Cold War and anti-communism, the neo-liberalism of Thatcher and Reagan, and the Third Way of Clinton and Blair. These arguments all belong to a common ideological tradition which is much broader than simply a national tradition. Some of its themes have been representative government, the corruption of empire, the nature of citizenship, liberty, equality, and justice, republicanism and community, authority and autonomy.

England and America have often functioned as poles of attraction and repulsion, offering at times rival models and rival doctrines. Particular events such as the Vietnam War have sparked fierce ideological contests.

But as with the war of Independence itself, the lines of opposition generally run across the two countries not between them, with representatives of all sides of the argument being found in both. The ideological communities, and the political affiliations they generate, are genuinely transnational in their scope. This is partly what gives them their power.

British national identity and political economy have been shaped by Anglo-America for over three hundred years. It has provided some of the most enduring features of British identity and British political and ideological debate. It has also been a fertile source for global projects, for ways of imagining the place of 'England' in the global order, which have often tended to prevail over alternatives. This has been of particular importance in relation to Europe. In the twentieth century in particular Anglo-America came to represent an alternative to involvement in Europe for the British state, a means of preserving its long standing ideal of an open, free-trade, liberal world order, and for many in the British political class it does so still.[12] For them the narratives of Anglo-America retain their potency.

The Rise of Global Hegemony

Anglo-America from the start was deeply intertwined with the expansion of England and therefore with the narratives of Empire and their preoccupation with the destiny of the Anglo-Saxon race. The American colonies were the most significant territory settled by Britons, and formed the key element of Great Britain's eighteenth century colonial trading system. The successful rebellion against the British Crown and the setting up of an independent state was a major setback for British power and its plans to consolidate its territorial empire, but it only checked and could not halt the continuing rise of the British power and global reach, based both on the continuing expansion of its territorial empire and military successes, but still more important its increasing commercial and industrial momentum.

After its break from Great Britain the United States for a long while was not a significant international player, and was content to stay on the periphery of world affairs, distant from Europe and preoccupied with its own internal concerns and its expansion over the continental land mass. After American independence trade continued to flourish between the two countries, and the United States became the most important component of the commercial empire which British industrial and financial supremacy now established in so many regions of the world. Politically however, there was little contact after the break and the new state was often treated with condescension and indifference.

This phase lasted up to the American Civil War. By this time the United States was an increasingly important economic partner for the UK, not just for trade but in particular because of the huge and growing inward investment of British capital into the American economy. At the same time, the British government was not keen to see the consolidation of American power across the whole land mass of North America. When the civil war broke out the British government equivocated. Many in the British political class sympathized with the Confederacy because its leaders belonged to a landowning aristocracy like itself, and at first it urged the Federal government to allow the Confederacy to leave the Union peacefully. During the war there was talk of the UK recognizing the Confederacy as a separate state, fuelled in part by pro-Confederate sentiment and in part by the perception that a fragmentation of the American state into two or more smaller states would suit British interests, by preventing the emergence of a power able to challenge the UK, and to that end the British government did nothing to stop the flow of arms to the rebel states. Many in the British political class cheered the defeats of the Union armies in the early years of the war.[13]

Once the war had been won by the Union side however, it became clear that there was no longer any political obstacle to the consolidation and extension of the power of the United States. The phase of rapid industrialization was about to start and this meant that before long the United States together with Germany was appearing as a serious competitor to British power and British interests. One of the most intriguing aspects of the history of Anglo-America is the way in which the increasing conflict between the two states was contained short of war, and indeed eventually transmuted into an alliance within which the British gradually relinquished their Empire and accepted a subordinate role to the United States in the organization of its global hegemony.[14]

A key feature of British political history in the twentieth century has been the way in which the global hegemony, first established and loosely organized by England in the course of its expansion over three centuries, was inherited and continued by the United States. There were major differences between England's nineteenth century hegemony and the American hegemony after 1945, but there are also some common threads. At the heart of the Anglo-American conception of global hegemony is the need for the leadership of one or more states to ensure the governance of the world economy and management of the international state system, and in particular to preserve the rules and conditions for an open, liberal world order. This idea was actively promulgated by leading sections of the political class in both the United Kingdom and the United States throughout the twentieth century, as well as by many outside Anglo-America who sought to resist it. The latest example is the anti-globalization movement.[15]

Hegemony understood in this way as a political statecraft for achieving and exercising world leadership has been at the heart of British politics for two hundred years. The British became used to seeing themselves as a world island, pioneering new developments and creating models which others have copied and adapted. The growth of a hegemonic outlook was closely related to the expansion of England and the British Empire, but was also more than this because it came to envisage the formation of a cosmopolitan order and not simply a territorial one.

Both the possibility and the need for global hegemony, whether exercised by one state or collectively, is closely linked to the emergence of a global capitalist economy since the sixteenth century, which has been associated with the unprecedented rise in output and productivity, as well as an increase in the interdependence of all regions and nations, a widening and deepening of the division of labour, and increasing complexity in its networks of production, trade and finance.[16] At the same time, this global economy has been constituted and propelled by politics, in particular the territorial nation-states. The differing capacities of these states and the economic and military competition between them are a major source of the dynamism and unpredictability of the system, as each seeks to shape the global economy to its advantage.[17]

As an economy, this global order has moved fitfully over two hundred years towards greater cohesion and interdependence. As a polity, it remains highly fragmented, never having been transformed into a single centralized political territorial empire. Its unity has come more from economics than from politics, its technological and organizational dynamism ensuring that no state has been able to stand aloof indefinitely. Every state has been forced eventually to come to terms with the global market, and to compete with other states for territory, resources and population. States seek to maintain whatever comparative advantages their national economies possess, and to protect their citizens as far as they are able from the insecurities that the global economy creates. Competition between states in the global economy has aided its expansion and led to a highly unequal distribution of resources and income within it. The hierarchy of states has not remained constant, however. States rise and fall. Those states that achieve dominance in one period frequently lose it in the next as rivals emerge to challenge them.[18]

The integration and complexity of the global economy has increased in the last hundred years but nation-states remain the seat of decision-making and the focus of legitimacy.[19] International institutions have been slow to develop, and have not kept pace with economic integration. This lack of balance has frequently been a source of instability, and has led to calls for the establishment of new political institutions that can foster and sustain the conditions for international economic order. Many have argued that global markets, no less than national markets, require central public authorities to establish international rules, institutions and norms of behaviour.[20] There has been a slow evolution of such rules, and repeated attempts to construct a durable world order, but progress has been swiftest when one state establishes such a lead over its rivals that it is able to create an order which other states come to accept and work within. Where such leadership is accompanied by a fair measure of consent it becomes hegemony.

Moments of true hegemony exercised by a single state are rare and do not tend to last long. Far more common are periods of great power rivalry and conflict, where leading states either aspire to be hegemonic by building alliances and common institutions or seek to impose their will unilaterally. The anarchy inherent in the international system, however, has been mitigated by the emergence of hegemony, in the past associated with a single state or group of states, but increasingly also with the rise of agencies and rules and norms which are slowly if uncertainly creating the basis for forms of collective hegemony and authority.

States often aspire to hegemony, and there have often been clashes between states in their conceptions of world order. The imposition of one conception of world order always involves coercion as well as consent. The opportunity for hegemony exists when one state achieves clear economic and military supremacy over all others. No second power or combination of powers is able to challenge its economic and military supremacy effectively. This economic supremacy is shown by a substantial lead in technology and productivity, by a commanding share of world trade and by decisive control of international finance. If a state gains economic and military supremacy it acquires numerous opportunities to consolidate this transient advantage, and make it permanent by winning the consent of other states to the order it seeks to build.

What is striking about the Anglo-American hegemony is that it combines territorial and cosmopolitan conceptions of order, so that the leading state, first England in the nineteenth century and then the United States in the twentieth have organized both territorial spheres of interest in the normal manner of great powers, as well as a commitment to maintain the liberal order of global capitalism. This has involved them not merely in attempts to secure their own interests, but also to promote institutions from the gold standard to Bretton Woods, which provide state functions for the wider global economy.[21]

In the sense of hegemony being used here, England emerged as a hegemonic power in the decades after 1815. It had established a clear dominance over all its rivals in finance, commerce and industry. London was now the undisputed centre of the world's financial and commercial system, and this supremacy was further enhanced during the period of British hegemony. By 1870 the London capital market was twice as large as all the capital markets of its rivals combined. Sterling was established as the leading international currency and this brought further prosperity to the flourishing financial and commercial sector. It was this sector too that provided the surplus which allowed a rising tide of foreign investment to be financed.[22] Despite the establishment of a huge new industrial sector, and in part because of it, England was still first and foremost a commercial and financial power.[23] The new wealth and opportunities which industry provided were fully exploited, but within the framework of the global network of relations which had already been established. The development of industry was viewed as the greatest commercial opportunity of all, because it permitted much greater specialization in the division of labour and a more ruthless exploitation of comparative advantage. As a result self-sufficiency in agriculture was abandoned between 1820 and 1850; the number of Britons fed on imported wheat rose from less than one million in 1820 to three and a half million in 1850, a five-fold increase.[24]

The commitment to free trade followed a commercial rather than an industrial logic. British prosperity and the feeding of its growing population came to depend on the maintenance of the network of trading relationships which now covered the whole world: its centre was London.[25] The British interest in preserving the free movement of goods, capital and labour in this world economy emerged when British manufacturing industries had a clear technological lead over all others. But it did not diminish when this lead began to vanish. The maintenance of an open world economy remained a vital British concern. The British position was, as a result, significantly different from that of the United States or Germany. Both the United States and Germany aspired to world power on the strength of their industrial manufacturing base. They pursued a policy of building up an export surplus, but trade was never a necessity for them in the way it was for the British economy. Autarky in many sectors and strictly regulated trade was also feasible. The world order which the British fashioned required a permanent deficit on visible trade which both stimulated economic development in other parts of the world economy and gave rise to increasing demand for British services – banking, shipping and insurance.[26] This made the British national interest ever more closely involved with maintaining the openness of the world system. The world order fashioned by the

United States, by contrast, required at first some means to offset the huge American export surplus, which reflected the overwhelming industrial and technological dominance the American economy had acquired by 1945. The solution was found first through the granting of credits, of which the Marshall Plan was the prototype,[27] and by increases in American foreign investment and overseas military spending.

Two further contrasts between England and America as hegemonic powers should be noted. The first lay in the type of territorial order they promoted. Both exercised great power in the world system because of their dominant market position. But in addition to this empire of trade, England had also acquired as discussed in the previous chapter a large territorial empire during its expansion, and greatly added to it between 1815 and 1918. British commitment to universalism and to the preservation of the open world economy was substantially qualified by the alternative attractions of protecting a vast but still bounded sphere of interest within the world economy. These attractions grew once England was faced with rivals claiming spheres of interest of their own. The existence of the British Empire made England's world position last much longer than it would otherwise have done, but it also made England less credible as an advocate of a liberal international economic order, since to its rivals the existence of the British Empire constituted a massive exception to its rules. The United States, always a strong critic of the European colonial empires on both economic and political grounds, was never inhibited in quite the same way. It was able when the time came to project itself as a believer in liberal universalism and liberal internationalism in a more convincing manner than the British, although America's ability to exercise hegemony has also been damaged by its own very strong conceptions of territorial order, and its pursuit of its own spheres of interest, even if it has not imposed permanent direct rule on other parts of the world.

The two powers were also very different in respect of the military supremacy which underpinned their hegemony. British military power was limited, resting mainly on naval power, although even here the 'Pax Britannica' in the nineteenth century required a naval budget of only £8 million.[28] The 'Pax Americana' saw the construction of an extensive system of overseas military bases, initially made necessary by the desire to contain the expansion of the Soviet Union, but increasingly by the desire of the United States after 1991 to extend their sphere of influence to the whole world. The Americans sought from the start to project their power and influence through a system of military alliances, organized first to contain the Soviet Union and the spread of communism, and after 1991 the activities of 'rogue' states and terrorists. The United States' hegemony has been far more active than England's ever was, involving attempts to win consent for its definition of world order, both in terms of security and the economy. In 1850, the high point of British hegemony, the British government was attempting to maintain a balance of power in Europe and a territorial conception of empire.

Challenges to British industrial and commercial supremacy were the first to develop in the decades before 1914. The challenge to British financial supremacy came later. The commercial challenge was the one which worried British political opinion the most, because the open-door policy allowed foreign exporters to invade the British market, while British exporters had to sell over high tariff barriers in an increasing number of countries, and there was a competitive scramble for colonies. Since the British state was unable to restore the conditions for an open world economy, it safeguarded its position by enlarging its own direct sphere of interest. A noted exponent of geopolitics, Halford Mackinder, claimed that England had been forced to abandon free trade when other countries tried to monopolize markets. In such circumstances, he argued, even democracies were forced to annex empires, conveniently ignoring the fact that England had had an empire long before it embraced free trade and was still far from being a democracy. Mackinder, however, insisted with the kind of insouciance that had infuriated many observers of England from Friedrich List onwards,[29] that the purpose of England's annexations had been benign. It was to 'support a trade open to all the world'.[30]

Mackinder was writing at a time, the beginning of the twentieth century, when British politics was gripped by a major debate on whether the policy of free trade, the linchpin of the cosmopolitan conception of world order, should be abandoned. The strategic issue at stake was whether in seeking to maintain its supremacy, priority should be given to the empire of territory or the empire of trade. This issue had been settled in favour of the latter at the time of the repeal of the Corn Laws fifty years before. Free trade made foreign nations valuable 'colonies' without imposing on the British the responsibility and the costs of governing them.[31]

In the second half of the nineteenth century free trade became a key component of the British conception of world order and claim to hegemony. Its universalism and idealism made it the model other nations sought to imitate, and made them more likely to accept British leadership. As the British Foreign Office put it:[32]

Second only to the ideal of independence, nations have always cherished the right of free intercourse and trade in the world's markets, and in proportion as England champions the principle of the largest measure of general freedom of commerce, she undoubtedly strengthens her hold on the interested friendship of other nations, at least to the extent of making them feel less apprehensive of naval supremacy in the hands of free trade England than they would in the face of a predominantly protectionist power.

This policy came under fierce attack from those who wanted to see the Empire developed as the priority, whatever the consequence for the open world economy. Leading imperialists such as Joseph Chamberlain and Lord Milner advocated naval supremacy in the hands of a protectionist England, and spearheaded the assault upon the policy of free trade. Milner condemned the 'insane delusion' that a nation could grow richer by buying outside its borders what it could produce within them, and the 'blind worship of cheapness' which was causing the British to undermine their own industries. It was time he argued for the British people to free themselves from the 'shackles' of free trade, and to establish new privileged and protected relationships with 'our fellow-countrymen' in the Dominions.[33]

The conflict between free trade and tariff reform reflected the extent to which by 1900 the British state was pursuing incompatible aims in a bid to maintain its supremacy. Protecting the British Empire and preserving a balance of power in Europe meant preparing for war. Safeguarding the open world economy meant maintaining peace. Only peace would ensure that the lines of world communication were kept open, international contracts honoured, and foreign investments secured. A Foreign Office memorandum in 1927 bluntly stated: 'We have got all we want – perhaps more. Our sole object is to keep what we have and to live in peace.'[34] But there were many powers who were not content with what they had, and were not prepared to live in peace. They either had to be fought or appeased.

After 1918 there was increasing awareness that England itself no longer had the resources to sustain the conditions for a liberal and open world order. Yet there was reluctance to abandon either of the two roles which the British state had acquired in the long expansion of England – the overextended British territorial empire (larger in extent than ever after 1918), or the central role British institutions like the City of London and the Bank of England had come to play in the governance of the liberal world economy. In these circumstances, the attraction of closer collaboration with the United States grew, and the idea began to grow of an Atlantic Union through which the governance of the liberal world economy could be shared.

The Special Relationship

England's undisputed supremacy in the international system lasted from 1815 until the 1870s. It was never as dominant as the United States was to become a century later, and its hegemony was much less organized. But it did possess a clear conception of the world order it wished to encourage and sustain, and its economic and naval supremacy enabled it to exercise hegemony through the persuasiveness of its example. The English model became the path of development from which to learn and British achievements those which rising nations wanted to surpass. In the last decades of the nineteenth century, England faced a rising industrial and military challenge from new rivals, particularly from Germany and the United States. The unification of Germany under Prussian leadership and the defeat of the secession of the southern states in the American Civil War created the conditions for rapid industrialization in both countries. Both resorted to policies to protect their new industries from British competition and both contested the inclusion of so much of the world in England's sphere of interest, whether as colonies or through the commercial and financial links England had established with them. Both also tried (with increasing success) to exploit the British policy of allowing open access to its markets. The British press became greatly alarmed by the success of American and German competitors. The first great bout of introspection about national decline was soon under way.[35]

The challenge to British power meant that either England had to come to terms with its new rivals or it had to fight them. If appeasement was chosen, a significant surrender of British power would be necessary. A negotiated balance of power and division of the world between spheres of interest would be very different from an undisputed hegemony, arising from supremacy in the world market. Using force, however, to resist the challenge and the reordering of world power would carry heavy risks and might ultimately weaken rather than strengthen England's position, even if England emerged as victor in the short run.

The arguments for appeasement of the new industrial and military rivals England faced by 1900 were persuasive. Yet appeasement could only be viable if the rivals in their turn were prepared to moderate the demands they were making on England, and bury, or at least postpone, their own aspirations for world power. The failure to reach an accommodation with Germany precipitated two world wars. England twice abandoned its policy of appeasement towards Germany, but at no time did it abandon its policy of appeasement towards the United States. Indeed, war with Germany made appeasement of the United States all the more necessary.

The struggles between the European powers made the rise of the United States swifter than it might otherwise have been. It also meant that the military contest between England and the United States, which many Bolsheviks confidently forecast as the next round of imperialist struggle after 1918,[36] never took place. Instead the United States emerged as the undisputed hegemonic power in the world system after 1945 with, on balance, more collaboration than resistance from the power it was displacing. This collaboration was most visible in the military sphere. The German challenge to England was only defeated with American help. But equally significant was the collaboration over the construction of a new world order, the re-establishment of an open world economy, and the attempt to remove existing exclusive spheres of interest in favour of multilateral trade and a unified international monetary system.

The transfer of hegemony went through three main phases. In the first phase, Britain acquiesced in the organization of an American sphere of interest. At this stage it was envisaged that British and American interests might be complementary, each dominating its own sphere of interest and cooperating to maintain international economic order. The second phase, during the 1940s, saw the development of the idea of a special relationship between Britain and the United States.

This notion was only intermittently accepted by the United States government, but it enjoyed much support in Britain. It became a crucial narrative for the British in reconciling them to 'England's' relegation from the front rank of world powers, and the surrender of its responsibility for so many aspects of global governance. From the British standpoint, the purpose of the special relationship was to allow Britain to act as broker between the United States and Europe. By this means, Britain expected to remain a powerful and independent voice with its own power base, while ceding the leading role in the world system to the United States. In the third phase, the United States moved to a new conception of an Atlantic partnership in which a united Western Europe, under the leadership of a revitalized West Germany, became the central objective. Britain was now relegated to a subordinate and dependent role within the alliance.

The decision to appease rather than confront the United States was crucial for later developments. In 1895–6 Washington intervened in a boundary dispute between Venezuela and British Guiana; the British conceded the Americans' right to do so. It led to further steps. The British abandoned their half share in the future Isthmian canal and withdrew their navy from the Western Hemisphere. No formal treaty was signed, but the unilateral declaration by the United States that this region fell within its sphere of influence was tacitly recognized. In 1901 the Admiralty was asked to advise on the feasibility of a war against the United States. It told the Cabinet that in order to place Great Britain in a position to acquire the command of the seas on the coast of America, it was essential for the neutrality of European powers to be assured.[37] The Admiralty's assessment underlined the weakness of the British position and the need to maintain friendly relations with the United States.

The arguments against fighting the United States, even if the neutrality of the rest of Europe could be assured, were many and compelling. Given the interdependence of the two economies it would have been a major economic disaster. There were vast British investments in the United States, and a huge volume of trade between the two countries. A war would have given great opportunities to England's other leading rivals to divide up the British Empire among themselves. Apart from these practical considerations, there was strong ideological distaste for a clash with America. The ideology of Anglo-Saxon unity was already potent, and was to become still more influential in subsequent decades, propagated by groups like the Rhodes Trust and the Round Table, and by intellectuals like Walter Lippmann.

The growing understanding between the two powers prepared the way for wartime collaboration in 1917–18. Germany was defeated, but the balance of power between England and the United States was decisively shifted. The Americans consolidated their advantage after the war at the Washington Naval Conference by insisting on naval parity with England. As a result of the war, they had overtaken England as the world's leading creditor nation, and were now without dispute the leading industrial power.

Despite the evidence of America's new dominance and Woodrow Wilson's commitment to the building of a new international political and economic order, the United States was not yet ready to take a leading role in the world system and relapsed into isolationism. The inter-war years demonstrated, however, that an international order could not be rebuilt without the United States. The collapse of the gold standard in 1931 under-lined this. The consequent fragmentation of the world economy into currency blocs and protected spheres of interest reduced trade and output, and contributed to the rise of regimes committed to the redistribution of territory in the world system by force.

The second phase began with the conclusion of the Lend–Lease Agreement. The establishment of the Coalition government in the United Kingdom and the decision to wage total war, brought a sharp break with both the domestic and the foreign policies of British governments in the 1930s.[38] The dependence of the British on the Americans was much more marked than in the earlier conflict, and from the outset the Americans demanded a high price for their support. The 1941 Atlantic Charter set out plans for a reconstruction of the international economic order on universal principles. Spearheaded by the State Department under Cordell Hull, the United States as the emergent hegemonic power in the world system had begun to redefine its interests.

A particular target was the exclusive spheres of interest which had been organized in the 1930s. Cordell Hull described the Ottawa agreements which established imperial preference within the British Empire as 'the greatest injury, in a commercial way, that has been inflicted on this country since I have been in public life'.[39] During the 1930s, the Americans had been content to accept the existing division of the world market and had toyed with the idea of organizing a new informal empire – the Grand Area – to include the Western Hemisphere, the British Empire, the Dutch East Indies, China and Japan. This bloc was intended to counterbalance Germany and the Soviet Union.[40]

The outbreak of the Second World War allowed more ambitious schemes to be floated. The Grand Area could be expanded to include both Western Europe and the Soviet Union. Britain and Japan could be forced to surrender their exclusive spheres of interest. The Americans were determined to remove imperial preference and to force the European powers to give up their colonies. The British, however, viewed their alliance with the Americans as a partnership and saw no need to abandon the arrangements which had perpetuated British world power long after British hegemony had disappeared. Opinion in the American government was split between those who favoured maintaining a special relationship with the United Kingdom in the interests of building a stable international economic order, and those who were against making any concessions that were not made to all other countries. Negotiations over the shape of the post-war order were protracted and many of the more ambitious plans were never realized. In particular, the hopes for an early resumption of multilateral trade and convertibility which underlay the 1944 Bretton Woods Conference were disappointed.

The British and the Americans put forward rival plans at Bretton Woods, and the final compromise owed more to the plan put forward by Dexter White for the Americans than to the plan put forward by Keynes. The compromise was attacked in the United States and in Britain. In America it was feared that the proposals departed too much from the canons of sound finance, and that America's interests would be best served by adhering to the principles of the gold standard, which did not permit discretionary rules aimed at maintaining activity in the world economy and easing the position of persistent deficit countries. In Britain, by contrast, painful memories of the collapse of the international financial system in the inter-war years had to be erased, and political opinion had to be convinced that abandoning the new security which a protected sphere of interest policy had given to Britain was justified. Keynes himself had been an advocate of bilateralism in the 1930s, but by 1944 he was once again a defender of the traditional liberal British policy of an open world trading order, suitably modified. He argued strongly against the feasibility of a system of bilateral and barter arrangements. Such a system, he thought, would never persuade the Dominions to make London once again the centre of their financial systems. It was a 'technique of Little Englandism', only to be adopted as a last resort when the country was facing autarky. He derided the supporters of the proposal for their lack of realism. They had little idea of how the Empire had grown or by what means it could be sustained. In particular, there was no prospect, he thought, that the rest of the Commonwealth would agree to cut their free commercial relations with the rest of the world.[41]

The Americans pressed hard for as full and as complete a liberalization of international economic relations as possible. The British held out for a period of transition, and important currents of British opinion, in both major parties, resisted what they saw as the forced liquidation of the British sphere of interest and, with it, British aspirations to global power, as well as the placing of severe constraints on the ability of British governments to pursue management of the national economy in the way they chose.

The policies of multilateralism and convertibility had failed by 1947, and the United States launched Marshall Aid in order to reconstruct the Western economy and help to underpin the new military alliance against the Soviet Union. Only much later were the objectives of Bretton Woods to be realized.[42] From the outset, American hegemony was marked both by universalism in respect of the international economic order and by a sphere of interest policy aimed at containing the Soviet Union. Britain had an interest in both, but British attempts to maintain an independent position within the world system which could continue to give it special privileges in dealing with the Americans eventually failed. Although interested at times in the special relationship, the Americans were still more interested in seeing the liquidation of what alone could give the special relationship credibility – the British Empire. The British failure at Suez in 1956 demonstrated clearly the impossibility of Britain pursuing a major policy independently of the Americans while remaining firmly within the American world order. Britain's peculiar post-war problem was that it failed to maintain the special relationship and therefore the basis for a continuing world role; but it also failed to reorganize its domestic economy and society sufficiently to compete effectively within the new expanding world economy. Hegemony was transferred, international economic order was eventually rebuilt, but the former hegemonic power was incapable of benefiting from it. Instead the relative decline in the 1960s and 1970s became more pronounced.

The Anglo-American Model of Capitalism

Why has the British political class been so attached to Anglo-America when it is this attachment which has played a major part in the demise of the British Empire? It is certainly true that it was not the first choice of the British political class, but they found first in 1917 and again and more drastically in 1940 that the British Empire could only survive with American help, and that the price of American help was the dismantling of the British Empire. What however made the choice palatable was that Anglo-America furnished an alternative, the continuance of the project of global hegemony, the idea of a global economy governed by free trade and sound finance and respect for property rights, and the idea of a global polity governed by the principles of democracy, human rights and the rule of law. These ideas were to come together in the concept of the Free World in the fight against Communism during the Cold War, and were important in the fashioning of new institutions such as the United Nations and the North Atlantic Treaty Organization (NATO), as well as the International Monetary Fund (IMF), the World Bank, and the World Trade Organization (WTO).

At the centre of these constructs was the notion that distinctive institutional features common to the United States and to Britain made their capitalisms and their states different from European models of capitalism, particularly from Germany and Sweden, and also from East Asian models, particularly Japan and Korea.[43] It was reflected in the collaboration by Britain and the United States in promoting a particular form of world order.

This order derived from England's nineteenth century hegemony based on free trade, sound money and laissez-faire. Part of this dispensation, concerning free trade, was resisted by the United States during its early phases of industrial development, but then became its own creed, although it was always more qualified. Certainly however, one of the greatest achievements of Anglo-America has been the liberal world economic order which has lasted now for more than a hundred and fifty years, although with some major interruptions during the First World War and again between 1931 and 1945. The exclusion of Russia and later the whole of the Communist world was a further restriction, but after the collapse of communist regimes in Europe 1989–91 and the gradual absorption of

China, by the end of the twentieth century the whole world was once more being governed by the Anglo-American conception of liberal world order. To its critics this represented the imposition of disciplinary neo-liberalism, exercised through the agency of the World Bank and the IMF, and underpinned by the financial and industrial power of transnational capital.

What made it possible was the willingness of the United States to endorse the rules and system of world order which England had earlier fashioned. Neither the United Kingdom nor the United States, however, always adhered to the principles. They were distorted by state interests, the determination of the British to run their empire as a protected sphere within the global economy, and the protectionist policies of the United States, which were modified but still present when the United States became the leading world power. What both states in succession were also prepared to do was to allow their currency, first sterling and then the dollar, to become international currencies, and therefore to assume the burden and advantages of being lender of last resort to the international system.

One of the important practical consequences of the Anglo-American conception of world order was that it ruled out a world order based primarily on territorial or regional principles. The period between 1916 and 1945 shook confidence in the ability of the liberal system to survive, and as a result many saw regionalism and the organization of closed trading blocs as the form which world order would take in the future. But the fifty years of American hegemony after the Second World War has restored a liberal world order. It has suffered various crises, but has not so far broken down, and in important respects its reach has been extended.

The survival of a liberal world order beyond the period when England could sustain it alone had important consequences for the United Kingdom, since it meant that although the American order was different in many respects from that which had gone before, it still meant that Britain was not forced to readjust its institutions or the basis of its economy in a radical way. Many of its crucial features, particularly the overseas orientation of so many of its largest companies and the importance of the financial and arms sectors, were preserved, and indeed strengthened.

The common understanding on global governance between the United Kingdom and the United States was reflected also in domestic institutional arrangements. There are of course important differences between the two capitalisms, but there are also sufficient features in common to make the idea of an Anglo-Saxon model plausible. These features include in particular the role of the state in the economy. Neither capitalism has had the kind of developmental state associated with Germany or Japan. The emphasis instead has been on individualism and minimal state involvement. There has also been a distinctive form of welfare provision, based on insurance principles, and a preference for targeted rather than universal provision. On labour the Anglo-Saxon model is known for its flexible labour markets, and for the way trade unions have not been successfully involved in corporatist arrangements to manage the economy.

The concept of Anglo-America helps illuminate the question of globalization and how British policy-makers and the wider political class has responded to it. The discourse of globalization from the standpoint of Anglo-America is merely the latest dominant discourse employed to promote the concept of a liberal economic order. Globalization from its inception has been predominantly an Anglo-American discourse and an Anglo-American project. It originated in the 1970s following the collapse of the Bretton Woods system. Monetarism emerged as the preferred solution to the problems of accelerating inflation and deepening recession, and was enforced through the international agencies of the global order, particularly the IMF, and backed by the financial markets.[44] Monetarism was not home-grown in particular countries. It was adopted first by the international agencies and the international consensus in Washington. In the 1980s this became formalized as the Washington consensus, and has since been referred to as disciplinary neo-liberalism,[45] which was accepted and adopted by national governments with varying degrees of ideological enthusiasm.

The Reagan/Thatcher partnership consolidated the hold of the new consensus and made it the new commonsense throughout Anglo-America. It drew further strength with the collapse of communism in Europe at the end of the 1980s and the vogue for the end of history,[46] with its suggestion that there were no longer any viable alternatives to the liberal capitalist model, and that ideological contestation was therefore at an end. The discourse of globalization has enlarged this idea, implying in some of its more extreme formulations that cosmopolitan order in the shape of transnational financial and trade flows has completely overwhelmed all forms of regulation based on territorial order, and that as a result all national governments are obliged to adjust their institutions and policies to those prescribed as the international norm.

There has been resistance to these ideas from within Anglo-America itself as well as from many states outside it, but it has not prevented the consolidation of neo-liberalism as the dominant framework for discussion of global governance. It is not a monolithic doctrine, and there are important variations within it, as there were with earlier dominant discourses; these included the rather ill-named 'post-Washington consensus' of the 1990s and the Third Way pursued by Bill Clinton and Tony Blair. But underpinning all such variations has been an acceptance of the necessity and inevitability of globalization, and the need for national and international governance to ensure that globalization is allowed to develop to its maximum.

Despite the ideological certainties of Thatcher and Reagan, the 1980s were a difficult time for Anglo-America because of the continuing weakness of the British economy and the challenges to United States hegemony. One particular form this took was the elaboration of arguments about the developmental state and models of capitalism which pointed to deep-rooted problems in the organization of the Anglo-American model of capitalism and argued that it was being outcompeted by other models, particularly those of Germany, Sweden and Japan.[47]

The key features of this Anglo-American model are traced back to the common ideals on liberty of the individual within a framework of the rule of law, which encouraged the development of capitalist enterprise which was fundamentally individualist and at arms-length from government. Although many historical details of this characterization have been challenged, the dominant Anglo-American understanding of the primacy of the market and civil society over the state has been sustained. The state played a much more powerful role than in some of the myths of spontaneous efflorescence of capitalism, but it was essentially an enabling role – removing the barriers to free market exchange and sustaining the institutions which could define and defend individual property rights. Many of the characteristics of the Anglo-American model have stemmed from this approach, in particular its voluntarism and short-termism, as well as the liberal character of its welfare system[48] and corporate governance,[49] and the relative importance of its financial institutions, particularly its stock markets.

During the years of the long boom in the 1950s and 1960s it became evident that there were several varieties of capitalism, and different ways of involving the state in the economy, although even then there were arguments that in practice there was considerable convergence towards a norm.[50] The models of capitalism which appeared to perform best were those of Germany, France, Scandinavia and Japan, all of which had markedly different institutions than Britain and America, and all involved a very different role for the state in defining and promoting the public interest as far as the economy was concerned. Criticism of the Anglo-American model and its shortcomings reached a crescendo in the 1970s and 1980s with the well-publicized difficulties of the British economy in comparison to its main competitors and with the apparent strains within the United States, which led many observers to predict that the United States was in irreversible decline, and that it was being overtaken by the economies of

East Asia. The hegemony of Anglo-America might be still pre-eminent in the security field, but it appeared to be under considerable challenge in the economic. Its model was regarded as obsolescent, in danger of being outcompeted.[51]

As the debate on globalization has gathered pace in the 1990s, the resurgence of the American economy and to a lesser extent of the British economy in the second half of the 1990s was proclaimed as vindication of the Anglo-American model, and of its particular suitability to the conditions of globalization. The economies which did less well in the 1990s – in Europe and East Asia – were roundly criticized in the Wall Street business press as sclerotic and inflexible, unable and unwilling to restructure themselves to meet the challenges of the new global economy. This turn of events has made the British and American governments the leading proselytizers for globalization, and has delayed British adjustment to the requirements of European integration. The renewed success of the Anglo-Saxon model of capitalism has been a vivid reminder to the British of their links to Anglo-America, and how these could be imperilled by absorption into Europe.

The globalization discourse in the 1990s became very much an Anglo-Saxon discourse, which was consciously used as a weapon against the opponents of Anglo-America as well as means of enforcing order through the global economy. It became a new means of hegemonic control. It took some time to emerge and be effective, but the foundations were already laid by the mid-1970s following the collapse of the Bretton Woods system. The new doctrines that emerged to guide the practices of the international institutions such as monetarism were designed to re-establish the conditions of international financial stability, at whatever cost to domestic spending programmes and domestic employment. The development of neo-liberalism as a set of doctrines and discourses took place first of all in the United States and was then imposed or accepted throughout the global economy. Sometimes the adjustments were painful, as in Britain, in France and in Sweden and most recently in East Asia. What was striking however was that having once succumbed to the medicine that was prescribed, the British political class, first Conservative and latterly Labour, became enthusiasts and proselytizers for the new dispensation. Denis Healey, Labour Chancellor in the 1970s, was described as an unbelieving monetarist when he took the first decisive steps to create a monetarist policy regime in the UK, imposing cash limits on public spending and monetary targets. There was nothing unbelieving however about the regime that followed.

British politicians became evangelists for the neo-liberal economic policies and for the superiority of the Anglo-American model. The belief in flexible labour markets, deregulation of business, privatization, low taxes, shareholder value and minimal state involvement became articles of faith which were pressed on the UK's European partners as offering the best way to create a prosperous and competitive economy. Globalization became an unreflective mantra which was used to argue that there was no alternative to the adoption of neo-liberal economic policies and the Anglo-American model. Resistance to globalization was futile because national governments no longer had the power to control global economic forces. States had to either work with globalization or be overwhelmed by it.

Anglo-America, considered as a special relationship between England and America, looks to be confined to a relatively short period in the middle of the twentieth century, and even then it was invested with more significance by the British than by the Americans. Anglo-America considered as a global hegemony and a powerful ideological tradition is still very much alive, and through its latest construct, the discourse of globalization, continues to shape our world.

6

The Reluctant Europeans

> England still stands outside Europe. Europe's voiceless tremors do not reach her. Europe is apart and England is not of her flesh and body. But Europe is solid with herself.
>
> John Maynard Keynes, 1919[1]

Europe is the fourth circle of England, and is both the oldest of the four and perhaps at the deepest level the most influential in shaping its identities and political economy. It is also the most troubled and least straightforward of the four in contemporary British politics, the source of deep divisions within and between parties. This is because although England has always been a part of Europe and is deeply European in its culture, its language, its institutions, its religion and its politics, the national identity first of England, and then of Great Britain and the United Kingdom, has generally been formed in opposition to 'Europe', or at least to some suitably frightening manifestation of Europe. It has often been convenient to make Europe the 'Other' against which the particular qualities of Englishness and Britishness are defined. One of the 'Metric Martyrs' (small shopkeepers fined in 2001 for refusing to introduce metric weights and measures in their shops) declared after the court hearing: 'I am British; I am *not* European', as though the one necessarily excluded the other. The belief that they could be, and should be, exclusive still fuels political debate.

Britain's relationships with the rest of Europe have been through many different phases and have undergone some major changes, most significantly since the end of the Second World War with the moves towards European integration which produced first economic cooperation and a common market, and culminated in the establishment of a European Union in 1994. European integration has transformed the European space and the place of the United Kingdom within it, but this phase of integration which has now lasted fifty years must be set in the context of many centuries of deep divisions, fragmentation, conflicts and wars.

English or European?

Although England's history has been closely intertwined with the rest of Europe, the dominant narratives of British politics have depicted England as a state and people apart from Europe. Since the sixteenth century when England first emerged as a separate nation-state it has fought wars with leading European powers – Spain in the sixteenth century, Holland in the seventeenth century, France in the eighteenth century, Russia in the nineteenth century, Germany in the twentieth century. England's self-image became that of the island people that stood alone against a succession of (European) enemies.

As noted in Chapter 3, the first Empire in which England was involved was a European one. The overthrow of the Anglo-Saxon Kingdom by William the Conqueror made England part of a wider network of territories controlled by the Normans which at times in the next few centuries incorporated large areas of France. Wars before the sixteenth century in which the English were engaged were not national wars, but conflicts within feudal jurisdictions which cut across any putative national boundaries. For several centuries after the Norman Conquest in 1066, Kings of England spoke French and often spent more time in their French lands than in their English ones. Only in retrospect were events like the Hundred Years War reinterpreted in nationalist terms as a war between England and France, rather than what it was – a war between rival appellants for the French throne and disputes over titles to French land.[2]

The first war which powerfully shaped a sense of national community and identity was the war of Protestant England against Catholic Spain, with its highpoint being England's defence of itself against the Spanish Armada in 1588. Successful resistance to foreign invasion by the dominant power in Europe became a major thread in English nationalist history – 1588, 1805, and 1940 being the three most memorable dates, when England resisted invasion from Philip II of Spain, from Napoleon, and from Hitler. In each case the threat came from the great power that dominated 'Europe', and against which England was pitted in lonely struggle.[3]

A cursory glance at English history however reminds us that this central image of popular nationalist history – England standing alone against Europe – is for the most part a myth. As a myth it does contain an important truth. England has at times been isolated, none more so than in May 1940, and the British people did experience their 'finest hour' in rallying to support those in the government and the political class who were determined to resist Hitler rather than sue for peace after the fall of France, even if the story is much more complex than it has often been presented.[4] But although such a policy was necessary for final victory it was not enough by itself. Isolation had to be temporary. Had it not been, victory could not have been secured. None of the European wars in which England was involved could have been won without major European allies – at different times Portugal, Holland, Prussia, Austria, Russia, Spain, France and many others. England's real policy was always divide and rule, rather than splendid isolation. It was isolated by accident, as in 1940, rather than by design. Yet popular nationalist history has refashioned the story of the world island to make it appear that England always defeats its enemies on its own, and does not require assistance. The only exception that is acknowledged, often grudgingly, is the help given by the United States in the two world wars of the twentieth century, although it is pointed out that it was provided late in the day, and only after England had borne the brunt and 'stood alone'.

Waterloo would not have been won, however, without the Prussians. If Blucher's army, forced into retreat at Ligny, had continued to retreat as Napoleon had expected, instead of returning to tip the scales at Waterloo late in the day, Wellington would have been defeated. The wider war against Napoleon could never have been won without the alliances with Prussia, Russia, Austria, and Spain. Germany could not have been defeated in the First World War without the alliance with France, or in the Second World War without the alliance with Russia. England has needed allies in Europe to overcome its enemies in Europe. These facts are obvious, yet somehow in the English nationalist imagination they disappear from view. Europe as a shifting patchwork of alliances and coalitions which England has always played skilfully to achieve its objectives, gets replaced by Europe as the monolith, dominated by forces inimical to England. A recent representative of this kind of English nationalism is Margaret Thatcher, who came to despise and detest everything 'European'. Only bad things, she declared, had come out of Europe in her lifetime.[5] The implication is that England – free, independent, peace-loving England – has always had to rescue Europe from itself.

The extent to which Europe has been characterized more often as enemy rather than as friend to England, despite the fact that it has always been both, owes a great deal to the fact that the wars which helped define first English and then British national identity were of two kinds. There were wars with colonial rivals for territory and trade, but there were also ideological wars, starting again with the war against Spain in the sixteenth century. Protestant England was pitched against Catholic Spain, and all the forces of the counter-Reformation. The sense of being a Protestant nation was further strengthened by the coup which placed the Dutch Prince William of Orange on the English and Scottish thrones in 1688 and continued as an important psychological and political reality through the eighteenth century. But it was superseded in the modern period by two further ideological wars – aristocratic England against egalitarian France; and liberal England against totalitarianism, first Nazi Germany then Soviet Russia. Fighting wars to defend what it considered right, and at the same time to prosecute its interests to the full, gave powerful extra momentum to England's sense of itself as a nation apart, moreover, a nation which in almost all its wars was rewarded with victory. Europe by contrast became the Land of Mordor, the place from which every so often dark powers arose which threatened England both militarily and ideologically.

The imagining of England as a land apart, somehow cut off from Europe and not fundamentally European at all, became the basis for one version of the national idyll and the celebration of a particular kind of Englishness; a green and pleasant land; a people slow to anger but resolute when roused; a nation essentially peace-loving and devoted to rural pursuits and simple pleasures; tolerant, kind, reserved, polite, self-effacing. All this may seem to fit rather oddly with that other England, urban and industrial, the great Empire, with its assertive anthems of national and imperial power – *Rule Britannia* and *Land of Hope and Glory*, the words of which used to boom out at Conservative Party Conferences and still do at Royal Jubilees: 'Wider still and wider may thy bounds be set/God that made thee mighty make thee mightier yet'; a nation renowned for its turbulence, its stubbornness, its disorderliness, drunkenness and slovenliness, its military prowess, its hard edge. But however different these two sides of the national character may seem to be, what they share is a common sense of a nation that is distinct from Europe rather than a part of it.

It is often argued that England was separated by its Protestant Reformation in the sixteenth century from the mainstream Catholic culture of Europe.[6] There is obviously some truth in this; the loss of the intellectual, political and religious links with France, Spain, Austria and Italy excluded England from the unified world of Roman Christendom, and encouraged the English increasingly to consider themselves a nation with its own distinctive institutions and doctrines and character. Before the Reformation the English thought of themselves as an integral part of European Christendom and its culture, but as Protestantism took hold, that sense of unity was lost. The English Reformation is therefore sometimes considered the moment at which England rejected not just Catholicism but Europe itself, and set out on a different path which over time accentuated the differences between England and Europe rather than smoothing them.

Yet the argument can easily be overstated. England was after all not the only Protestant country in Europe; the Reformation took root in many countries. Protestant England became integrated into a new network based on the interchange of science, religion and politics across Protestant Europe.[7] England was never as isolated in the way that is sometimes suggested, and still in any case retained a sizeable Catholic minority. Ireland too remained predominantly Catholic. But one of Protestantism's lasting effects on the English state was that it encouraged the development of a state church, which was to leave a profound imprint on English institutions. England would have developed differently had it remained a mainstream Catholic country, but its Protestantism reorganized its links with Europe rather than breaking them altogether.

Out of the endless series of wars in which it was engaged, the English state emerged in the nineteenth century as the dominant world power, but it was a power gained through its global territorial conquests and acquisitions and the new liberal economic order which it established, rather than through its control of Europe. Unlike other great European powers England was never in a position to attempt to dominate Europe militarily. Towards Europe it pursued its traditional goal of maintaining a balance of power, and preventing any one power from dominating the European land mass. A crucial part of this strategy was finding appropriate allies in the rest of Europe. It was never a strategy of splendid isolation or withdrawal.

So powerful were the new forms of political nationalism in the modern era, and so successful was England as a nation-state, especially after the creation of Great Britain in the eighteenth century, that the importance of Europe in the construction of British identity can easily be forgotten. But a very powerful sense of Europe has long existed, shaped by two other major transnational political spaces, the Roman Empire and Christendom.[8] The common culture and common institutions which these supplied are the traditions which have fashioned the modern concept of Europe. It is a diverse political space but one which after the enormous destruction and conflict of the first half of the twentieth century has begun to be unified and integrated through the project of a European Union.

This European Union is a new form of political association which constantly confounds attempts to pronounce exactly what kind of political regime it is. Since 1994 it calls itself the 'European' Union, to emphasize the plans which emerged at the Maastricht Treaty for further integration and the creation of new institutions, in particular those to realize the plans of economic and monetary union and to enlarge the Union to include the countries of East and Central Europe.[9] But since Europe is not an island and has no natural borders either to the East, there is immense confusion as to where Europe begins and where it ends. The present plans for enlargement envisage a Union of twenty-five countries and there are more beyond that seeking membership, including Turkey. One of the problems with 'Europe' is that there is no sure means of defining which nations belong and which do not.[10]

The creation of such a Union has posed major new strategic and ideological problems for British governments, and a choice which they have spent fifty years attempting to postpone, but it is a choice which keeps returning and is being posed ever more urgently. England and the other nations that make up the United Kingdom can no longer relate to Europe in the old way, through the British state. This is because 'Great Britain' itself can no longer be preserved in the way that it once used to be, as the instrument of English power and interest. England's position in each of the other circles – Union, Empire, and Anglo-America – is changing, and a reordering of priorities and choices has become possible, and many argue, necessary. A significant part of the British political class has accepted the logic of giving priority to the European circle, but there is a strong body of opinion adamantly opposed, much of it within the Conservative Party.[11] Even many of those who do welcome further European integration and see this Union as the project on which England should embark, still shrink from it in part because of the difficulty of persuading their fellow-citizens of the desirability of accepting a much more positive conception of being European.

The European Question

The British relationship with the European Union has been one of the dominant issues of British politics in the last fifty years. It has also been one of the most divisive. The debate has moved through a number of phases. In the first phase up until 1961 the debate was whether Britain should participate at all in the negotiations to set up the first agreements on European cooperation, and on how it should respond to the existence of the Common Market after the signing of the Treaty of Rome in 1956. In the second phase from 1961 to 1975, the debate centred on whether Britain should apply to join and on the terms of entry. Twice rebuffed, Britain finally became a full member in 1973, endorsed by a referendum in 1975. In the third phase from 1975 to 1990 the debate focused on what the benefits of membership were. Labour in government was suspicious of Europe, and in opposition proposed withdrawal after only ten years of membership. Thatcher demanded a substantial rebate on the British contribution to the budget , and resisted for as long as she could, British membership of the Exchange Rate Mechanism, but she also signed up to the most important programme of European integration since the Treaty of Rome, the creation of the Single Market. In the fourth phase, debate has focused on the plans for deeper integration through the Maastricht Treaty in 1991, particularly economic and monetary union through the establishment of the single currency, and wider integration through enlargement.

Europe is the issue that never seems to go away. Controversy has continued to rage not only over the type of Europe the United Kingdom should be seeking to promote, but also at times (particularly in the early 1980s and the late 1990s) over whether the United Kingdom should remain a member at all. Both parties have shifted their position on the European Union, and in recent years have changed places. The Conservatives used to be the party of Europe, while the majority of the Labour Party was opposed to it. In the 1970s Labour was more divided on Europe than the Conservatives and it was one of the factors in the split in 1981 which led to the creation of the Social Democratic Party. By the 1990s however Labour had become the more pro-European party while the pro-European wing of the Conservative Party lost control of policy towards Europe against a background of a rising tide of anti-European feeling in the party. This trend was confirmed with the election as Party Leader of William Hague in 1997 and Iain Duncan Smith in 2001, both prominent Euro-sceptics. Duncan Smith had been a leading rebel against ratification of the Maastricht Treaty, and during the 1990s had been sympathetic to the case for withdrawal. Kenneth Clarke, the leader of the pro-European wing of the party, was defeated on each occasion, and largely because of his stance on Europe.

The reason why the issue of Europe has been so persistent and so divisive is that there is a lot at stake. For the future of British politics there is no more important issue, involving as it does a reassessment of British identity, security and political economy, and a judgement about the relative priority to be given to Europe as opposed to other relationships, particularly those with America. Such choices occur rather rarely but when they do they often trigger political realignments which can constitute major turning points in the life of parties and states. The nature of the British political system with its tradition of executive government and simple plurality constituency voting rules impose heavy penalties on parties which split or become deeply divided. Only eight splits occurred in the one hundred and fifty years since the Great Reform Bill of 1832.[12] Some of the most important have involved a strategic global political economy choice – particularly those in 1846 and 1903. Each involved a fierce clash between rival visions of the best future for the Union and the Empire. Parties which split suffered subsequent electoral defeat, ideological marginalization, and in most cases a lengthy exclusion from office.

Europe is this kind of issue. It divides parties because it fuses together questions of sovereignty and identity with political economy in a novel and powerful way. It can be compared with previous major conflicts over strategic choices in political economy, the Repeal of the Corn Laws in 1846 and Tariff Reform before 1914, but they did not involve questions of sovereignty directly, but rather the balance of interests within the state, and the basic orientation of policy. The European issue however has managed to involve both, and it has succeeded in splitting the two major parties of the state and helping to cause not one but two electoral collapses, in 1983 and 1997.

European Cooperation after 1945

In the immediate post-war period, British governments acknowledged the importance of Europe and the moves being taken to set up new European institutions. But they continued to give greater priority to the Empire and Commonwealth relationships and to Atlantic relationships. Churchill's three circles argument also gave priority to the Empire and to America over Europe. British governments encouraged moves to European unity but had no intention of playing a leading role in European institutions, because they believed Britain had a different role and status from other European countries.[13] Economic cooperation was in any case considered less important than security cooperation, which was handled through the Atlanticist framework of NATO.

Despite therefore the warm words of encouragement given by Churchill and other British leaders to the early moves to European economic and political union, support at this stage for any serious involvement of the UK was limited to a small band of European enthusiasts. The British government withdrew from the negotiations which led to the European Coal and Steel Community which was established in April 1952 following the Paris Treaty in April 1951, and also from the negotiations which established the European Economic Community (EEC) in January 1958 following the signing of the Treaty of Rome in March 1957. Part of the reason was the strong attachment of the political class to Britain's continuing global responsibilities, and to their desire to combine leadership of Europe with leadership of the Commonwealth. In the 1950s the British government tried to persuade other European members of the Organization for European Economic Cooperation (the OEEC, established in 1948) to embrace a programme of unilateral reduction of import controls, currency convertibility, and non-discriminatory trade. The other European states however wanted to move towards the establishment of a customs union, regulated trade, and to maintain the power to discriminate against imports from countries outside the common external tariff, notably the United States. To many in the British political class the kind of community which many advocates of European cooperation wished to create seemed protectionist and inward-looking. They continued to argue for open, multilateral trading relationships, and began to reduce the import controls which had underpinned post-war reconstruction in the mistaken belief that British industries were now strong enough to compete in global markets without any support.[14]

The decision of British governments to stay aloof from the early attempts to build European union was hardly a surprise and the Treaty of Rome was duly signed without the participation of the United Kingdom in 1957. But only four years later, in July 1961, the British government submitted its first application for full membership of the community it had scorned. The change was brought about by a substantial reassessment by important sections of the political class of Britain's economic and security interests. The Suez episode in 1956 was one catalyst, since it painfully brought home to the British government how limited were the possibilities of independent action in pursuit of British interests abroad when support from the United States was lacking.[15] Another factor was the evidence that British trade was growing very rapidly with advanced capitalist economies, particularly those in Western Europe, but was growing much more slowly with the Empire and Commonwealth. The dynamism of the Common Market in comparison with the fitful progress of the stop–go British economy seemed marked, and growing awareness of this began to win many converts in British industry and the British media to the need for the British economy to be a part of the EEC. After the British government had pulled out of the negotiations at Messina in 1956, it had organized the European Free Trade Association (EFTA), an association of smaller European countries designed to promote the removal of trade barriers between them. But this was quickly seen to be no substitute for a closer association with the powerhouse of the European economy based round France, Germany and the Benelux countries.[16]

Entry to the European Community

The initial application in 1961 formed part of a more general reassessment of Britain's place in the world, and the need to modernize British institutions.[17] After Macmillan took over as Conservative Leader following the failure at Suez, he moved to repair the damaged Atlantic relationship and to speed up the withdrawal from Empire. Macmillan had been one of the early supporters for a more positive European policy, and with the full backing of the Americans he was able to persuade his party that member-ship of the EEC was the logical next step. It could not be a substitute for Empire, because it commanded little of the emotional and ideological pull which Empire had for Conservatives.[18] But it was accepted as an expedient policy, serving the interests of British industry and Conservative electoral interests. Maintaining a growing economy and rising living standards made it sensible to attach the British economy to one of the fastest growing regional economies in the world.[19]

A formidable coalition of business, media, and political opinion was assembled in support of the application, but it encountered substantial opposition. Conservative opponents from the start stressed the threat to national sovereignty as well as to the Empire. These rebels sought to construct an alternative political economy around what remained of impe-rial preference and the need to bind the Commonwealth together.[20] But given the trends in trade this alternative rested more on sentiment rather than on any serious calculation of economic interest. Opposition also came from the Labour Party under Hugh Gaitskell, who famously claimed that 'Britain' would lose its national sovereignty and its distinctive national tradition and that one thousand years of history were at stake,[21] although since 'Britain' had existed for only just over two hundred and fifty years it was clearly England that he meant. Apart from the loss of national identity, Gaitskell also attacked the proposal to join the Common Market because he argued it would entrench market criteria as the arbiter of public policy and threaten the possibility of socialism in Britain, and with it the hard-won gains on welfare and employment of the British Labour movement.[22] This was to become the heart of the anti-Common Market case in the Labour Party.

The first British application failed because of the French veto. De Gaulle had decided that Britain and its political class were not yet sufficiently European in their policy and outlook, by which he meant that they did not share France's strategic view of Europe, and were likely to be serious obsta-cles to its achievement.[23] Since the British political class still gave priority to its relationship with America in both security and political economy, it was unlikely to accept the direction in which the rest of the member states, and especially France, wished the Community to develop. De Gaulle's insight was as usual acute, although what he was advocating was not a federal vision of Europe, but a Europe of nation-states under French leader-ship. The different preoccupations and traditions of the British political class he saw as a threat to that leadership. Until it was ready to choose Europe over America, it was not ready in his view to join the European Community.

By the middle of the 1960s most of the British political class, including the Labour leadership, had come to share the assessment made by Macmillan at the end of the 1950s that it was now in the British national interest to join the Common Market. Once in government after 1964 the Labour Party reversed its earlier opposition, and made a second application in 1967 which like the first was also turned down by De Gaulle. Membership was not finally secured until after De Gaulle's death and a political deal between his successor, President Pompidou, and the new Conservative government under Edward Heath.[24] There is little doubt that Harold Wilson would have accepted the same terms that Heath negotiated had he been re-elected in 1970. But in opposition once again, the internal politics of managing the Labour Party forced the leadership back into a position of public opposition to the EEC. Labour voted against the terms of entry negotiated in 1971, and were joined by 39 Conservatives. The government only won the vote with the support of 69 Labour MPs led by Roy Jenkins who resigned as Deputy Leader of the Labour Party, while twenty others abstained.[25]

Under pressure from the Labour left, Wilson in opposition promised that a future Labour government would renegotiate the terms of entry and then put them to a referendum. This was done in 1975. The Labour Cabinet approved the 'renegotiation' and voted to support continued membership 16 votes to 7, but a majority of the parliamentary party voted against, and a special Labour conference voted 2 to 1 against. In the Referendum Campaign that followed, the Labour government allied with the Conservatives and the Liberals to campaign for a yes-vote while the bulk of the Labour movement campaigned against, but it was the yes-campaign which won by 2 to 1.

Early Membership

Despite the successful negotiation of entry in 1973 and the winning of the Referendum in 1975, the British did not embrace their new European identity with any enthusiasm. The British government proved 'an awkward partner',[26] an awkwardness which began with the Heath Government, and continued with every succeeding administration. British governments acted in a very Gaullist manner from the start, seeking to promote their own interests in isolation from other member states and with little regard as to how Community institutions might be strengthened.

The reluctance which the British showed to become full members and really engage with the European Community owed much to the Atlanticist preferences and priorities of so much of the political class. At the outset this was most in evidence on the Labour side. James Callaghan in particular never made any secret of the priority he accorded to the relationship with the United States. His government blocked proportional representation for elections to the European Parliament, with the result that each European election produced a contingent of British MEPs which was wildly unrepresentative of the British electorate and out of line with European practice. This was not rectified until the constitutional reforms of the Blair Government. Similarly Labour's reluctance to participate in moves to greater economic and monetary union led to the decision not to put the pound into the new European Monetary System approved at the Brussels Summit in December 1978.[27] There was little positive enthusiasm for Europe in the Labour leadership (especially following Roy Jenkins' departure to be European Commission President in Brussels), and a majority of the Labour movement remained hostile to the European Community, and deeply suspicious of any moves towards further European integration.

The Referendum had been expected to settle the issue once and for all. The UK was now a full member of the European Community, and membership had been explicitly endorsed by the electorate and by the leaderships of the three main political parties. The Labour movement, however, was not reconciled to the UK being in the European Community, which it continued to denounce as a capitalist club whose rules prohibited socialist policies.[28] The deep political and economic crisis of the 1970s kept the Labour Party moving to the left and developing a new socialist programme, the alternative economic strategy, which aimed at guaranteeing full employment and extended welfare through protectionist and interventionist policies.[29] Since these policies contravened the rules of the European Community, the implementation of the alternative economic strategy required withdrawal from the European Community, to which the party duly committed itself in its 1983 Manifesto.

The Labour left argued that the rules of the Community prevented a Labour government adopting the measures it would need to revive the British economy. Reclaiming full national sovereignty was seen as essential to implement a radical interventionist programme, targeting investment to create a technologically advanced and high productivity industrial base. The radicalism of the left did not stop at questioning British links with Europe. The post-war Labour Atlanticist tradition was also rejected, with the commitment to unilateral nuclear disarmament and a radical revision of the British role in NATO. Labour became committed to a radical revision of British stances in both political economy and security, seeking to disengage from both Europe and America.[30]

While Labour hostility to the Community was expected, other European governments and the European Commission hoped that the return of the Conservatives to government in 1979 would herald a more constructive policy. Margaret Thatcher had supported continued membership of the European Union at the 1975 referendum as vital for the British national interest (even though she had not played a prominent part in the campaign). Thatcher had also criticized the decision of the Labour government not to join the European Monetary System in 1978. Once in government, however, a different pattern asserted itself.

The first cause of friction was the British contribution to the budget, a problem left over from the original negotiations. It had not been solved then, and the issue had not been resolved in the renegotiation either. The difficulty was a structural one reflecting the way in which the Community budget was financed. The UK was a major contributor through the Common External Tariff and through VAT payments, the two main sources of Community revenues. But the main programme which the budget supported was the Common Agricultural Policy from which the UK received relatively little. The subsidies provided to small-scale agricultural production through the CAP were a political priority for several of the leading members of the EC, but not for the UK with its relatively efficient and large-scale agriculture. The solution for a British government with a positive European agenda would have been either to accept the higher budget contribution as the price of belonging to the club, and enjoying the benefits for British companies of unrestricted access to European markets; or to press for the enlargement of the budget and the development of programmes such as the regional development fund which could be expected to provide much greater benefits for the UK.

Thatcher rejected both 'communautaire' solutions and pressed instead for the British government's money back.[31] The stridency of her negotiating style eventually won a compromise solution at the Fontainebleau summit in 1984, but it further strengthened the attitude in much of the British media that 'Europe' was an alien force, hostile to British interests against which British governments had constantly to struggle. Yet the Thatcher Government for all its apparent antagonism to Europe signed up to the single market programme and pushed the Single European Act through Parliament in 1986. This represented a major move to deeper integration, and included the concession of qualified majority voting, and therefore a significant pooling of sovereignty, but which was considered by the British in this instance acceptable in order to overcome the veto of some states on measures to increase competition in particular sectors. The British supported the single market because it was in line with British interests,[32] and there were other signs under the Thatcher Government that the British were becoming more adept at playing the internal EC political game.[33]

Despite this, however, the 1980s were in retrospect the decade when the great Conservative schism on Europe, explored further in Chapter 8, became serious. The basis of the new divisions in the Conservative Party after 1985 was a splintering of the Thatcherite right into pro and anti European factions. All the Thatcherites supported the vision of the European Community as a free trade area, but they increasingly differed as to how the single market was to be achieved and maintained, and the extent to which it was desirable to create common economic institutions to underpin the single market. The immediate flashpoint was the Exchange Rate Mechanism (ERM) and whether Britain should join it. Lawson and Howe urged membership on pragmatic grounds, but Thatcher increasingly came to interpret the ERM as an unacceptable loss of sovereignty and the preparation for a much more far-reaching economic and monetary union, the creation of a federal state.

Thatcher's increasingly strident denunciations of Europe fuelled Euroscepticism in the Conservative Party, and connected with the new conservative political economy already sketched out by Powell. The political economy of socialist protectionism had no echoes on the right in the 1970s and 1980s. The older national protectionist tradition which had once been so strong in the Conservative Party, in support of imperial preference and before that of agricultural duties, had almost disappeared. Instead opposition to the European Community came to be orchestrated by the free market nationalist right. The first and most brilliant exponent of this position was Enoch Powell. Although originally a supporter of the Common Market, he had become a dedicated opponent by 1970, subsequently resigning from the Conservative Party at the 1974 election and advising his supporters to vote Labour because Labour was promising a referendum on EC membership, and therefore a chance for the British people to reject Europe. He then took a prominent part in the referendum campaign on the 'No' side. Powell was not just anti-Europe but also anti-America. Like the Labour left he wanted Britain to disengage from both Europe and America, as the only way to restore full national independence. The Thatcherites were to take his anti-Europe lead, but remained resolutely Atlanticist. For them America was increasingly the model they sought to promote.

The huge seismic shift in British politics during the Thatcher years also saw Labour completely change direction. The scale of Labour's election defeat in 1983 created a new dynamic in the party which discredited the

alternative economic strategy and led to the abandonment of the commitment to withdraw from the European Community. The party swung
increasingly to a pro-European stand, already foreshadowed by the pragmatic stance of many trade unions towards European cooperation.[34] The
ideological onslaught of the Thatcher Government against many key
aspects of post-war social democracy convinced many in the Labour Party
that many of its social and economic objectives could best be realized
through the European Community, and caused a reappraisal of the virtues
of European social democracy. The more Atlanticist and pro-American the
Thatcher Government became, the more Europe commended itself to the
left. It was thus in the Reagan/Thatcher years that the ideological opposition of Europe and America as two different models of political economy
became firmly established.

Ever Closer Union

The most recent phase of Britain's relationships with Europe has been
dominated by the creation of the European Union by the Maastricht Treaty
in 1991, and the setting of goals for economic and monetary union, for
enlargement, and for a common defence and foreign policy. The achievement of a genuine single market was seen to require corresponding development of supranational institutions, in particular a single currency, and
corresponding developments in social programmes and forms of accountability so that it might achieve its full potential. A larger community budget
and more programmes and legislation at the European level were required,
accompanied by the transfer of more decision-making power to the
European Parliament to give greater legitimacy to the decisions of the
European Commission, and to make it more independent of the Council of
Ministers.

It was these consequences of the creation of the single market in promoting new moves towards economic and political union which so divided the
Thatcherite wing of the Conservatives. Many of them like Geoffrey Howe,
Chancellor and then Foreign Secretary under the Thatcher Government,
accepted the logic that a single market needed in due course the creation of
a single currency and such other agencies as were necessary to regulate it.
The Thatcherite programme in Britain had targeted the political obstacles
to the working of the free market and had endeavoured to sweep many of
them away. It followed that if there was to be a real single market at the
European level there had to be supranational administrative and legal institutions to ensure that local political obstacles in the various nation-states

were exposed and overcome. The problem for many Thatcherites however, including Thatcher herself, was that although they agreed with the goal they were not prepared to will the means if this meant transferring what they regarded as core aspects of British national sovereignty to Brussels.[35]

The central point of opposition was the proposal for a single currency. Many Conservatives feared that the transfer of monetary responsibilities to a European Central Bank would be followed by the transfer of fiscal responsibilities to the European Commission, and the loss of control by British governments to influence conditions in the British economy.[36] Economic policy would be determined at European level, and might well be more interventionist and social democratic than the Conservatives wanted. In this way socialism could be imposed through the backdoor on the British people without them having voted for it. The Thatcherites saw themselves as part of a conservative revolution in Anglo-America which had made great strides in the 1980s on both sides of the Atlantic.[37] But Europe with its very different traditions now appeared to threaten those achievements.

In her celebrated Bruges speech in 1988 Thatcher argued that national sovereignty should always be given priority over supranational institutions. Europe should be no more than an association of nation-states, agreeing to set up institutions and common programmes where these were in the interests of all states. The implication of this view was that qualified majority voting sanctioned under the Single European Act should be abolished, and certainly not extended; that the powers of the European Court to interpret the terms of the treaties which had established the European Union should be limited so as not to override the national courts; and that the European Commission should have no independent power to initiate legislation but should be subordinate to the Council of Ministers.

After leaving office Thatcher came to regret that she had ever accepted the Single European Act, and became ever more extreme in her denunciations of Europe, until she had reached the point where in common with a growing number of Conservatives she was prepared to advocate renegotiation of the treaties, and if that failed, then outright withdrawal.[38] Those Conservatives that agreed with her argued that if the rest of the Union would accept the British view of the way the Union should develop, then there would be no need for Britain to leave, but so long as the other member states still accepted a role for supranational institutions which are not entirely subordinate to national governments, then there would continue to be conflict. Conservative supporters of continued UK membership of the European Union regard the anti-European drift of opinion in the Conservative Party as based on a fantasy that there is an alternative political

economy available, an alternative way of reconstructing the four circles of
the British state, which would reveal the European project pursued during
the last fifty years to have been a false trail and allow it to be discarded.

Thatcher's resistance to making a commitment to membership of the
European Monetary System was eventually overcome by the insistence of
her colleagues, but she succeeded in defining the new terrain of anti-EU
sentiment within the Conservative Party and in the country. After her
forced departure her successor John Major, who as Chancellor had finally
taken the decision to join the European Monetary System in September
1990, was at first expected to strike a new note and chart a fresh direction
for the relationship with the European Union. He clearly intended to do so,
speaking of his wish to see 'Britain' at the heart of Europe. But his awareness of the tide of opinion in his own party was already apparent in the way
in which he conducted the negotiations for the Maastricht Treaty, insisting
on crucial opt-outs from the social chapter (on the grounds that this would
raise British business costs) and from the commitment to participate in the
third stage of economic and monetary union.

He presented the outcome of the negotiations at Maastricht as a considerable triumph for British diplomacy, but his efforts were undermined by
the catastrophe of Black Wednesday, on September 16 1992. The forced
suspension of sterling's membership of the Exchange Rate Mechanism
(ERM) knocked away one of the crucial supports for the government's
economic policy. If sterling had stayed within the ERM then the ground
would have been prepared for the British government's eventual acceptance (without the need for a referendum) of a single currency and of
economic and monetary union. The forced exit ignited the opposition to the
Maastricht Treaty and gave the government nine months of parliamentary
battles to secure passage of the Bill. It also permanently damaged the reputation of the government for economic competence and led directly to the
eruption of a civil war within the party over its leadership and future direction. Given his increasingly precarious majority as a result of by-election
losses and defections, Major was obliged to adopt a vacillating and inconsistent policy in order to hold the factions of his party together. He steadily
however grew increasingly negative in his attitude towards Europe because
of the growing strength of anti-European opinion in the party and in the
Conservative media.[39] In 1996 the House of Commons vote which saw 74
backbenchers support Bill Cash's motion for a referendum before any
further moves towards European integration, revealed just how far the party
was moving away from its former pro-European stance.

By 1996 the other members of the European Community were increasingly despairing of the British Conservatives as likely to develop a

consistent and positive European policy, and rather as they had done in the 1970s, they transferred their hopes to the opposition, and the new Labour Party of Tony Blair. The Conservatives were quick to seize on this and attempted to portray the Labour Leader as 'the poodle of Brussels' and Labour as a federalist party which would abandon British sovereignty. Tony Blair was the first Prime Minister since Edward Heath to be unequivocally pro-European, and even then he was frequently at odds with other members of the EU. Under Blair Britain exercised its opt-out not to go in the single currency, and pressed for radical reform of the Community Budget and programmes such as the CAP. Even under Heath there were some early difficulties in the British government's relationships with its European partners. It raised the question of whether there are reasons regardless of which party is in government why friction is likely to persist between the British government and the rest of the Community.

Political Economy

This question is related to another. What kind of political space will Europe turn out to be? European integration has been analysed as deriving from fundamental shifts in the organization of the European and world economy. As national economies have become more interdependent so interests have been formed in support of further and deeper economic integration. The continued political separation of Europe into nation-states is an obstacle to this process of economic integration, which is gradually overcome through the development of supranational institutions. On this view it is the trends towards regionalization of the European economic space through trade and investment flows which is the central reality of the past fifty years. The setting up of the original communities reflected an early grasp of this new political economy of the European economy by the founder states. Once the governments of other countries including the British government recognized the same logic they applied for membership.

European integration is here understood as a long-term process which can be hindered or delayed by political decision-making, but not halted or seriously diverted. Sooner or later the political opposition to the next stage of integration will be overcome because of the irresistible pressure which arises from the new structure of interests in the European economy. Progress towards further integration is regarded as cyclical. It is fastest in periods of economic prosperity and economic growth; in periods of economic recession and stagnation it is halted or slowed. But each new period of advance starts from a higher base so that the development of integration appears cumulative, an inexorable process leading to deeper and wider political and economic union, and the transfer of key functions from national governments to supranational institutions.

Opponents of European integration often argue that the end-point of this process will be the creation of a United States of Europe – a strong centralized state which replaces the existing nation-states as a focus of legitimacy, identity, and executive competence. An alternative view, however, is that a new kind of political system is emerging, the first post-modern state, in which there are overlapping economic and political spaces, jurisdictions, and institutions.[40] Government functions are distributed among several different levels – European, national and local. The nation-state transfers some functions to European institutions and others to regional and local institutions, but it still retains an important range of decision-making powers. National sovereignty is qualified and limited but not dispelled. Most of the key issues in the debate over Britain's relationship to the European Union are over the extent to which national sovereignty should be limited by the transfer of decision-making to supranational institutions.

If the trend towards European economic integration is so powerful what explains Britain's troubled relationship with the European Community, the reluctance to get involved in the first place, the constant fretting about the terms of entry, the friction over particular issues, and the unwillingness to accept the way in which the Community operates? Are these transitional problems which reflect particular historical legacies, and which will all in time be overcome? Are they symptoms of post-imperial trauma from which Britain will eventually emerge? From this standpoint the intensity of the European issue in British politics and the conflicts around it are part of the process of adjustment.

But what if the process of European integration is not either irresistible or irreversible, but the result of decisions made by national governments in line with their perceived national interests and in response to changing political and economic conditions in the world economy? From this perspective although long-term economic and social trends exist which have given rise to various kinds of interdependence and interconnectedness in the global economy, governments and other political actors have important degrees of autonomy in managing and adjusting to these pressures. Government decisions both sustain and modify the structures within which they operate.

There can indeed be no presumption that the trend towards economic integration and political union is inevitable or irreversible. The calculations by government of their national interest or of their domestic political pressures may change as a result of external as well as internal factors. The

European Community has often been viewed as a political project based on a political understanding between France and Germany,[41] and shaped in the particular political and economic context of the cold war and the long post-war boom. The debates in the 1990s on the future of the European Union took place in a very different context; the collapse of communism in Europe, the disintegration of the Soviet Union, the reunification of Germany, and the relative stagnation of the European economy relative to other parts of the global political economy.

For Britain too the context of the debate about the EU has altered, particularly as the choice between Europe and America in British politics has sharpened. In the 1950s the Empire was still a potent influence on the thinking of the British political class, and the Atlantic Alliance was the linchpin of thinking on security. In the 1990s the ending of the Cold War and the new drive to European integration symbolized by the processes of economic and monetary union and enlargement made a reappraisal of Britain's involvement with both Europe and America overdue.

At the centre of this debate is whether there really is no other choice for Britain than deepening economic and political integration with Europe, as many of the enthusiasts for integration contend. Sceptics have argued that the regionalization of the European economy which occurred in the forty years between 1950 and 1990 was closely related to the division of the world economy between the United States and the Soviet Union. The disintegration of the Soviet Union and its command economy opened the way for a new era of a unified global economy. The future patterns of regionalization in this global economy may be different and may fragment rather than further unify the European economy. The disappearance of the former superpower confrontation brought into focus the economic division between East Asia, North America, and Western Europe, but the fears that a new world of regional blocs and inter-bloc rivalry were about to emerge have so far not materialized.[42] What has occurred is a further enhancement of the power of the United States, and an increasing tendency of the United States to resort to unilateralism, abandoning multilateral solutions to problems of global security or global economy.

The biggest question facing the EU is whether the contradictory tendencies of deepening integration through economic and monetary union and widening it through enlargement can be successfully managed. Reaching decisions and a common will in a Union of fifteen nation-states has been hard enough, but reaching it in a Union of twenty-five will be much harder, unless the Union can agree fundamental constitutional reforms. The European Convention was set up under the chairmanship of Valery Giscard d'Estaing precisely for this purpose. But huge obstacles remain. The euro has been successfully launched and in its first three years confounded the critics, but the Union has appeared more divided than ever on security and foreign policy questions, particularly over Iraq in 2003. Chirac's scolding of some of the applicant countries for signing a letter supporting the US position on Iraq revealed French irritation that countries who wanted to be part of the EU, as well as countries that were already members of the EU, such as Britain and Spain, were prepared to have bilateral relations with the US rather than first forge a consensus on foreign policy within the European space.

Whether the EU can advance further and become a counterweight to America in global governance of security and political economy will depend on whether there is the political will in Europe to make it happen. European union has advanced as far as it has because of domestic political calculations by the various national political classes. The political, administrative, business and media components of the political class in the UK have always predominantly supported membership of the European Union. No Cabinet of either party has ever come out against membership since the first application in 1961. Several key government departments, particularly the Foreign Office, have become very committed to making Europe work. Business opinion has remained broadly in favour of membership and of further steps to integration. The media is more divided, with the Conservative press since the 1980s becoming steadily anti-European, but the overall picture suggests that there remains a strong bias as far as the political class is concerned for continued membership of the Union. Membership confers significant benefits which could not be realized in any other way.

Despite the growing strength of the anti-European wing of the Conservative Party, therefore, there remains substantial consensus in the political class about the desirability of continued membership to safeguard essential national interests. Does membership still make sense, however, in terms of domestic politics? The earlier disagreement between Labour and the Conservatives on the desirability of membership reflected different estimates of the gains and losses from entry. The defensiveness of the Labour movement sprang from a desire to protect the arrangements which had guaranteed full employment and collective welfare. The successful national political economy which they saw as one of the achievements of the 1945 Labour government was threatened by the free market ethos of the Common Market. The Conservatives however believed that membership of the European Community would help to sustain prosperity and expansion, and that although there were some costs in the form of higher food prices, these would be easily outweighed by the faster rate of economic growth which being a full member of the Community would be expected to promote. This standpoint was that taken in the other member states. Transfers of sovereignty in building the European community were acceptable if they helped promote the domestic policies on which the post-war political order was based.[43]

Within the UK the Conservatives' post-war electoral strategy of seeking to align themselves with the growth sectors of the economy and society consistently gave them the edge over Labour. This difference became a chasm after 1979 when Labour became identified with declining regions and sectors of the economy. The puzzle remains however. It is easy to see why the national protectionist strategy which Labour adopted in the 1970s and which was already implicit in its earlier suspicion of the Common Market was a weaker electoral strategy than the strategy of the Conservatives. But why then did so many of the Conservative Party and its media allies begin to turn away from that strategy in the 1980s and 1990s? In the 1960s only *The Daily Express*, still wedded to the ideal of the British Empire, opposed the application to join the Common Market. In 1996 *The Times, The Daily Telegraph, The Daily Mail, The Sun*, and *The Star* had also all become strong critics of the European Union. The vehemence of their criticism has begun to cast doubt on whether the UK should continue to be a member.

One explanation is that the balance of costs and benefits had altered, particularly as a result of the long recession which had affected the United Kingdom and the rest of Europe at the beginning of the 1990s.[44] The costs of the common agricultural policy continued to loom large and were only just offset by the benefits from increased trade and increased inward investment. The anti-European wing of the Conservative Party increasingly argued that there was an alternative political economy to the one associated with membership of the European Union, which was capable both of guaranteeing British security and of obtaining greater prosperity than could be secured within the Union.

They believe that as a result of changes in the global economy and the policies adopted by the Thatcher Government in the 1980s, England has an opportunity to become the 'Hong Kong' of Europe, with a policy regime which emphasizes deregulation, low taxation, flexible labour markets, and open trade and investment.[45] This policy regime is contrasted with that likely to be imposed through the supranational institutions of the EU – regulation, high taxation, inflexible labour markets, and restrictive policies on trade and investment. Europe's position, it is argued, has changed. From being one of the powerhouses of the growth of the world economy in the 1950s it has become relatively stagnant. The fastest growing markets are in other parts of the world, particularly East Asia. The policy of British governments should not therefore be to tie itself to an inward looking bloc whose instincts are restrictive and protectionist, but to pursue its traditional open seas policy of seeking the most rapidly growing markets and the cheapest sources of supply. Such a policy would also be Atlanticist in continuing to entrust the security of Britain to NATO and the Atlantic Alliance rather than any arrangements within the European Union. It would also renew the close relationship and understanding between the governments of Britain and the United States on the organization of the world economy. In this connection membership of the North American Free Trade Association (NAFTA) is seen as more relevant to long-term British interests than membership of the EU.

This alternative political economy is what makes the divide within the Conservative Party so serious. The majority of the party and its media allies has swung behind this alternative strategy, even if its business allies for the most part remain unconvinced. But the alternative is plausible enough to give the political class pause, and the resonance with popular chauvinism against Europe orchestrated by the Conservative tabloids makes it look electorally attractive also. The Euro-sceptics calculate that there is now a gulf between how the political class perceives the European Union and how the people do. This populist tactic however ignores the ambivalence in the electorate. The European Union is less popular among British people than it is in most other member countries, but that did not prevent the referendum result in favour of continued membership and the hard-headed calculation by many voters that although they may not like Europe they still regard it as the best option for maintaining employment, growth and living standards. The emotional attachment to the pound sterling will be of less significance in the evaluation of a single currency than whether it is likely to make certain outcomes which voters want, such as low inflation, more likely. The political economy of currency union may well be more complex than many of the anti-Europeans allow. They portray it as an issue of the political class versus the people, but really it is another question of different elements of the political class fighting one another, and which group the people will trust more. The credibility of the alternative political economy of the right then becomes crucial, against the more tested political economy of the left. The present division in the Conservative leadership makes it very difficult for the free-market nationalists to persuade the electorate that a radical shift is either safe or sensible.

It has been argued in this chapter that in recent decades the European issue has had a greater capacity to split British political parties than any other. This is because there are key strategic political economy choices involved. The opponents of European Union have tried to formulate an alternative political economy which would both command the support of the political class and of the electorate. The success of the European Union in the past is due to the fact that the European project secured both. The question for the future is whether a new consensus in the political class on the desirability of further European integration which can command popular support will become established, or whether the balance will swing to new national-populist elements in the political class which will favour a much looser association between the European nations if they favour one at all.

7
The English Model

No unbiased observer who derives pleasure from the welfare of
his species, can fail to consider the long and uninterruptedly
increasing prosperity of England as the most beautiful phenomenon in the history of mankind. Climates more propitious may
impact more largely the mere enjoyment of existence, but in no
other region have the benefits that political institutions can
confer been diffused over so extended a population; nor have
any people so well reconciled the discordant elements of
wealth, order and liberty.

Henry Hallam, 1818[1]

The choice between Europe and America which has come to dominate the
future of British politics is not only a matter of identity and security.
Europe and America have also come to represent different models of
economic, political, and social organization as far as political debates in
Britain are concerned.[2] As argued throughout this book, the debates are
often as much within Anglo-America, or within Europe, as between them.
But Europe and America have increasingly been used on both sides of the
debate in British politics as convenient terms to denote rival ideals to be
promoted or avoided.

At one time England itself was renowned for being a model for others,
an object of imitation, and an exemplar of particular forms of excellence.
What lay at the root of the English model were specific forms of liberal
capitalism, representative government, and collective welfare. Together
these comprised a distinctive political economy, and a particular interlink-
ing of the institutions of state and civil society which, despite many blem-
ishes and failures, helped create a successful economy, an effective and
representative state and a flourishing and relatively stable civil society
through the eighteenth and nineteenth centuries, and a comprehensive
welfare state in the twentieth century. At the middle of the twentieth
century the English model was still very much intact, and was celebrated

for securing the gradual extension of civil, political and ultimately social rights, which promoted forms of citizenship and self-government throughout British society.[3]

In the last fifty years, however, England has more often been held up as an example to be avoided, a warning of what not to be, a model to be shunned rather than copied, even by other nations in the Union. *Die Englische Krankheit* was a term applied originally to the poor record on strikes and industrial relations which afflicted the British economy in the 1970s.[4] But in the wider decline literature it came to be applied to all English and British institutions, in particular to Britain's underperforming capitalism, its anachronistic *ancien régime*, and its underfunded and failing public services.[5]

This decline was in part a real process, most marked in relation to British military power. British jurisdiction contracted in absolute terms in the course of the century, and the UK lost its former naval, financial and industrial pre-eminence, and with it went many strategic capacities which the British state had formerly possessed. British power and global reach and imperial responsibility were very different in 2000 from what they had been in 1900. But in other respects the decline was a matter of perception; it was relative rather than absolute. British living standards were much higher in 2000 than in 1900, the bulk of its population had 'never had it so good', as Harold Macmillan observed in 1959. The talk of decline which reached a crescendo in the 1970s and 1980s was often about relative rather than absolute loss, deriving from anxieties in parts of the political class that there had been a falling away in cultural and moral standards, in economic performance, in social solidarity and a sense of community compared both to the past and to other countries.[6]

The pervasiveness of writing on decline particularly in the second half of the twentieth century reflected a strong sense that the old political economy which had functioned so smoothly and so well for so long was falling apart, and that the new political economy which was replacing it was increasingly dysfunctional and malign. Few in the political class, however, agreed on the diagnosis of the problem or on what should be done to put it right,[7] and this created a period of some turbulence and polarization in the 1970s and 1980s, accompanied by many apocalyptic predictions, most of which turned out to be exaggerated, but some of which did nonetheless highlight changes that were to come.

The decline debate reflected a loss of confidence by many in the British political class about the future of the British state and in its own capacity or desire to manage the process of adjustment necessary to establish a new identity and orientation of policy. This mood of resignation was intensified by the growing realization that England in most fields was no longer a model for the rest of the world. From the 1960s onwards it came to be viewed as an increasingly dysfunctional political economy. Instead of the virtuous circle of a dynamic capitalism, stable and representative political institutions, and a strong public sector and sense of public interest, Britain was seen by the end of the 1970s as having entered the vicious circle of a sluggish and underperforming capitalism, a polarized political class, a state that was no longer effective or representative, and a government that was overloaded, and no longer capable of defining a public interest against the claims of increasingly powerful sectional interests.[8] These perceptions created the political crisis of the 1970s, out of which has come the new course which has transformed British politics, a revolution in two stages, the first initiated by Thatcher, the second by Blair, and a political discourse in which the choices have increasingly come to be dominated by the stylized alternatives represented by Europe and America.

English Capitalism

The English model of capitalism was the work of many nationalities – Scots, Welsh, Irish, Italians, Flemings, Huguenots – as well as the Anglo-Saxons themselves. It was by no means the first model of capitalism in Europe, the Italian city states were much in advance of it, but it became the crucial model partly because it was the first example of capitalism becoming the dominant mode of production in a large national economy, and also because from the outset its development depended upon the wider development of a global capitalist economy. The territorial space of the United Kingdom was large enough to create a sufficient internal market, and England's global reach meant that the economy developed through the network of trading relations across the world; tradeable commodities such as cotton, sugar, and slaves became the lifeblood of this economy.[9]

Capitalism and Empire were inseparable. Each was a means to the development of the other. The British state was highly rapacious and built a formidable military machine, particularly its navy, which by the end of the eighteenth century had superior equipment and superior seamanship to any other.[10] It underpinned the conquest and consolidation of England's first colonial empire, and encouraged, in line with the thinking of the time, a mercantilist policy towards maximizing the wealth and the territory of England. In pursuing this course the British state was imitating what had already been successfully accomplished by Spain, Portugal, the Netherlands and France. Great Britain in 1760 was a prosperous economy, with a productive agriculture and an expanding commerce. It was emerging as one of the more successful European states, but there was nothing strikingly different in the way in which its political economy was organized.

That was to change in the next hundred years. Some of the foundations were already in place; the external trading networks, the unified state and internal market covering the whole land area of the British Isles, key institutions including the Bank of England and the stock exchange, above all the clear specification of property rights and the sweeping away of many legal obstacles to the emergence of a commercial society. What now emerged in addition were new industries, new technologies, new political doctrines, and a new political dispensation. Together they created the English model of liberal capitalism.

English capitalism was proclaimed as liberal in the nineteenth century, even though many of the means by which it had been created, such as the slave trade and land enclosures, were far from liberal. It was regarded as liberal because of the relative freedom of its civil society from the state, and because property rights were individual and therefore alienable.[11] A strong sense of civil rights, of equality before the law, of rights of self-government and voluntary association, were key components in the emergence of what was for the time a comparatively fluid and open civil society. Many blockages to civil and still more to political rights remained, particularly the distribution of educational opportunity, discrimination against women,[12] and discrimination against Protestant Dissenters, Jews, and Catholics. But even with these limitations the civil societies which had emerged in England and Scotland by the end of the eighteenth century had created a form of citizenship which gave (male) individuals a high degree of autonomy and flexibility in accumulating wealth. Many of the Dissenters in particular took full advantage. Barred from the universities in England and from holding public office, their energies were deployed elsewhere. Scientific, technological and industrial advance was often pioneered by them, and they contributed disproportionately to the new class of capitalists which spearheaded the industrial civilization of the nineteenth century.[13]

This enterprise and dynamism of civil society, this restless individualism, operating within a framework of law, but creating such extraordinary changes in society and business through the application of new technologies, lay at the heart of the English model. The role of the state was important, especially in the development of military technologies, and frequently underplayed in later panegyrics to economic liberalism, but in much of the economy the state played essentially an enabling role, rather than a directing role.[14] It removed obstacles, and facilitated change, rather than in the early stages deliberately planning and leading them. This social and technological dynamism of English capitalism was what so struck outsiders, along with the enormous contrasts of the new industrial civilization; unimaginable wealth coinciding with poverty and squalor; dazzling design and technology coexisting with sprawling ugliness and meanness of spirit.[15]

The English model of capitalism owed a great deal to Scotland. It is indelibly associated with the political economy of the Scottish Enlightenment, Adam Ferguson, David Hume, and Adam Smith; it was also shaped by the utilitarian philosophers, Jeremy Bentham and James Mill, and with the classical political economists of the early nineteenth century, David Ricardo, McCulloch, and John Stuart Mill. Out of this came the doctrines which critics were quick to label 'the dismal science', because of its iron laws and inexorable necessity, and its establishment of utility or efficiency as the chief criteria by which all economic, political and social arrangements should be judged.[16]

Liberal political economy represented a revolution in thinking about how best to manage an economy. In his *Inquiry into the Nature and Causes of the Wealth of Nations* Adam Smith sought to advise statesmen on the best principles for maximizing that wealth.[17] If the state restricted its role to enforcing competition and property rights, and removing obstacles to free markets, he concluded, the result would be to liberate enterprise and create much greater prosperity and ultimately much higher revenues for the state. The idea was an extraordinarily simple one, but like all the most successful ideas one of enormous power. It meant that wherever possible policy should be aimed at freeing trade and enterprise rather than restricting it. The watchwords of liberal political economy in the nineteenth century became free trade, sound money and laissez-faire.[18]

This was a system of universal ideas of great range and scope, implying as it did the idea of a minimal state, a governing intelligence whose activity was restricted to ensuring that the rules governing free exchange were in place and were upheld, but which otherwise removed itself from as much involvement as possible with economic decisions. This was ceded to the 'individual', who was conceived as a sovereign agent, enjoying rights and autonomy, and owning property, even if for most of the population this property amounted chiefly to the labour power they could sell on the market for whatever wage it could command.

It took some time for the full implication of these ideas to be understood and for their practical effect to be felt. There were many other ideas and many interests which opposed them. In the course of being implemented the deficiencies of a purely liberal view of political economy and the new industrial capitalist economy were to be starkly exposed. But this was only appreciated much later. What liberal political economy achieved was the delineation of an ideal political economy to which English capitalism was the nearest approximation, and promoted this as the ideal to which all countries which sought to become developed in the English manner should aspire. What made it liberal was its concept of the individual and its sanction for individual autonomy acting within a framework of general rules as the basis for a capitalist order.[19]

This English model has often been caricatured as celebrating rampant individualism, a libertarian vision of a society without restraints, which in the context of capitalism means accumulation without limits, private greed and selfishness, the subordination of moral principles to the pursuit of self-interest through market exchange. But the individualism and the market promoted by the English model and the liberal political economists were always understood as existing within the rule of law, the framework of general rules which the state existed to enforce and which defined and promoted the public interest and ensured that the pursuit of private interest was consistent with it. This was always an ordered liberty, and the public power existed to ensure that it remained ordered – enforcing competition, breaking up monopolies, ensuring that contracts were honoured, and that money was stable in value.[20]

Another strong feature of the English model was the attention it gave to voluntary association and self-government, and the development of citizenship. The English Common Law recognized the existence of corporate personality and English civil society became peopled by a myriad of associations which were able to act as legal individuals. Two of the most important examples of such corporate personalities for the English model were the limited liability public company and the trade union. Both were at first resisted on the grounds that they denied the responsibility of the individual. Only unlimited liability preserved the principle that those launching an enterprise were prepared to accept all losses as well as all profits. Similarly trade unions were viewed as conspiracies against property, seeking to interfere with the process of individual exchange by making themselves monopoly sellers of labour.

In the second half of the nineteenth century however both limited liability and trade unionism were legalized, and a way found of reconciling them with the provisions of Common Law. The strength of the idea of voluntary association alongside the idea of the individual was demonstrated. The English model of capitalism was never simply about individual agency but also about forms of collective agency. The public company with limited liability was promoted by those who argued that such cooperation was a perfectly reasonable expression of laissez-faire principles and that to deny it would be an unreasonable restraint of trade. They were joined by those who argued that without legal instruments to make joint stock companies possible many of the most important opportunities for industrial investment such as railway construction could not be accomplished.[21] Many liberals who also wished to see a much wider dispersion of property ownership saw joint stock companies as a vehicle for small investors, and limited liability as a principle that could protect their capital.

It was however quite typical of the English model, and in marked contrast to legal and political developments elsewhere, that in the case of both companies and trade unions, they were conceived fundamentally as private associations outside the state, rooted in civil society, which by acquiring corporate status and corporate personality acquired certain legal privileges as well as certain legal obligations. The German approach of starting from first principles and defining constitutionally the public nature of associations such as companies and trade unions was not adopted.[22] In this way the self-governing character of civil society and its independence from the state was protected. The vitality of English civil society, its wealth of corporate personality and voluntary association, and its degree of independence from the state were essential ingredients of the English model.

In the course of the nineteenth century the English model of capitalism became fully established. The doctrines of liberal political economy became political and administrative orthodoxy, and the validity of its basic principles was not thought to be open to doubt. Even those who criticized the new doctrines recognized the power of the principles and their hold on both the imagination and the practice of the nineteenth century. In England the decisive political moment which consolidated the hold of liberal political economy upon the state was the Repeal of the Corn Laws in 1846. Free trade had been conceded in principle twenty years before, but the Repeal of the Corn Laws in 1846 showed that no political coalition was now strong enough to stand in the way of the application of free trade principles, not even the landed interest.

More than anything else free trade came to symbolize the English model of capitalism. It stood in sharpest contrast to the mercantilism of the colonial system, and it pushed the British economy across one of the great divides between modern and traditional societies – the movement from self-subsistent agricultural communities to urban, industrial communities dependent on trade and advanced division of labour. England became the first country to abandon the security of self-subsistent agriculture for the greater wealth and opportunities offered by industry and international trade.

Its prospects and its survival became indissolubly linked to the global economy which it had helped create.[23]

Many critics of British power in the nineteenth century saw the doctrine of free trade as a cynical device which served British interests, because of the superior productivity of British industry.[24] The British could outcompete and undercut the rest of the world, so it was naturally in their interest that all markets should be open, and that protectionism should be outlawed. There was some truth in this, but it failed to explain why the idea of free trade had such power and attraction across the world. By projecting the ideal of a liberal global economic order framed by a common set of rules, the English model came to represent a universal interest. It set out the goal of a self-governing, spontaneous order which maximized freedom, equality and prosperity. The grandeur of its cosmopolitan vision was admired by Marx and Cobden alike.[25]

The two other maxims – sound finance and laissez-faire – were also vital components of the English model. Sound finance meant that the people could trust the value of the currency. It would be managed in accordance with rules which ensured that although there might be price movements there would be neither sustained inflation or sustained deflation. A stable standard of exchange meant that all economic agents could have confidence in buying and selling, in investing and consuming, because the calculations they made would not be erroneous because of a currency that fluctuated widely in value. A large part of the prestige of the English model of capitalism derived from the pound sterling which became a rock solid currency, linked to the gold standard from the 1820s, and so stable that it was treated in practice as equivalent to gold, and an international medium of exchange in its own right.[26] The price level in the UK was still liable to go up sharply during wartime when the state greatly expanded its exactions from its citizens, and the normal restraints were relaxed. But in the hundred years which elapsed between the final defeat of Napoleon at Waterloo in 1815 and the beginning of the First World War in 1914 the UK price level actually fell slightly. This extraordinary financial stability created a remarkable level of trust and confidence, essential foundations for a liberal capitalist order.

Laissez-faire was also an important aspect of the English model, not because it signified an inactive or weak state, but because it implied a small state, a state with strong powers, which was required to be decisive and vigilant in exercising them, but which was content to remain within well-defined limits.[27] This idea of a trade that was open and free to all comers and a currency that was not routinely devalued to provide additional revenue for the state was novel. Europe was crammed with states which grew ever larger and more dominant in their societies. These top-heavy authoritarian, bureaucratic and military states, exemplified by the empires of Germany, Austria and Russia made the idea that national success and military power could be based on a small state seem far-fetched to the Chancelleries of Europe. Yet the success of England and the English model could hardly be disputed. In the nineteenth century this was the most successful capitalism that had ever been and its success had transformed the world, in the process creating the economic forces and the political powers which would soon challenge and later eclipse it.

Critics of this image of liberal England have ridiculed it as an illusion. England after all had become a major military and imperial power, had fought successive wars against the leading European powers, and the British state had given significant and sustained support to its naval dock-yards and other parts of its military infrastructure. But while it might give a very different picture of itself abroad, at home the English state was still remarkably undeveloped, compared to so many of the states elsewhere in Europe.[28] The idea that reducing state functions to a minimum and trusting in the spontaneous activity of the people and the web of corporate bodies and voluntary associations in civil society was the best way to create successful capitalist development was something few other societies were able to match, but it remained an alluring vision, not just for domestic policy but for the organization of the global political economy as well.

The English model of capitalism proclaimed that a successful capitalist economy should be society-led rather than state-led, policy should be subordinated to the general interest of wealth creation, and society should be encouraged to become a commercial society, a society in which every-one is a buyer and a seller, a society of strangers in which there is respect for the rule of law, a high level of trust in others, and respect for property rights and contractual obligations. Such a model is founded on certain basic citizenship rights, particularly freedom of labour, freedom of association, and freedom of speech. It depends on a flexible labour market in which all citizens are in principle free to sell their labour services.

This commercial society of the English was much derided by other Europeans, as being obsessed with the pursuit of pleasure and happiness and material comfort, rather than more uplifting objectives of military glory and spiritual and intellectual achievement. Napoleon famously called the English a nation of shopkeepers, who put material comforts ahead of ascetic martial virtues. In the First World War British soldiers were mocked in the German press as unmanly when safety razors were discovered in captured British trenches. But although the English were shopkeepers they were a nation of sailors and soldiers as well, the Scots even more so.[29]

England could hardly have expanded as it did if its citizens had been devoted entirely to the arts of peace and domestic comfort. But there was enough in the jibe to make it stick. The English were remarkable for the importance they gave to their civil society and to the subordination of the state to its needs. Adam Smith codified this new political economy, and launched a new doctrine on the world, a new way of understanding the relationship between the state and the economy.

Critics of English Capitalism

There were other features of the English model which were not essential to it, but which came to be thought characteristic, particularly by its critics. One was the particular form which industrialization took in England, another the separation of industry and finance. The industrial revolution although it utilized new technologies was also very labour intensive, and dependent on huge armies of unskilled labourers as well as highly skilled artisans.[30] England celebrated its status as workshop of the world in 1851, but it was a workshop in which there was still a very high premium on individual skill. Only in a few branches of industry was the shape of the future organization of industry glimpsed: the integration of science and continuous technological development into the heart of the production process, the scientific management of labour, the exploitation of company forms of organization, the vertical and horizontal integration of the chain of production, marketing, and sales – in short the creation of the mass consumer industries of the twentieth century.[31]

From the standpoint of what came afterwards, British industry in the nineteenth century, although hugely impressive to contemporaries, and the pioneer for the rest of the world, was eventually to be judged only a stage on the way to the full development of capitalism rather than that full development itself.[32] At a certain point British industry in sector after sector began to lose its technological and organizational lead and ceased to be a model for development.[33] The famous guarantee of quality of British manufacture was taken first by German and American companies, later by Japanese. In the twentieth century the English model no longer delivered the superiority it once had in technology. There were exceptions to this rule, particularly in fields related to defence such as aeronautics, and in pharmaceuticals, but in general other states, particularly Germany and Japan, now proved much better at organizing industrial production and developing new products and technologies.[34]

The inability of so much of British industry to maintain its competitive advantage in the twentieth century was once ascribed to the costs of being a pioneer. There had been heavy costs in developing industries such as the railways and heavy engineering which had not previously existed, and the sunk capital costs meant many businesses were reluctant to make new investments to modernize their plant, while industries in newly industrial-izing economies had no such handicaps and were able to adopt the latest technology and the best methods of organization.[35] This failing of British industry to maintain its leadership in the twentieth century has to be kept in perspective. The failure was relative rather than absolute. The British econ-omy remained a highly successful and productive industrial economy, and its industrial sectors were eventually restructured and modernized. But so great had been the nineteenth century investment in specific industrial districts and in the cities which grew up around them that it shaped prac-tices and attitudes very deeply. It has taken an extremely long time to change that legacy. Even today images of the industrial North as a grim land of slagheaps, dereliction, chimneys, back-to-back housing, and unem-ployment are still potent.

The cultural failure to maintain the momentum of the industrial revolu-tion and the glamour of the great technological innovations, the new machines, the scale of enterprise and above all the confidence and the dynamism which were so much part of nineteenth century England, the land of Isambard Kingdom Brunel, was one of the most noted features of twentieth century England. Traditionalism and conservatism were hardly absent from England in the nineteenth century, but their presence became much more obvious in the twentieth.[36] England was now being compared with other societies, particularly America, which were much better adapted to embrace modernity and let it rip. The dynamism of English civil society was inherited by the United States, but it was pushed much further, exploit-ing the full potential of mass production and mass consumption and mass culture in a continental economy. The comparison with America, and to a lesser extent with Germany, made the English appear defensive and inward-looking in cultural terms,[37] even though the forces which continued to transform the lives of the English had been unleashed by the English themselves, and had once been a cause for celebration and congratulation. But a key strand in the diagnosis of British economic problems in the twen-tieth century was held to be the decline of the industrial spirit,[38] and the triumph of 'gentlemanly capitalism'.[39]

This peculiarity of the English has often been linked to another, the insti-tutional separation of industry and finance in British capitalism and the continued success of the City in the last seventy years amidst the relative decline of industry.[40] The reasons for this separation lay initially in the origins of British capitalism in the trading and financial networks which were established long before industry. The advent of industry enormously increased British wealth and power, and had the effect of making the financial and trading network still more important rather than less. London became the financial and commercial hub of the new global economy, and sterling its currency. The expertise of the City and the trust placed in it were assets which gave it competitive advantage through the twentieth century. Aided too by a state which placed far fewer restrictions on its financial sector than were common elsewhere, the City succeeded in surviving huge challenges to its position, including the suspension of the gold standard in 1931 and the decline of sterling as an international currency after 1967, and retained its position as a leading financial centre.[41]

The contrast in fortunes between the industrial and financial sectors in the UK made many suspect that the relative decline which the economy as a whole was suffering was because industry was being sacrificed to the interests of finance.[42] This charge was levelled in every major financial crisis of the twentieth century. The case against the City was that it had starved industry of finance before 1914 choosing to maximize its returns by diverting funds to more profitable opportunities overseas, and that it had always prevailed on British governments to maintain deflationary policies to protect the value of sterling and therefore the value of the City's investments. An alliance between the substantial class of rentiers in the UK who depended on their financial investments for their income, and the industrial and political and bureaucratic interests associated with the British state and British Empire, ensured that the City view was upheld in major crises.[43] This did not prevent the steady decline of sterling, since the UK no longer had the industrial base and industrial productivity to sustain the high levels common through the nineteenth century, which had been the basis for the huge outlay on foreign investment in the forty years before 1914. When the Conservative government in 1925 decided to put sterling back on the gold standard, it chose the pre-war parity of \$4.86. By 1950 the rate was \$2.80. By 2000 it was \$1.50.

The alternative model for industry–finance relations since 1945 has been increasingly that of other European countries, notably Germany. The close links between finance and industry in Germany have made possible a degree of sustained long-term investment considerably greater than anything achieved in the UK.[44] The practices of the City, most importantly the dependence of the price of shares floated on the London Stock Exchange on company performance, backed up by the sanction of takeover and merger, creates a bias against long-term investment, in favour of actions that maximize short-term financial returns.[45] The market for corporate control came to be relied on as the means for enforcing efficiency, but did so at the expense of the long-term productive strength of the economy.

This argument is not about the flow of funds from the City to industry. There was no reason why the City should have discriminated against British industry. If there had been profitable opportunities in Britain, funds would have flowed. There were also examples of long-term support for particular industries from City institutions. The problem was rather that industry as whole was expected to generate its own funds for investment, and except in a few fields, notably defence, finance and government was not organized in Britain to give sustained long-term support to British industry.[46] British capitalism had become set in a mould which was difficult to break. It had many highly profitable and successful sectors, many of them geared to opportunities in overseas markets. What was so difficult to revive was a new entrepreneurial spirit and dynamism in the domestic economy, particularly in the former centres of heavy industry, which could create new long-term competitive industries to replace the old.[47]

The relative decline of the British economy might have continued indefinitely if the rising levels of personal prosperity and consumption of the period of the long boom had been sustained. But the dislocations of the global economy in the 1970s forced adjustments on all economies and exposed the accumulated weaknesses of the British economy, so that unemployment, inflation, and the public finances all tended to be much worse than in other countries.[48] During the impasse of the 1970s the critique of the underperformance of the British economy hardened into three rival programmes. On the left the failings of the economy were ascribed to too little investment in new technologies, in skills, in education and research, as well as to a structural imbalance between industry and finance. The remedy sought was through national planning,[49] the revival of the model of the 1940s, which would put the state firmly in control of the economy, replacing private ownership and markets where necessary to achieve its objectives of full employment, and equal citizenship through redistribution and a universal welfare state. This model of an independent British socialism inspired the different versions of the alternative economic strategy in the 1970s and 1980s.[50] They represented a final attempt to put socialist protectionism into practice.

Socialist protectionism envisaged an independent national economy, which would be run according to socialist priorities. It was formulated by leading socialist intellectuals in the 1920s and 1930s, including the Webbs, G.D.H. Cole, and Harold Laski,[51] and received great practical impetus from the war economy of the 1940s and the physical controls which were applied. The Labour Party began to scrap many of the controls after 1945, but its conception of the economy it wanted to create was one in which the markets were largely replaced by forms of planning, which were democratic and accountable, avoiding the waste and inefficiency of markets. Above all the national planning model promised to ensure equality, and collective rather than individual freedom.[52]

A very different line of argument developed on the right.[53] The shortcomings of the economy were blamed not on too little intervention by the state but too much, and ways were sought to restore the English model of liberal capitalism by rolling back state involvement in the economy and breaking trade union power. Restoring profitability and managerial authority in the enterprise, re-establishing sound money, transferring public enterprises and public services to the private sector, and reducing the burden of taxation by deep cuts in public spending were seen as the main ways of recreating the virtues of the English model. The imbalance between finance and industry in the British economy, the level of investment, or any other forms of active industrial policy were not seen as proper concerns for government. If a free market were restored, the economy would perform well again.[54] Setting the economy free meant strengthening the state, in order to shatter the compromise between capital and labour that had been painfully worked out in the political struggles of the first half of the twentieth century, and consolidated in the new policies and institutions of the Attlee Government in the 1940s.

Restoring the English model of capitalism became the centrepiece of the reform programme of the Thatcher Government. But although the Thatcherites talked a great deal about Victorian virtues and recapturing the spirit of entrepreneurship and economic dynamism that had existed in the nineteenth century,[55] the model they drew upon was less the English model – so distorted by the ravages of fifty years of collectivist economic policies inspired by imperialists, New Liberals, and socialists – as the American model, particularly the version advocated by the new conservative movement in America, and so triumphantly paraded by Ronald Reagan.[56] The doctrines of monetarism, shareholder value, privatization, deregulation, flexible labour markets, cuts in taxation and welfare spending added up to a new model of capitalism, which proclaimed its superiority over other models, and was set out as the template for all the world's economies to copy, including those in Europe. In this way America became the ideal for the Thatcherites, and in economic policy they sought to copy the Americans, in the hope of reviving the English model that had been lost.

In reaction to the onslaught of Thatcherism, there developed alternative models and alternative perspectives, centred in particular on the idea of a developmental state,[57] drawing on the success of those European capitalisms, such as the German and the French, and Swedish, which had been notably more successful than the British, and which offered greater hope of combining a dynamic economy with high levels of spending on public services and social security.[58] These alternative models of capitalism underpinned the rethinking of Labour Party economic policy in the 1990s. A great deal of their inspiration came from European examples, reflecting the new recognition on the British left of the superior performance in so many ways of the European model. But another source of these ideas was also Anglo-America itself. Liberal critiques of the conservative model produced a different version of the Anglo-American model, which was to flourish briefly in the form of the Third Way.[59]

The English Constitution

One of the conditions for the success of English capitalism was long regarded as the English Constitution. The great virtue of this Constitution which made it a model for the rest of the world in the eighteenth and nineteenth centuries was that it achieved a balance of powers between the different parts of the state and upheld the rule of law and civil liberties, so checking the power of the executive and protecting citizens from arbitrary government. Tendencies to authoritarian and absolute government remained, and could reappear, as in the 1790s during the scare that the French Revolution might cross the Channel, but they often encountered vigorous resistance, which together with legal and customary obstacles were generally sufficient to moderate them.[60] England was considered exceptional for the relative degree of liberty enjoyed by its citizens; this was a state which had risen to be the most powerful and wealthy state in the world, yet maintained no large standing army or large bureaucracy, and upheld the principles of Common Law which offered a measure of protection to traditional liberties and customary ways of life, despite a rapacious and corrupt political class.[61]

The British political class in the eighteenth century was indeed rapacious, corrupt, oligarchic and cruel, as well as often obdurate, short-sighted and stupid, and fortunate on more than one occasion to survive. Revolution was never far away.[62] But even in the eighteenth century the English Constitution had admirers, such as Montesquieu, who noted its virtues when it compared with constitutions elsewhere. But it was in the nineteenth century when the British political class had managed to stifle its deeper instincts and become more skilled at preserving its interests and privileges that enthusiasm for the English Constitution and its political class really set in. Writers from Tocqueville to Schumpeter praised it for its sagacity, its ability to manage change, to make concessions when concessions were needed, to be pragmatic about its principles, and to share power. The decisions to permit gradual widening of the right to vote between 1832 and 1928 was seen as a prime example of this ability. There were many misgivings in the British political class at every stage of this process, because it meant first diluting the power of the landed oligarchy and then empowering individuals without any kind of property stake in the country at all. There was also disquiet about the replacement of *functional* representation, the representation of interests and communities in Parliament regardless of their strict numerical size, by *mathematical* representation, the representation of individuals, divided up into equal constituencies, on the assumption that every individual should count the same. But the changes were made, and despite the popular agitation for much more radical measures, relatively smoothly, so that Whig historians were able to hail them as a further example of the English genius, the ability to manage change within the framework of inherited institutions.[63]

At its best the English Constitution promoted self-government. This was its secret, and it was why it became a model for others. It encouraged citizens to form associations and corporate bodies, to pursue collective purposes alongside their individual purposes, but to do this within the broad framework of law established and underpinned by government, rather than through government itself.[64] This sense of a vigorous civil society pursuing public goods separate from government was very strong and in marked contrast to many states elsewhere. Government might be small in England but the wider public realm was large. What was novel in comparison with states elsewhere was how much of the public realm was self-governing and self-funding.

The English Constitution has been called many things, not all of them flattering. It was Old Corruption in the eighteenth century, but by the end of the nineteenth as a result of the flood of reforms following the Great Reform Bill of 1832, the English Constitution had metamorphosed into the *Westminster Model*, a model suitable to be exported around the world. At the heart of the Westminster model is Parliament, and the conventions which define the roles of Monarch, Prime Minister, Ministers, civil servants, MPs, and Lords. At its height the Westminster model was the exemplar of representative and responsible government,[65] combining *popular sovereignty* in the rules governing election of MPs to the House of Commons, and the formation of governments with strong popular mandates, and a *strong executive* in the shape of a professional, career civil service implementing the policies of the party forming the government. The idea of ministerial accountability, the separation of the roles of Ministers and civil servants, the first taking decisions and the second giving advice, was central to this model, as was the idea of an incorruptible and non-partisan civil service.

English institutions have been renowned for their continuity, their legitimacy and for their stablility when compared with the political institutions of most other countries. This continuity has been traced by some historians back to the twelfth century or even further back to the Anglo-Saxon period. Stubbs, Maitland and generations of Whig historians argued that English institutions were formed very early, and provided a framework in which all subsequent economic and political developments have been contained.[66] The longevity of English institutions was frequently held to be a sign of their virtue. The frequent changes of regime and political upheavals common in other countries were blamed on their defective political institutions and contrasted with the balanced constitution of England which permitted orderly change.

The settled form of English institutions over so long a period is, however, deceptive, concealing the fact that English history has always been marked by change, upheaval and conflict, as well as by stability and continuity. Major discontinuities, including the Norman Conquest itself in 1066, the Tudor Revolution in government under Henry VIII, and the Republic of the 1650s which abolished the Monarchy and the House of Lords, tend to be obscured or forgotten. The period leading up to the Great Reform Bill of 1832, and the period between the 1880s and the 1920s were times of major upheaval and structural change for the British state.[67] The 1970s inaugurated another such period, which has not yet run its course.

What has struck so many observers has been that the English and then the British state has managed to be highly centralized and decentralized at the same time. The Norman Conquest imposed a strong central state and transformed England into the purest form of feudal society, in which all land was held as a grant from the King, and made all landholders a vassal of the King, obliged to give him service.[68] The old Saxon landowning class was dispossessed, and Norman appointees filled all the important offices of Church and state. This new alien governing class spoke French and was more interested in its ties with Normandy and its dynastic and territorial ambitions in France than its possessions in England. But this Norman Yoke, although often brutal and savage, was in important respects superficial. It did not fundamentally transform the habits or customs of the people over whom it ruled. It had to come to terms with institutions such as the Common Law and the widely practised habit of self-government. The innovation of a strong, centralized Monarchy was not challenged, and this became one of the key ways of binding the different parts of the kingdom together under one rule. But this authority was exercised within the Common Law, which meant that anyone, including kings, were subject to it. Resistance to the Monarchy produced Magna Carta, a written constitution of a kind.[69]

Out of the long struggles between centralized authority concentrated in the person and office of the King, there developed a constitution that was balanced between the Crown and the two Houses of Parliament. In the course of this struggle the supremacy of the Commons was eventually established, but it remained qualified by the existence of the royal prerogative, and a hereditary second chamber, comprising the landed aristocracy and the Bishops. No republican constitution ever endured in England – the brief episode of republican rule during the Commonwealth ending with the restoration of the Monarchy in 1660. Despite periods of heightened republican sentiment as in the 1870s and 1990s, the Crown has seemed a safe and permanent part of the Constitution, a symbol of the Union, and the legitimation of the centralization of authority.[70]

To help the Monarchy survive in the modern era Walter Bagehot's advice was not to let the daylight in on magic,[71] but magic has often been in rather short supply where the English Monarchy is concerned. It has been a thoroughly political rather than a sacred institution, designed to serve the purposes of the state. There may have been almost unbroken continuity in the institution of Monarchy, but there has been little continuity in the dynasties that have made it up. There have been numerous breaches in the strict law of succession, weak monarchs have been disposed of, and whole new dynasties inaugurated when this has been in the interest of the political class. The line of descent has often been broken, as with the accession of Henry IV, Henry V11, and George I, representing gaps in legitimate succession which sometimes amount to a chasm. So anxious was the political class in the early 1700s to ensure a Protestant succession and to keep out the legitimate dynasty, the Stuarts, that they settled on a minor German prince, the Elector of Hanover, who spoke no English, and who was fifty-eighth in line to the throne.[72] In the last thousand years, the English throne has hardly ever been occupied by anyone English. This most quintessential English institution has been the preserve of foreigners.

But the Crown has played a vital part in the balanced Constitution which was so much admired in the eighteenth and nineteenth centuries. The doctrine of Crown-in-Parliament reaffirmed the importance of strong central authority as the basis of the British state; at the same time it allowed for this authority to be exercised within the context of a representative assembly. For most of its history Parliament has not been democratic, but it has been representative, and there is a long line of Conservative commentary on the Constitution which has argued that it is more important that it should be the latter rather than the former, because greater democracy is often achieved at the expense of representation.[73] The role of Parliament is to represent all significant interests and opinion within the nation. In this way it can best fulfil its role of exerting checks on the executive, obliging it to be responsible and to operate within the rule of law. The means of electing Parliament is secondary to this purpose.

Critics of the English Constitution

The Westminster model of a balanced Constitution and a self-governing civil society has come under increasing attack since the 1970s. Critics complained that it had become unbalanced, that it was undemocratic, and that it was over-centralized. The Constitution was no longer working as it should, and its shortcomings became an important strand in the writing on decline. The apparent weakening of the long tradition of self-government was regarded as one of the main causes of all the other ills that were afflicting British politics.[74]

In the original conception of the balanced Constitution, no single institution dominated. The executive had the leading role in proposing legislation, but was accountable to both Houses of Parliament, and had to obtain consent for its measures. The charge that the Constitution had become unbalanced claims that the conventions and checks which had preserved balance have been eroded or destroyed.[75] One of the chief causes, it is claimed, has been the growing power of the Prime Minister.

The office of Prime Minister was a natural development once the titular sovereign was no longer in any real sense the head of the executive. No titular sovereign has vetoed an Act of Parliament since 1707. The office of Prime Minister formally does not exist in statute, which is why the Prime Minister also has to have another title, First Lord of the Treasury. At state occasions such as royal funerals and royal marriages and the State opening of Parliament, the formal Head of State, the Queen, takes precedence over the executive Head of State, the Prime Minister. Protocol rules, and due weight is given to every minor royal and aristocrat in the Queen's household as well as from the far-flung corners of Europe, ahead of democratically elected politicians from Canada, Australia, and New Zealand, not to mention the UK. But these minor slights are bearable for British Prime Ministers, who have in their grasp the much more valuable prize which is the unhindered exercise of the royal prerogatives, including the right to sign treaties and to declare war, as well as powers of patronage, including the appointment of the Cabinet and other Ministers in the government, as well as a vast array of public appointments, all without direct reference to Parliament.

Formally the Prime Minister is merely the Minister who coordinates the work of the executive on behalf of the Crown, but in reality he has become much more than this. What the doctrine of Crown-in-Parliament conceals is that the supremacy of Parliament over the King which was definitively achieved in the seventeenth century has meant that the English Constitution has not one but two monarchs. The first is the person who is the titular sovereign, but the second is the real sovereign, the leader of the executive, the Prime Minister. There has been much talk in recent time about Prime Ministers becoming more like Presidents, but the Prime Minister has no need to become a President because he is already a Monarch, a position of considerably greater scope.

The titular sovereign has long ceased to be an effective check on Ministers, and both Houses of Parliament have lost their power too.[76] In the case of the House of Lords their veto power over legislation was removed after the Peers' refusal to pass Lloyd George's 'People's budget' in 1910. Their power to delay legislation was limited to two years, reduced to one year in 1948. The composition of the House was changed by the addition of Life Peers in the 1950s, but there remained an in-built Conservative majority. But although it could be an irritant, especially to Labour governments, the House of Lords in its truncated form could not prevail if there was a clear majority in favour of a particular measure in the House of Commons. This might not have mattered if the House of Commons had retained an ability to restrain the executive. But with the rise of party and party discipline, the executive has learnt how to control the Commons. The party majority in the Commons makes the Chamber an arm of the executive rather than a part of the legislature seeking to hold the executive to account. Governments have become 'elective dictatorships'.[77] So long as they can command a majority in the House of Commons, they can push through whatever legislation they wish, over the resistance of the House of Lords if necessary, and however unpopular it may be in the electorate or among groups most affected.

The charge of elective dictatorship was first made against the Labour government between 1974 and 1979. Despite lacking an overall parliamentary majority for three of the five years it was in office, and being supported by a minority of the electorate, the government was still able to push through a great deal of controversial legislation. A determined executive appeared to have no effective constraints on its power.[78] But the problem was about to become far worse. In the 1970s, governments despite being elective dictatorships appeared weak, unable to manage the pressures on them, or govern effectively. The reassertion of a very strong executive during the Thatcher years reawakened (for some) all the fears that had been expressed about elective dictatorships, and the absence of constitutional checks to the actions of an over-mighty executive. The disregard of constitutional conventions and the spurning of any search for consensus or compromise heightened the sense of a constitution which had become unbalanced, and was no longer a model to be imitated, but a system in need of quite drastic reform.

A second line of attack, although often linked to the first, has been that the English Constitution is a pre-modern constitution, devised before the era of democracy and popular sovereignty, which fails to guarantee the basic citizenship rights which are enshrined in all modern constitutional democracies. British citizens are subjects not citizens, sovereignty does not reside with the people as in the United States Constitution or the French Constitution, but with the Crown-in-Parliament. From this flows the excessive secrecy and lack of accountability of the central executive, and the campaigns for Freedom of Information, a Bill of Rights, and more effective checks and balances, both parliamentary and legal. The aim is to overturn the doctrine of unlimited and undivided parliamentary sovereignty. A written constitution it is argued would give much better protection to citizens of their civil and political rights.

Subordinating Parliament and the executive to the will of the people also requires some fundamental democratic reforms to the electoral system and the House of Lords. The reformers around Charter 88 picked up the cause of electoral reform, arguing that there was a huge disproportionality in votes cast and seats won in the Westminster Parliament, due to its adherence to the simple plurality rule and single member constituencies. What made the electoral system such a target was that it ensured that most governments elected since 1945 had been elected on a minority of the popular vote, yet because of the voting rules were rewarded with a majority of the seats in Parliament, which allowed them to use all the unchecked powers of the executive in pursuit of their programme.[79]

Electoral reform was demanded by the reformers to stop governments pushing through unpopular minority policies on the basis of a bogus parliamentary majority. Proportional representation of whatever kind was chosen would ensure coalition governments, and a different style of conducting politics, less adversarial and more consensual. PR should also be applied to voting for local councils, devolved parliaments and assemblies, the European Parliament, and was also an integral part of proposals for the reform of the House of Lords. Abolition of the hereditary principle and curbing the Prime Minister's powers of appointment would require a directly elected second Chamber, and the redefinition of its powers in the Constitution.

The role of the Monarchy and of the Courts also became a target for criticism. In the written constitution favoured by the reformers, the office of Head of State would be subordinate to popular sovereignty, and its powers and duties would be defined in the constitution. The question of whether the Head of State should be a hereditary monarch or directly elected was considered a secondary question to be determined by a referendum. Similarly, many argued that the Courts needed to be part of the constitutional mechanism for checking the executive, and that a new Constitutional Court would be needed to oversee the constitution. This was the key change which the critics fastened on – a written constitution was required to entrench certain guarantees of citizenship, which the old constitution no longer seemed able to secure.

The third line of criticism of the English Constitution has already been surveyed in Chapter 2. The doctrine of unlimited and undivided sovereignty meant that there was only one supreme source of authority in the state – the Crown-in-Parliament. In practice this could not be sustained, and led the centre into making many different local arrangements for governing the three kingdoms. But the state remained unitary in principle; forms of local administration and decentralization were not guaranteed by the Constitution; they were at the whim of the Westminster Parliament, and might be withdrawn as easily as they were granted. The truth of this was shown most starkly when the Northern Ireland Parliament at Stormont was abolished in 1971 and direct rule introduced. Voters in England were reminded of it with the concerted attack on the powers and responsibilities of local government, particular under the Thatcher Government in the 1980s. The territorial code of British government which for so long had meant that the centre gave considerable freedom and flexibility to the periphery, so long as in return it affirmed the autonomy of the centre,[80] seemed no longer adequate to the times. The highly centralized character of the British polity on London and the south-east of England helped fuel further the demands for effective devolution and the constitutional entrenchment of the powers of subordinate authorities.

The different strands of criticism coalesced in the constitutional agitation which grew enormously after 1970 and helped discredit many aspects of the Westminster model. The English Constitution was no longer a model to be imitated but a model to be avoided, found wanting on numerous counts. But what was to replace it? As with British capitalism, the models that became influential were no longer English models, but models from

America and from Europe. The American model was to keep certain aspects of the British system, such as first-past-the-post elections and adversarial politics, but to accept popular sovereignty as the basis of the constitution, and subordinate government to citizens, ending secrecy and deference, and the closed worlds of Westminster and Whitehall. On this view the American revolution and the democracy and civil society which had resulted from it was the revolution which had been born in England but never consummated here. Being the fulfilment of the English model, the American model needs to be 'brought home'.[81] Another view, however, while not dissenting from some of that, has argued that the constitutional revolution that is required is a move towards European styles of democracy, in which the emphasis is upon consensus building, consociational politics, corporatism and partnership between associations in civil society and government. In a map of contemporary democracies, Britain has become an outlier with a mix of institutions found almost nowhere else.[82] Constitutional reformers want to see movement towards international norms – to improve representation, openness, and accountability – and to ensure greater protection of civil rights, and the decentralization of powers.

British Socialism

The English model was associated at its height in the nineteenth century with both liberal capitalism and self-government, but in the twentieth century it also became associated with the welfare state, which was the particular achievement of British socialism, built around campaigns and struggles for civil, political and social rights. Many of the early struggles were for the right of the working class to organize, to develop its own institutions and its own unions, and for the right to vote. As the movement grew in strength and confidence, so socialist demands for the reorganization of industry and for social justice began to be advanced.[83]

At the core of British socialism and its formidable Labour movement was a model of the self-organization of the working class, and a model of social and economic citizenship. The recognition of the independent civil associations of the working class and the extension of welfare, came to be supported by all parties, particularly after the widening of the franchise made it expedient to do so. British socialism became a key factor in twentieth century politics, and all the main parties of the state helped shape the new collectivism, the welfare state and the public services and public sector, which by the middle of the century had become a dominating feature of British politics. The forms it took were influenced in particular by Liberals such as Keynes and Beveridge, by Conservatives such as Neville Chamberlain, and by Socialists such as Sidney and Beatrice Webb.[84]

From a liberal perspective the extension of social rights to the whole population through public funded schemes of universal welfare entitlements could be treated as another sign of liberal progress, the latest stage in the evolution of the British state, and evidence that the threat of class war had been overcome through the incorporation of labour through the development of a notion of democratic citizenship.[85] From the perspective of the Labour movement the achievement of universal programmes of welfare, in particular the National Health Service, were evidence that socialism could work through democratic means, that capitalism could be regulated and tamed, that power could be redistributed, and markets rebalanced in favour of working people and their families.[86]

The British Labour movement had many setbacks in its progress towards power and the reshaping of the British state in accordance with the principles of social justice. But the victory in 1945 of the Attlee Government seemed to demonstrate that a party with a socialist programme could triumph in a leading capitalist country, and that substantial reforms could be achieved without the need for violent revolution. A peaceful revolution which would lay the foundations for socialism was after all possible, despite the experience of so many other socialist movements in other parts of the world in the first half of the twentieth century. Britain appeared to have demonstrated that a democratic transition to socialism could be achieved, and that the successor to the British Empire in binding the state together would be British socialism.

The main elements of this British socialism were the size and organization and unity of the British Labour movement, and its adherence after 1918 to a socialist programme.[87] Key to this programme were new welfare guarantees which broke decisively with earlier liberal models, and sought to incorporate the working class through the granting of new citizenship rights. The adoption of Keynes' macroeconomic policies to promote full employment and growth and of Beveridge's social policies to guarantee security for all citizens, combined with a considerable extension of public ownership of utilities, was widely seen as inaugurating a new form of capitalism. This 'mixed economy' preserved the benefits of the free enterprise system while conceding the claims of the Labour movement for a new political settlement guaranteeing much greater equality, security and inclusion for all citizens.[88]

The Keynesian welfare state as it later became known was regarded as the great achievement of British socialism, and for a while placed British

Labour in the vanguard of social democracy worldwide. Liberal England had given way it seemed to socialist England, which nevertheless built upon and incorporated much of the liberal inheritance. It could still be presented as a continuation of the long development of English history rather than any kind of rupture with it. Proof of this was that it had required no great constitutional change other than the extension of the suffrage to be brought about.

British socialism was however notably different from that in many other European countries, partly because of the marginal influence of Marxism in Britain, and partly because of its unified labour movement. In this respect the British Labour movement was a mirror image of the British state; formally unified, locally decentralized. The world of labour was a highly diverse, stubbornly local, resolutely sectional group of self-governing associations, which nevertheless established a single peak organization, the Trades Union Congress, and a single working-class party, the Labour Party. Its focus like that of so many British institutions was firmly upon the central institutions of the state. There were no significant religious or political divides in the British Labour movement which produced the kind of separate organizations common elsewhere in Europe. Even the Communist Party worked within the ambit of the Labour movement, and sought several times without success to affiliate to the Labour Party. This gave British Labour enormous strength, both as the working-class movement of the first industrial capitalist country in the world, and a working class which comprised a majority of the population. British Labour acquired great prestige and weight within the international working-class movement. The trial of strength between labour and capital in England, the birthplace of modern capitalism, was seen as a testing ground for the prospects of socialism in the rest of the world. The split in the ranks of international socialism between Communists and social democrats after 1918 meant also that Britain, with its relatively weak Communist Party, became the site of one of the major experiments in building a socialist programme of gradual reform, seeking to achieve a transformation of capitalism into socialism through constitutional means.[89]

Labour's triumph in 1945 and the legislative programme on which it then embarked came to be seen as one of the most important watersheds in the history of the British state; a defining moment in the way that 1832 had been; the moment of passage from one kind of political order to another. What seemed striking about the new political settlement was that in a very English way it combined universalism with voluntarism. The self-governing Labour movement remained rooted in a voluntarist culture, and guarded its independence from the state jealously; at the same time it became a key pillar of the new state, for a time a 'governing institution'.[90] But this in time also came to be seen as its greatest weakness. Within thirty years the welfare state and the public sector which Labour fashioned were more often criticized than praised, and blamed by an increasingly vociferous right as the root cause of decline.

Critics of British Socialism

By the 1970s the first phase in the development of the British welfare state was complete and it was clear that it had reached an impasse. It either had to go forward or be trimmed back. A powerful socialist critique of welfare states and their role in sustaining capital accumulation rather than serving human needs[91] was accompanied by a feminist critique of the way in which the welfare state was founded on certain assumptions about the nature of families, in particular about the central role accorded the male breadwinner.[92] The conclusion of both types of argument was that more democratic and more extensive forms of welfare needed to be developed, to counter the charge that welfare programmes were mainly concerned with controlling the behaviour of the poor and limiting their demands. Households, it was argued, needed additional kinds of support to provide for child care and parental leave, disability, special educational needs, and higher pensions. Taking social rights seriously meant new programmes had to be developed to counter all forms of inequality and disadvantage. It was argued that the early promise of the welfare state had been blunted and steps had to be taken to regain its momentum if it was to remain in the vanguard of social democratic welfare states around the world.

Such stances led naturally to the advocacy of much higher spending on the welfare programmes as well as a reorganization of many of the principles on which the welfare state was based. So important had the welfare state become that for many in the British Labour Party its preservation and extension had become the most important goal in politics, and provided principles which could not be compromised. If there was a clash between the welfare spending and financial stability the natural instinct was to give priority to welfare spending. It was what drew people into politics on the Labour side. For the new right it was always the other way round. A successful economy was the priority, and welfare was a residual, the level of which was to be determined by what the economy could afford.[93]

By the 1970s the new right assault on welfare had been extended. The welfare state was now blamed for inflation and dependency, the destruction of an ethos of enterprise and the impoverishment of society. The new right

programme which helped shape some of the actions of the Thatcher
Government proposed the containment of welfare spending, and where
possible its reduction. The Thatcherites argued that England had taken a
wrong turning and had ceased to be true to itself. The extended state of
social democracy which Conservatives themselves had helped to build was
acknowledged as the heart of the problem; it was profoundly un-English
because it had moved away from self-reliance and from self-government. It
had established huge bureaucracies and had required ever higher levels of
taxation to support it, destroying in the process an important part of what
the English understood by liberty.[94]

From this angle what the Thatcherites proposed was a counter-revolution, an undoing of the settlement with the Labour movement, a proclamation that this was a mistaken path, a false turning in English history. It
sought instead to return to the liberal welfare policies of the nineteenth
century with their emphasis on work, and self-reliance. Under the 1834
Poor Law, attitudes towards the poor had been punitive, particularly
towards the female poor,[95] and welfare had been provided selectively and
only under strict conditions, which included attendance in the workhouse.
The new right wanted to return to the spirit if not the letter of the old Poor
Law, rejecting any notion of a right to welfare or any universal entitlement.
By minimizing expenditure on welfare, taxation could be reduced, and the
state slimmed, so making private initiative and private action once more
central. In this way the Thatcher Government was determined to reverse
decline. In its 1979 manifesto, overcoming decline was a central preoccupation,[96] and central to its vision of how to do it was to return to the principles of limited government and individual enterprise which had been such
important features of the English model in the past. The extended state had
to be dismantled and the special interests which had come to infest it
disarmed. In this way, it was imagined, a dynamic economy could be
rebuilt on the principles that had once made England great.[97]

This struggle over the 1945 political settlement and its outcome came to
dominate the last decades of the twentieth century and is still a defining
ground of British politics in the twenty-first century. At stake is the issue of
how far the attempt to extend social rights through the welfare state and
public services of the post-war era was a legitimate application of the principles of the English model, and how far it represented a repudiation or betrayal
of them. What is undeniable is that the conflicts of the 1970s put a halt to the
development of more expanded forms of welfare. There was a significant
retrenchment, although more limited than many supporters of the Thatcherite
counter-revolution wanted, and which significantly did not seriously touch
the National Health Service or several of the other major programmes.[98]

The results were contradictory. The UK did go through a period of financial retrenchment, and the welfare state stopped growing. At the same time many of the features of universal provision were retained. There was no wholesale dismantling of the structures of the extended state. What took place was a steady squeeze on the resources given to the welfare state and a steady deterioration in service levels, which government tried to mitigate by attempting to reorganize the way in which services were delivered. The result was that by the middle of the 1990s the UK had fallen considerably behind the level of welfare services provided by many other European countries, particularly those in Scandinavia.[99] In the 1940s the UK had achieved the most advanced welfare state in the world, but this was not sustained and developed in the decades that followed. As a result of the economic difficulties of the 1970s the key political decision was taken that the way to build a strong economy was not to extend welfare but to reduce it, or at least contain it. Under the Thatcher Government the UK moved back towards a liberal model of welfare, although many social democratic elements, particularly the commitment to universalism in several areas, remained. The influence of American conservative thinking on welfare became very strong under the Thatcher Government, and the same discourse of dependency, the underclass, and workfare became established. The Thatcher Government however found it much harder to move to an American style welfare system, than to create American style labour markets or to deregulate the financial markets. One of the main reasons for Labour's success in the 1990s was that the squeeze on resources for the public services pushed the quality of public services below the level the electorate wanted, and allowed Labour to mount a strong campaign for major investment in the public services. But as over its economic plans, the Labour leadership set aside the European models which had influenced the early stages of the policy review in favour of the American models developed by the new Democrats in response to the conservative revolution in America. What Labour was to find in office, however, was that public aspirations for public services required a move in the direction of European models rather than American ones.[100]

Conclusion

By the end of the 1970s England was no longer regarded, even by the English, as a model for the rest of the world; serious doubt had come to be cast on the viability of its capitalism, on its capacity to govern itself, and on its ability to deliver effective public services and social justice. Of the three, the English Constitution had always been most quintessentially English. Capitalism and the pursuit of Empire had been British projects, shared with the other British nations, as had the project to transform Britain into a welfare state and establish democratic socialism. Other parts of the United Kingdom, notably voters in Scotland, were to resist more strongly than many English voters the abandonment of the commitment to a progressive expansion of welfare, and were to fall foul of the Thatcher Government as a result.[101]

The disintegration of the English model had a profound disorienting effect on British politics, contributing to the mood of crisis and polarization that was a marked feature of the 1970s and the first part of the 1980s. It directly produced the radical projects of right and left for remedying the problems and restoring capitalism and socialism to their former pre-eminence. The two projects were clearly incompatible, and both required tearing up the old compromise between labour and capital, and left and right, that had emerged after 1945. The battle to launch its project was won by the right, and produced the Thatcher Government, which administered partly by design and partly by accident a series of shocks to the British state and the British economy. These have transformed the landscape of British politics, its identities and its political economy, as well as creating conditions for a new politics of the left. The first phase of the political revolution which Thatcherism launched tackled head-on the power bases of British socialism: the unions, the local councils, the public sector, and the welfare state.

The universalism of the welfare state which the Labour party stood for was also one of the key institutions binding all parts of the United Kingdom together and promoting a sense of Britishness. One of the problems for the Conservative Party was that in its efforts to resuscitate English capitalism using the full powers of the English Constitution, its appeal became more and more directed towards England and it lacked a project for Britain. This party of the Union and the Empire helped undermine the things it most wanted to preserve. The Thatcher revolution was to prove a very English affair, bent on preserving or reviving particular kinds of Englishness. But what it also came to represent was a clear choice between Europe and America. Thatcherism was fiercely Atlanticist in security and foreign policy, and increasingly Anglo-American in its thinking on economic and social policy. Europe came to be the model the Thatcherite wing of the Conservative Party did not wish to adopt.

8

Conservative Schisms

> One of the greatest of Romans, when asked what were his politics, replied, *Imperium et Libertas*. That would not make a bad programme for a British ministry.
>
> Benjamin Disraeli, 1879[1]

The Conservative Party has long seemed one of the great certainties of British politics. So dominant had it become in the 1980s that the twentieth century was dubbed the Conservative Century,[2] and there was some speculation after the party won its fourth election in a row in 1992 that Britain now had a dominant party system like Japan.[3] But soon after that election the party was plunged into a deep schism over its policy towards Europe, and lost its reputation for economic competence. Its poll ratings plunged and in 1997 it suffered a major election defeat, and then a second defeat of similar proportions in 2001, the first time the Conservatives had experienced this in the democratic era. After every election defeat in the twentieth century, however serious it seemed at the time, the Conservatives at the subsequent election had made a strong recovery in both seats and votes, and created a platform which carried them back into office at the next attempt. The election result in 2001 gave no sign that a Conservative recovery had begun.

The blight on the Conservative Party after 1992 has puzzled many observers, since in the past the protean nature of the party has always served it well. Surely this oldest of political parties would in time adjust to the new political conditions and adapt its message and appeal, as it had done so often before, drawing on one or more of the many diverse strands that historically make up Conservatism?[4] Others argued however that the party's future was far from secure, because the Thatcher years had changed the party fundamentally, allowing the party to be captured by an alien ideology, neo-liberalism, which had so damaged Toryism and the traditional statecraft of the party that it had finally rendered the party unelectable,[5] while entrenching a membership and a party leadership which were unwilling to take the steps needed for recovery.

161

Thatcher's legacy has not only become highly contested inside the Conservative Party; it has come to dominate debates about the future of British politics. The reverberations of the political revolution which Thatcher inaugurated are still being felt. Some Conservatives still insist that Thatcher represented the return of the party to its lost traditions and principles (after an absence which stretched back seventy years)[6] while others have derided it as an alien import which divided and ultimately destroyed the party as a governing force.[7] The party which at the end of the nineteenth century had been so closely identified with the Union and Empire and the expansion of England, found it hard at the end of the twentieth to adjust to a quite different political landscape. Dominating this landscape has been the choice between Europe and America, and it was this choice which overshadowed Conservative politics by the end of Thatcher's premiership, creating the great schism which destroyed the party as a governing force in the 1990s.

The Conservative Century

The Conservative century began with a landslide defeat for the Conservatives in 1906, and ended with another in 1997. In between there were notable interruptions to Conservative rule, particularly between 1945–51 and 1964–70. Nevertheless between 1916 and 1997 the Conservatives were in government either alone or in coalition for sixty one of the eighty one years. Between 1945 and 1997 the Conservatives formed majority governments for 35 of the 52 years or 67 per cent of the time. Governments of the centre left have been uncommon, and have rarely lasted long. The Liberal government of 1906 stayed in office ten years; the 1945 Attlee Government and the 1964 Wilson Government only lasted six years. In sharp contrast the Conservatives generally enjoyed long, uninterrupted spells in office (1931–45, 1951–64, 1979–97), winning three consecutive general elections between 1951 and 1964, and four between 1979 and 1997. In the twentieth century Labour never lasted in government for two full parliaments.

This ascendancy of the Conservatives was remarkable, because it took place after the suffrage was widened. Many Conservatives had feared that widening the suffrage would overwhelm the defences to constitutional order and the rights of property.[8] But the Conservatives were to thrive in the new mass democracy and more often than not commanded electoral majorities, despite the social structure being heavily weighted against them. Parties of the right elsewhere in Europe relied above all on the votes of the peasantry and the rural areas; by the end of the nineteenth century the British electorate was overwhelmingly urban and working class. The Conservative Party by contrast was the party of rural England, and the party of the established institutions of England – the Monarchy, the Aristocracy, the Church, the Law, the Universities, the Army and the Navy. Composed primarily of country gentry, the party resisted moves to reform the constitution and the widening of the franchise to the towns which culminated in the Great Reform Bill, and fought bitterly to maintain agricultural protection in the shape of the Corn Laws. When Robert Peel proposed the repeal of the Corn Laws in 1846 he split his party, two-thirds of his MPs refusing to support him. The party did not secure a firm parliamentary majority again for almost thirty years.[9] Why such a party of hereditary and traditional privilege and the landed interest should not only survive into the era of mass democracy, but thrive in it, and indeed dominate it, needs some explanation.

Another curiosity is that the century which the party dominated was not a period of great national success. In sharp contrast to the Liberal century from 1815 to 1914, which saw the consolidation and expansion of the British Empire, and the recognition of British military, economic and ideological hegemony, the Conservative century, despite victory in two world wars, was also the century of decline, imperial retreat and economic failure. But despite presiding over such a long drawn-out period of national decline, the Conservatives were not blamed for it. They were re-elected again and again. Even when they suffered major election defeats, as in 1945 and 1966, within a few years they were back in office.

The dominance of the Conservatives over British politics in the twentieth century and their remarkable resilience, despite the narrowness of their social base and their unpromising association with a period dominated by the contraction of England rather than with its expansion, has been ascribed to many things – their statecraft or governing strategy, their close relationship with the English people, the divisions among their opponents. But there is also something deeper at work. What all these reflect is a command and understanding of the British state which during the twentieth century far exceeded that of any other party. This state survived into the second half of the twentieth century with many of its more idiosyncratic features still intact, the last major *ancien régime* and multinational imperial state left in Europe.[10] The identity of the Conservative Party is inseparable from the history of this state. It has been its supremely flexible and adaptable instrument, and also one of the most important articulators of the narratives that have sustained and defined it. Conservative ascendancy was founded on a special political tradition, an intuitive grasp of the difference between the two kinds of politics necessary in a modern democracy, the politics of support and the politics of power, as well as of their necessary relationship.

Conservative Political Hegemony

The reason why Conservatives faced a harder task in rebuilding their electoral support after 1997 than after any of their three major electoral defeats in the previous fifty years – in 1945, 1966 and 1974 – was that they had lost not just short-term electoral popularity, but also the political hegemony which they had exercised more or less continuously since the advent of the wider franchise in 1885, and which accounted for their previous rapid recoveries after electoral setbacks. The foundations of this Conservative political hegemony were laid in the period between 1886 and 1926,[11] which saw the creation of a new identity and a new strategy for the Conservative Party in response to rapidly changing political circumstances. These included the achievement of universal suffrage (1885, 1918, 1928), the suffragette campaign for women's rights, the battle over Home Rule for Ireland which ended in the dissolving of the Union, the breaking of the power of the House of Lords with the Parliament Act in 1911, the huge upheaval of the First World War, the development of new forms of media including mass circulation newspapers and radio, and the growing political importance of the Labour movement.

A party of traditional country squires and great landed proprietors, closely tied to the interests and symbols of Old England, might have been expected to dig ever deeper trenches of reaction faced by this onslaught of changes, most of which were deeply unwelcome to them. At times, particularly over Ireland, the party came close to doing this and precipitating a constitutional crisis of quite unpredictable outcome.[12] But in time, and helped crucially by the First World War, the Conservatives mastered the new politics more surely than their main rivals, the Liberals, and following the Bolshevik Revolution in Russia and the growth of militancy in the British Labour movement during the First World War, they emerged in the 1920s as the leading party for all the interests of the established order and of property to oppose the rise of Labour, displacing the Liberals in the process.[13] The Liberals had resisted Labour by seeking to co-opt them into their progressive coalition; the Conservatives by contrast treated the rise of Labour as signalling a struggle between imperialism and individualism on one side and socialism and collectivism on the other, presenting themselves as the only political force which could save Union, Empire, Constitution and Property from the socialist onslaught. They reclaimed the political hegemony that the Liberals had taken from them in 1906, and began to treat Labour rather than the Liberals as their main challenger, redefining the central question of politics as the confrontation between labour and the established order. Many Liberals, including Churchill, found their way into the Conservative Party in the 1920s as part of a united front against socialism.[14]

Conservative political hegemony like all political hegemony depended on mastery of a particular statecraft, the politics of power and the politics of support, which in the democratic era in England has focused on how to combine winning elections and maintaining parliamentary and party support with how to govern effectively and competently.[15] It required also the ability to win political arguments and to present the party as the embodiment of particular interests and identities. For the Conservatives the narratives which defined their politics became the dominant narratives of British politics itself. In Disraeli's famous formulation in his speech at the Crystal Palace, the three great objects of the Conservative Party were to maintain the institutions of the country, to uphold the Empire of England, and to elevate the condition of the people.[16]

When Disraeli declared these three objectives in 1870, however, the Conservatives were far from enjoying political hegemony. They began to emerge as the leading force in British politics only after Disraeli's death in 1881. The establishment of an enduring Conservative political hegemony through the twentieth century came to rest on five pillars – Union, Empire, Liberty, Property, and Welfare. The Union was especially important. One of the crucial events in the formation of the modern Conservative Party was the decision by Gladstone and the Liberal leadership to attempt to settle the Irish Question in British politics by proposing Home Rule for Ireland. The split in the Liberal Party which this caused was the major reason for the almost unbroken rule of the Conservative Party between 1885 and 1906. Gaining the support of the Liberal Unionists led by Joseph Chamberlain ensured parliamentary majorities for the Conservatives. Unionism became one of the great rallying points of modern conservatism, dividing it sharply from its opponents, and to emphasize its importance the party changed its name to the Conservative *and Unionist* Party. Maintaining the Union of the United Kingdom became one of the central tasks of Conservatives. They remained essentially the party of England, but believed that if England was to continue to expand, and maintain its position in the world, a Union of all the nations in these islands, including the Irish was essential. The Conservatives wanted the hegemony of England within the Union to be consolidated through the acceptance of the jurisdiction of the Westminster Parliament over the whole of Britain and Ireland, and for all nations to give their allegiance to it by accepting a Unionist and British identity.[17]

The second pillar of Conservative political hegemony was Empire. After some earlier ambivalence among Conservatives about the desirability and the costs of expanding the Empire, by the beginning of the twentieth century the Conservatives had emerged as its key defenders and cheerleaders. Like the Union the Empire became a crucial way for imagining and defining British political identity. The extension of British rule in India, the colonial expansion in Africa in competition with other European powers, and a succession of imperial wars, above all the Boer War, 1899–1902, helped consolidate the new imperialism.[18] The story of English expansion and British imperial destiny now became central to Conservatism, and once more it established a key dividing line between themselves and their opponents. Large sections of the Liberal Party and in time of the Labour Party were branded by Conservatives as pacifists and little Englanders, opposed to both Union and Empire. By such means the Conservatives proclaimed themselves the patriotic party.[19] Empire also came to be linked to the wider position of hegemony which England enjoyed in the world, the empire of trade and finance as well as the empire of colonies and fortresses. British commercial and financial power were seen as the natural counterpart of British military and administrative power. The projection of British power through so many spheres and in so many different ways at the end of the nineteenth century made a deep impression on the Conservative mind. It made the Union still more important as the foundation of the entire edifice, and the risk of disengagement by the Irish all the more threatening.

The Union was not the only part of the Constitution which the Conservatives sought to defend. It was part of the wider defence of the old constitutional state, which became a third pillar of their political hegemony, and involved a particular understanding of that Constitution and its place in English history.[20] This old constitutional state, which stretched back to the settlement of 1688, comprised the key institutions of Crown-in-Parliament – the Monarchy, the House of Lords, and the House of Commons – and also included major institutions of the public realm, such as the Law, the Church, the Army, the Navy, the Civil Service, and the Universities. The Conservatives increasingly proclaimed themselves as the defenders of England's ancient institutions and their privileges, with the assumption that the members of these institutions were on the whole natural Conservatives. The divide was between the established and the disestablished (the latter comprised all those forces which coalesced into Liberal Britain) – Scotland, Wales, and Ireland, the North and West of England, the nonconformist Churches, the commercial and manufacturing classes, the artisans, and the new industrial urban areas. From their defence of traditional institutions came the Conservative emphasis on order, hierarchy and authority. They were supporters of liberty but it was an ordered liberty, and an ordered liberty of a particular kind, which put great weight upon the framework of ancient institutions and ancient traditions which comprised the British state. Anything which threatened this state tended to be opposed by Conservatives, which is why so many of them resisted the extension of the suffrage and the reform of representation, as well as any encroachment on the position of the Established Church, or any change to the powers of the House of Lords. Wiser counsels generally prevailed, but the Conservatives fought a determined rearguard action. Many of the big questions of nineteenth century politics revolved around constitutional issues, and although the Conservatives in the end had to concede defeat on the House of Lords, on the extension of the suffrage, even on the separation of the Irish Free State from the Union, it is remarkable how much of the old constitutional order survived into and through the twentieth century.

A fourth pillar was property. The Conservative Party was originally one branch of the landed interest; during the nineteenth century it emerged as the general protector of the landed interest against the coalition of the great Whig landowners and their allies in the new class of industrialists. Helped by the defection of most of the remaining Whig landowners to the Unionist side over Irish Home Rule and by the growing political and industrial strength of the Labour movement, the Conservatives during the early decades of the twentieth century became the general protector of all property interests. The gulf between capital and labour, the propertied and the propertyless became a central divide in British politics and one of the central ways used by Conservatives to define their identity against their opponents.[21] During the 1920s the party consolidated its close relationship with the City of London, as the leading sector of British business, but its position in relation to manufacturing was more equivocal. The party always had strong support from some manufacturing sectors, particularly in the defence sector, but in the dispute between free traders and tariff reformers, many sectors of British manufacturing and finance which depended on free trade and open markets continued to back the Liberal Party. Only later when the Conservatives appeared as the best political bulwark against socialism did the party come to command almost universal support from all sections of capital.[22]

The final pillar of the Conservative Party in the twentieth century was welfare. Elevating the condition of the people has been interpreted in a variety of ways, and promoted by various forms of Tory paternalism and collectivism. The Conservatives contrasted their approach with the unfeeling and harsh attitudes of the new factory owners to their workers, although the record of their own treatment of agricultural labourers was little different.

Conservative attitudes to the working class were shaped by the laws governing the relationships between masters and men, which did not treat the relationship as one between free and autonomous and equal individuals. This did not preclude a concern for welfare but it tended to be thought of either in prudential terms, as the ransom that property had to pay to remain secure, or in military terms as the expenditure necessary to ensure that the manpower available to the Empire was healthy and good quality.[23] The Conservatives were as a result one of the principal architects of the welfare state as it developed incrementally from the nineteenth century into the twentieth. But even here the Conservatives injected a hard political edge. They sought to protect their friends and to shut out their enemies. They made much play with notions of the deserving and the undeserving poor. The deserving poor were those who depended on the Conservative Party. To a much greater extent than the Liberals the Conservatives were instinctively a protectionist party, seeking to protect not only the interests of property but the interests of a wider Conservative electorate, dividing the working class in particular, and seeking to provide material as well as ideological reasons for identifying with the Conservatives.[24]

These five pillars of Conservative political hegemony took shape in the early decades of this century, and defined the identity and the appeal of the party. It became organized around the defence and promotion of the Union, the Empire, Liberty, Property, and Welfare – and developed into a formidable electoral machine, with significant support in all parts of the United Kingdom. Liverpool and Birmingham were Conservative cities, and there was a strong Conservative presence in many others. After the division of Ireland in 1922 Northern Ireland was firmly integrated into the Conservative coalition through the alliance with the Ulster Unionists. There was likewise a strong Unionist presence in Scotland. This was a party which at its height in the 1930s polled 55 per cent in 1931 and 54 per cent in 1935, shares of the vote which gave it overwhelming parliamentary majorities, and reflected its ability to win votes and seats in all parts of the country and from all social classes.

The success of the Conservatives was not uninterrupted in the twentieth century. Their political hegemony was challenged by the Liberals between 1906 and 1916, by Labour between 1940 and 1951, and by Labour again between 1964 and 1979. The most serious challenge came in the first decade of the twentieth century when the Conservatives were weakened by a split in their own ranks over tariff reform, and the Liberals were united and resurgent. The argument over the merits of tariff reform as against free trade was damaging to the Conservative cause for a time, although by driving free traders out of the party it further consolidated the identity of the party as the party of the territorial Empire, already established through the rhetoric of Disraeli, the Boer War, and the colonial policies of Chamberlain. When Conservative hegemony was challenged, however, the Conservatives always recovered strongly and were soon back in government. Electoral defeats stimulated reorganization of the party.[25]

The fortunes of the Conservative Party over the last one hundred years have followed a series of cycles of the two-party system, in each of which one party has been broadly dominant, although sometimes the other party held office briefly as in 1924, 1929–31, and 1970–4 or was in coalition as in 1916–22, 1931–5, and 1940–5. These cycles consist of four long periods of almost unbroken Conservative rule, separated by three shorter periods when the Conservatives not only lost office, but faced a struggle to recapture their political hegemony.

The pattern of Conservative dominance through the period as a whole is clear enough, but to call it hegemony would surprise some Conservatives who have argued that the Conservative Party for the first three-quarters of the twentieth century was on the defensive and retreated before the pressure of the Labour movement and collectivist ideas.[26] Friedrich Hayek in 1960 explaining why he was not a Conservative criticized Conservatives for lacking firm principles, and therefore being unable 'to offer an alternative to the direction in which we are moving'.[27] Keith Joseph spoke of the 'socialist ratchet'. Each period of Liberal and Labour government in the twentieth century had increased the scope and scale of the state; each period of Conservative government until 1979 had failed to reverse it.[28] The cumulative trend of the twentieth century had been towards ever higher levels of public spending and taxation and ever more intrusive state control of individuals. From this standpoint the success of the Conservative Party for much of the twentieth century was an illusion. They were in office but not in power, because they consistently sacrificed Conservative principles,

Table 8.1 Dominant parties in British politics 1886–2003

1886–1906	Conservative
1906–1916	Liberal
1916–1940	Conservative
1940–1951	Labour
1951–1964	Conservative
1964–1979	Labour
1979–1997	Conservative
1997–	Labour

continually making concessions and accepting the changes introduced by their opponents.

An alternative argument, however, is that the success of the Conservative Party and the secret of its political hegemony in the twentieth century lay precisely in its readiness to develop its own distinctive collectivist and interventionist programme.[29] The Conservative leadership proved sufficiently flexible and farsighted to reposition the party when it became necessary, and accept changes in the role of the state, justifying them in terms of the Conservative tradition of using the state to promote welfare and security. The Baldwin–Chamberlain Governments of the inter-war years and the Churchill–Eden–Macmillan Governments of the 1950s and 1960s fall recognizably into this pattern. If it had been successful the Heath Government from 1970–74 might well have inaugurated another phase in the development of this tradition. But the defeat of the Heath Government amidst industrial unrest and a world economic crisis not only helped discredit its programme but also led to a reaction against that entire tradition within the party. The new line of the Thatcher leadership, although resisted at first by many of the old leadership group, was successfully imposed.[30] Three consecutive electoral victories under Thatcher not only ensured that she became the most dominant leader since Churchill, but also legitimated the new anti-collectivist turn in the party and rewrote the party's script.

Thatcherism

The Thatcherites justified their anti-collectivist programme as a return to true Conservatism, and as the only way to rebuild a Conservative political hegemony. Indeed some argued that for the first time in the collectivist era the Conservative Party was building a genuine political hegemony instead of being content to administer within parameters established by its opponents.[31] Conservative critics of Thatcherism argued that post-war leaders of the party would have regarded the Thatcherite programme as entailing a huge political risk, endangering Conservative political hegemony by pushing the party out of the mainstream of British politics and British sentiment.[32] They believe that the real cause of the collapse of support for the Conservative Party in the 1990s is directly attributable to what took place during the Thatcher era. The electoral and political success which the Conservatives enjoyed at that time concealed the long-term damage that was being done to the Conservative position. The Major Government in reaction to this sought to return to a more traditional style of Conservative leadership, but it was unable to overcome many of the problems it inherited, in particular the factional divisions within the party over Europe.[33]

In the 1990s the Conservatives were convulsed by a bitter internal dispute over the meaning of the Thatcherite legacy,[34] and whether it should seek to reject it or to build upon it. Critics of the legacy contended that neoliberalism was corrosive not just of the Conservative party and its distinctive governing tradition and statecraft, but also of the institutions which had formed the bedrock of Conservative political hegemony in the past.[35] Not all the problems the Conservatives faced after 1990 were due to Thatcherism, but many Conservatives agreed that during the Thatcher years the 'hollowing out' of Tory England had accelerated.[36] Many of its familiar landmarks had been eroded, making it harder for the Conservative Party to rally the kind of support it once enjoyed and re-establish its political hegemony. The failure of the Conservative Party at the 2001 election to register any kind of recovery in either votes or seats meant that the electoral unpopularity of the party had remained constant and at historically low levels since the exit from the Exchange Rate Mechanism on Black Wednesday in September 1992. By 2001 this could no longer be passed off as a temporary turndown in the party's electoral fortunes; rather it appeared to reflect the undermining of the pillars which had sustained Conservative political hegemony in the previous hundred years. The difficulty for the party was that it found itself cast adrift, searching for a new identity and a new narrative in unfamiliar political circumstances. It had to find a way to make itself popular again, but what seemed to be required was a re-invention of itself which was much more profound than any re-invention it had previously been called on to make. The big question for the future of the Conservative Party in 2001 remained how to move on from the Thatcher era. Thatcher brought the Conservatives remarkable success and extraordinary political victories, but the cumulative impact of her policies and her legacy was to signal the end of Conservative hegemony rather than to renew it. She restored the Conservatives to dominance but by means which were to undermine that dominance, altering the political terrain in ways that would create the opportunity for a resurgence of the left.

The Unionists' Last Stand

The relationship of the Conservatives to the Union was already under strain when the Thatcher Government took office. It was further weakened in the Thatcher and Major years. The territorial politics of the Conservative Party had been one of the most consistently successful aspects of its statecraft,[37] ever since the priority given to the Union had helped re-establish the party as the leading party in the state at the end of the nineteenth century. In the struggle over Irish Home Rule the Conservatives became the focus for Unionist opinion particularly in Ireland and in Scotland and major cities such as Glasgow and Liverpool. Playing the Orange card became a key weapon in the Conservative political armoury. The lengths to which the Conservatives were prepared to go were demonstrated before the outbreak of the First World War when the Conservative Party encouraged elements of the army to refuse to obey the orders of the Liberal government to 'coerce Ulster' by making it comply with the provisions of the Home Rule Bill.[38]

Conservative intransigence over Ulster made the breakup of the Union with Ireland much more certain, but when it happened the settlement was shaped by the Conservatives, and six counties of Ulster were retained for the Union. The circumstances surrounding the separation cemented the alliance between the party and the Ulster Unionists, who dominated the new Northern Ireland Parliament, Stormont, and for fifty years provided a small but very reliable component of the Conservatives' parliamentary majority at Westminster. The Irish crisis and its resolution had long-term consequences for the Conservatives. If the whole of Ireland had remained within the UK and had continued to send representatives to the Westminster Parliament, the balance of political forces in that Parliament would have been much less to the Conservatives' advantage in the twentieth century. A stronger centre/periphery cleavage would have existed alongside the class cleavage, and would have helped create a different dynamic to British politics, one which would have provided greater opportunities for the formation of centre-left coalition governments.

As noted in Chapter 3, the basis of the Union was different for each of the four nations in the British Isles, and this was reflected in the different arrangements for governing them.[39] There was no uniform pattern imposed from the centre. This highly flexible system of rule was a crucial component of the old constitutional state and its legitimacy. So long as the centre retained control over the policy areas to which it attached most significance, it was prepared to allow considerable decentralization and local autonomy.[40]

This Conservative governing strategy faced serious challenge in Northern Ireland. The breakdown of public order forced the Heath Government to suspend the Stormont Parliament in 1972 and impose direct rule, and begin the long search for a new political basis for governing the province which involved the minority republican community as well as the Unionists. These decisions destroyed the alliance between the Ulster

Unionists and the British Conservatives at Westminster. After the February 1974 election the Unionists no longer took the Conservative Whip,[41] the Conservatives ceased to be the single largest party in the House of Commons, and Edward Heath was forced to resign.

The breach with Ulster Unionism was not healed. Under both Thatcher and Major the Conservatives pursued a strategy of disengaging from Northern Ireland, which involved intensive negotiation with the Irish government and secret negotiations with Sinn Fein and the IRA, culminating in the 1993 Downing Street Declaration, the 1994 ceasefire, and the establishment of the peace process which Labour inherited and continued.[42] The signal in the Downing Street Declaration that the British government had 'no selfish or strategic' interest in Northern Ireland, and that if ever the Ulster people wished to separate from the United Kingdom the British government would not oppose it, was not lost on the Unionists, and obliged them to recognize that there was now no party at Westminster which was committed in principle and in all circumstances to the maintenance of the Union, and to the acceptance of the Ulster Unionists as a British nation.

The same pattern is observable in relations with Scotland. Since the 1955 election when the Conservatives won 50 per cent of the Scottish vote and 50 per cent of the Scottish seats, support for the party has halved. The rise of Scottish nationalism prompted the Heath Government and the Scottish Conservative Party to support devolution in the 1970s.[43] If devolution had been implemented then it might have halted the erosion of the Conservative vote and allowed the Conservatives in Scotland to build an independent Scottish identity fighting the other parties for representation in a Scottish parliament. Once Thatcher became leader, however, in 1975, she changed the party's line to one of total opposition, not only to Labour's proposals for devolution but also to any plans for devolution at all, against the opposition of many leading Scottish Conservatives, including Alick Buchanan Smith and Malcolm Rifkind, both of whom resigned in protest as Shadow Ministers.

Under the Thatcher Government the deterioration of the Conservative position in Scotland accelerated. Although the existence of the Scottish Office still provided a buffer, many Thatcherites were keen to impose Thatcherite policies on Scotland, believing that they would prove as popular as they were in England. Scotland was widely seen by English Conservatives as a burden.[44] The Scots were always demanding subsidies for their industries and extra privileges which were not available to the English regions. Thatcherism came to be viewed in Scotland as quintessentially English, and a series of flashpoints developed – the closing of

Ravenscraig, the imposition of the poll tax (a year before England), and the privatization of the water industry. Conservative support began to ebb away, some of it going to an increasingly assertive and confident Scottish National Party.

John Major reaffirmed the Conservative commitment to the Union, but with support for an independent Scotland having risen to 35 per cent of the Scottish electorate by 1995, the Conservatives had become a marginal political force in Scotland, and had no viable strategy for rebuilding their position. They were more than ever the party of England and in particular of southern England and its metropolitan heartland. That had always been their core identity, but Unionism had allowed them to project themselves as a credible political force throughout the United Kingdom. By 1997 this was what they had lost and lost decisively. In the general election they failed to win a single seat in either Wales or Scotland. They then campaigned for a No vote in the referendums the Labour government organized for a Welsh Assembly and a Scottish Parliament. Only when these were lost did the party reconsider its policy and accept devolution. But the road back appeared long and hard. In the 2001 election the party managed to win back one seat in Scotland, but its share of the vote declined still further to 15 per cent.

Empire, Anglo-America and Europe

The Conservatives approached questions of world order and England's place within it as the party of Union and Empire, the party of the British state. For much of the twentieth century the Empire and how to protect it had a profound effect on Conservative thinking. At the beginning of that century Joseph Chamberlain and his Conservative allies in the Tariff Reform Campaign advanced a programme of imperial protection to guarantee military and economic supremacy, and help weld the dispersed and fragmented territory which England controlled into a cohesive political and economic bloc, which could stand against the great continental empires of Germany, Russia, and the United States. In domestic policy the Chamberlainites favoured using the proceeds of the tariff to pay for welfare programmes. The emphasis was on security, creating through the tariff both higher employment and the funds to finance welfare programmes.[45]

The Chamberlainite tradition in the party dominated the perspectives of the leadership until the Thatcher era. The ability to link external and domestic policy, and to provide a positive programme of domestic reform, instead of merely negative and defensive anti-socialism, was a key factor in the electoral appeal of the Conservatives, and the blunting of the class message of its opponents.[46] It was the means by which the party could proclaim itself the party of One Nation. The conception of England as an Empire, with a global role which went far beyond the British Isles themselves, was the basis of an idea of citizenship which legitimated the extended role for the state to ensure basic welfare and security to all.

The Conservatives however proved unable to preserve the Empire from disintegration. Instead they had to preside over its decline. Much of the party found it very hard to reconcile itself to this loss, and the leadership strove very hard to postpone it. The policy of appeasement in the 1930s (much derided since) was a deliberate and very Conservative strategy to avoid British entanglement in another European war, because Conservative leaders were all too well aware of the huge costs involved and the inevitable consequences for the British Empire and the domestic balance of power if a war had to be fought.[47]

In the post-war years, however, the Chamberlainite tradition proved able to adjust to the loss of Empire. The alliance with the United States became the new linchpin of Conservative policy. The Conservatives hoped that a partnership with the United States would allow parts of the global hegemonic role which Britain could no longer sustain to be transferred to the United States, while permitting Britain to remain a great power and able to protect its global interests. The relationship was always unequal, and the continuing decline in British power after 1945 exposed the limits of British influence. It convinced many in the Conservative leadership that Britain's security in the world order was best achieved by joining the European Economic Community. Entry into the European Community was bitterly opposed by many of the old imperialists in the party, but for some of the Chamberlainites it became a logical step.[48] They argued that the nature of the world economy created a strategic necessity for the United Kingdom to be part of a political and economic network broader than the British Isles. The attraction of the Empire from this geopolitical perspective had been that England was at its centre and dominated it. The disadvantage of the Atlantic Alliance was that the relationship was so unequal between the United States and a United Kingdom which was being forced gradually to disengage from its colonial possessions and military bases. The European Community implied a pooling of national sovereignty and the creation of a partnership in which the UK would be a leading but not a dominant player. Gradually the Conservatives under first Macmillan and then Heath transformed themselves from being the party of Empire to being the party of Europe. The motives were partly economic, to take full advantage of the rapidly growing European market, but the overriding reasons were political, the defence of

Western Europe, the protection of British security, and the maintaining of British influence.

One of the successes of the Conservatives has been their ability to project themselves as a national party while at the same time accepting the United Kingdom's involvement in wider institutions and relationships designed to safeguard British interests. During the Thatcher era the Conservatives renewed their identification as a national party, but they also opened a major debate about what Britain's role in the world should be, and in particular whether it had to choose between Europe and America. Before Thatcher the Conservative leadership had argued that there was no choice to be made. Britain could be both European and Atlanticist. Thatcher's lasting effect on the Conservatives was to deny that that was possible.

Yet although Thatcher in retrospect sounded a clarion call to her fellow citizens against the European danger, her policy in office was deeply ambivalent, and produced a deeply inconsistent policy. The drive to create a single market was promoted, and culminated in the signing of the Single European Act in 1986, which for the first time introduced qualified majority voting to prevent one country vetoing progress. Thatcher strongly supported QMV as a means of accelerating progress towards the single market, but equally strongly opposed the UK joining the ERM and succeeding in delaying it for five years. Towards the end of her premiership she became deeply worried about the moves towards further integration and the possible creation of a federal union. Her attempt to sabotage any further moves to deeper European integration created open division in the Cabinet, three cabinet resignations, and directly triggered the events which led to her resignation in 1990 after she had failed to win enough votes to prevent a second ballot.[49]

John Major inherited a deeply divided party on Europe and struggled to keep the great schism within bounds. Following the conclusion of the Maastricht Treaty,[50] and Major's victory in the 1992 general election, the government seemed to have a free hand to develop policy in a more pro-European direction, reviving the trajectory of past Conservative governments which had been interrupted under Thatcher. But there was considerable unease in the party about the constitutional implications of the Maastricht Treaty. A total of 22 MPs voted against the second reading of the Bill in May 1992. After the Danes voted No to ratification of the Treaty in June 1992, 84 Conservative MPs signed a Commons early-day motion, calling on the government to make a fresh start and rethink the British position on Maastricht.[51]

Following Black Wednesday in September 1992 there was an explosion of anti-European sentiment in the party. Margaret Thatcher, Norman

Tebbit, Cecil Parkinson, Kenneth Baker and other senior figures in the party encouraged the rebellion. The party conference in October saw open conflict over Europe. A total of 65 MPs signed another 'fresh start' early-day motion, and ratification of the Maastricht Treaty became the focus for dissidence. A long and laborious parliamentary battle took place, in which the future Conservative Leader, Iain Duncan Smith, played a prominent role, during which the government narrowly escaped outright defeat on several occasions. In the vote on the Paving Motion in November 1992 the government survived by three votes. Right at the end of the process in July 1993 the government lost a vote on the Social Chapter by 324 to 316, with 26 Conservative MPs voting against the government. Major's response was to call a vote of confidence and threaten a general election if defeated. The rebels voted with the government, but the government's difficulties proved far from over. The divisions continued to deepen within the party, and numerous issues, particularly concerning the European Court and its powers of jurisdiction and revisions to the rules governing qualified majority voting (QMV) became flashpoints. In November 1994 the patience of the leadership snapped and the whip was withdrawn from eight Conservative MPs; a ninth gave it up voluntarily.

The leadership's problem was partly due to its small majority. But the strength of the Euro-rebels' position reflected the balance of feeling within the parliamentary party as well as the party outside Parliament. A survey of the parliamentary party at the time of the 1994 European Parliament election showed that on the key issues that were being debated the balance of party opinion was closer to the position of the Euro-rebels than it was to the European wing.[52] A total of 59 per cent agreed that the disadvantages of EC membership outweighed the benefits (32 per cent agreed) while 64 per cent agreed with the statement that sovereignty could never be pooled (30 per cent disagreed). In subsequent surveys the existence of a small but significant minority of the parliamentary party indicated its support for withdrawal from the EU altogether, and this position came close to being endorsed by Margaret Thatcher. In her book *Statecraft*, she demanded a fundamental renegotiation of all the European Treaties, to restore British sovereignty and argued that if the negotiations could not be concluded satisfactorily the option of withdrawal should be considered.[53] Similar sentiments had been voiced by other senior Euro-sceptics, including Norman Lamont and Norman Tebbit.

After Black Wednesday, Major moved the public position of the party closer to what he correctly perceived to be the centre of party opinion, and his speeches became much more Euro-sceptic, but he also had to keep the support of the majority of his Cabinet and the support of the group of very strong pro-European MPs. The difficulty in managing the party was the contrast between the leadership and the MPs. The Cabinet was divided 2:1 in favour of a more pro-European policy; the MPs were divided 2:1 against. In addition the Conservative press, particularly the *Sunday Telegraph, The Times, The Daily Mail,* and *The Sun,* were all urging a much stronger anti-European line. Business, although divided, was predominantly pro-European.[54]

The reason for the depth of the split that emerged in the party was a direct result of Thatcher's leadership of the party. She legitimated opposition to Europe in a way which the leadership had hitherto successfully avoided. She suggested that there was an alternative – the English adventure was not over, provided English sovereignty was not given up. Priority should be given to America over Europe, because this was the guarantee of preserving an open seas, open trade policy, cultivating links with all parts of the world, rather than being focused on Europe. She pointed to the trade deficit the United Kingdom had with the EU and to the location of the bulk of British overseas investments in countries outside the EU. True internationalism, she argued, meant avoiding entanglement with a protectionist, inward-looking, interventionist, high cost continental economy.[55]

Turning Britain into the Hong Kong of Europe, a deregulated, free-market offshore paradise gave a new and pointed meaning to the notion of the world island. But its realism was much disputed and split the Thatcherites themselves. Those who supported the logic of the free-market policy could see the advantages not only of completing the single market, but also of putting in place central powers adequate to police it, remove obstacles to its functioning, as well as facilitating its smooth operation by, for example, providing the stability of a single currency. Michael Heseltine argued for the more extended state powers at European level to develop a coordinated industrial policy.[56] A strong European economy would be the foundation for a strong European security and external policy, the means by which European influence could be projected, and the interests of European capital defended against the challenge of North American and East Asian capital.

The opponents of closer European integration argued instead that national sovereignty must take priority over economic integration. If national sovereignty were weakened, the legitimacy of the state would be weakened, and with it the legitimacy of national political organizations like political parties. The Thatcherites reacted so passionately against Europe because they came to see Europe as a fundamental threat to England and to national identity. They realized that they felt much more in common with America than with Europe, and they polarized the choice in that way. They attacked the political class of Europe for having lost touch with the peoples of Europe, and for embarking on a project of creating a state which had no natural legitimacy, because it lacked its own nation. The irony that the British state had never had its own nation either was lost on them.

Capitalism and Decline

The Conservatives had not always been the party of capitalism, but they became so in the twentieth century. One of the strangest features of the Thatcher/Major years was the weakening of that association. The party had emerged in the 1920s as the standard bearer for all property interests against the threat posed to them by the Labour movement at home and by revolutionary socialist and national liberation movements abroad. It developed a particularly close relationship with the City of London. But this identification of the Conservative Party with the general interests of capital went hand in hand with policies to support the national economy. The challenge of the Labour movement was in part blunted because the Conservatives accepted an interventionist role for the state.[57] The Conservatives became the party of collectivism and of protection, quite prepared to see an extension of welfare programmes and the provision of certain kinds of economic security to particular sectors of the economy. In the 1930s, following the collapse of the gold standard and the dislocation of world trade in the slump, the Conservatives moved to extend intervention much more generally throughout industry and supported many 'market closing' arrangements in order to safeguard profitability and jobs.[58]

The National government, dominated by Conservatives, also at this time introduced imperial preference, (the Ottawa Agreements) establishing a trading bloc around sterling which covered the countries within the British Empire as well as some other countries within the British sphere of influence. The dream of the Tariff Reformers at the beginning of the century was thus partially realized. British economic policy became linked to a policy of strengthening links within the Empire aimed at increasing both its economic and military security. It was accompanied at home by policies which extended welfare provision.

The Conservatives successfully contained both the political and the industrial challenge of organized Labour in the inter-war years, blunting the class challenge of militant Labour in the early 1920s, defeating the General Strike in 1926, and weakening the legal position of trade unions. But this was not accompanied by an adoption of laissez-faire policies. The doctrines of economic liberalism had never had much influence within the Conservative Party since the days of Peel. The party had always been a strong defender of the rights of property and had resisted any form of encroachment on those rights, but its dominant tradition in macroeconomic policy had been predominantly protectionist. The split over the proposal to repeal the Corn Laws entrenched in the party a strong hostility to 'Manchester Liberalism'. Many in the party were not prepared to put free-market principles above the interests of their particular communities.[59]

This tradition explained why it was relatively easy for the party to recover so quickly to reposition itself after the shock of 1945, and accommodate itself to the further extension of the state which Labour introduced. So long as the dividing line between public and private sectors was clearly marked the party had no difficulty accepting most of Labour's reforms and the new style of economic management which was introduced. The Keynesian approach to economic policy was essentially pragmatic, and this was very much in line with those Conservatives who favoured finding a 'middle way' between collectivism and laissez-faire and for governing in the light of particular circumstances rather than doctrines.

This One Nation tradition of Macmillan and Heath contained a corporatist bias in the sense that it treated the problem of economic management as one of governing a political community and therefore of finding the policies which could command wide assent, particularly from organized producer interests. Heath appeared at the beginning of his government to be steering a very different course, one of disengaging the state from many of its responsibilities and adopting a much tougher line towards organized labour. But the difficulties he immediately ran into soon prompted a change of course, and a return to an interventionist programme which relied on partnership with the employers and the unions. It was the shipwreck of this policy and the extraordinary political alarms and anxieties of the mid-1970s which created the conditions for the Thatcherite ascendancy.[60]

In the Thatcher period, the party renewed and consolidated its identity as the party of capital. With Labour moving to the left, the support of all sections of business for the Conservatives substantially increased. The Thatcher Government succeeded in pushing through tough anti-union measures in stages and the effect of these measures combined with the huge shake-out and high unemployment of the early 1980s to break the back of union resistance to the restructuring of the economy.[61] Tax reductions on higher incomes and deregulation and privatization also helped create a speculative boom in the late 1980s.

Superficially the Thatcher decade appeared a huge economic success, and Conservative Ministers certainly proclaimed it as such. The party had been elected on a pledge to reverse economic decline, and by the end of the 1980s there was talk of a British economic miracle, and of the British economy now outperforming all the other economies in the European Union.[62] But although there were substantial improvements in the United Kingdom's economic position in the 1980s, many of the claims that were made proved unfounded.[63] The long and deep recession which began in 1989 punctured the hopes that had been expressed and exposed the limitations of the British economic recovery. Yet despite this setback the Thatcher decade represented a decisive repudiation of the Chamberlainite tradition on economic policy, and an explicit abandonment of an interventionist strategy for the national economy as a proper object of government policy. The inspiration was the new commonsense of Anglo-America, the ideas of the New Right.[64]

Naturally there were exceptions to this. Agriculture and defence remained protected sectors and continued to flourish under the Thatcher Government. Some regions, notably Wales, under more dirigiste political management, also had a different experience.[65] But for the bulk of the economy the key stance adopted by the Thatcher Government was symbolized by some of their first actions, the abolition of all exchange controls, and the announcement of the phasing out of regional aid and industrial subsidies. The Thatcher Government accepted the shake-out imposed by the world recession which saw the reduction and in several cases the disappearance of many industrial sectors. Given the low investment over so long a period in so many industries such a restructuring had become almost inevitable.

Critics of the government pointed to the failure to develop a successful supply side programme to close the gaps in investment, training, research and development, and finance which had crippled British industry in the past. The Thatcherite economic miracle was too dependent on a few sectors, particularly financial services. When the recession came in 1989–91, the economy appeared only marginally better able to absorb it than before 1979. Despite this setback, however, progress was resumed after 1992 following the exit from the ERM, and a long period of steady if modest expansion ensued, which Labour inherited and continued. By the end of the 1990s the British economy was no longer in relative decline, in comparison with other countries in the OECD group. Britain had moved on to a new and more sustainable path of development, and the turning point had occurred during the Thatcher years.[66]

The success of the Conservatives was double-edged for their political hegemony however. It removed one of the most powerful reasons to vote for the party. The Thatcher decade seriously weakened organized labour as a significant factor in national economic policy, and forced Labour to rethink its economic policy. With the shift of the Labour Party to a policy agenda which accepted the constraints on national economic management imposed by international financial markets, and the removal of any threat from organized labour, the urgency of the need for business to support the Conservative Party as the main defender of their interests diminished.[67] The Thatcher decade thus saw a loosening of the ties between the Conservatives and their supporters in industry, but also a weakening of the ability of the Conservatives to project themselves as the defenders of the national economy.

Another key aspect of Conservative strength in the past had been their reputation for economic competence, the feeling that they were much more in tune with business than Labour was, and therefore that they knew how to run the economy successfully. Conservative governments presided over their share of economic crises, but relatively few, and until 1992 none that compared with the major storms that so damaged Labour governments – in 1931, 1947, 1949, 1967, and 1976. The Conservatives never had the same difficulty as Labour in winning the confidence of the financial markets, reconciling their spending commitments to the principles of sound finance.[68] The fiasco of Black Wednesday helped undermine in the minds of the markets and the voters the Conservative reputation for economic competence. Labour seized the priceless mantle which the Conservatives had retained for so long.

Another legacy of the Thatcher period was that the Conservatives seemed to be offering less to their supporters, in terms of tangible material benefits. Rhetoric about the benefits of competition and enterprise in the abstract failed to gain much response. Conservatives had always favoured the widest possible extension of property ownership, but they had often done little to bring it about. In the 1980s the sale of council houses to their tenants and the offer for sale of shares in the former nationalized industries were partly aimed at broadening the base of Conservative electoral support, but with limited results.[69] The more competitive environment which the Conservatives created also increased insecurity, much of which then came to be blamed on the Conservative government. The enormous financial rewards which went to a few privileged groups made a sharp contrast with the distress of many new property owners suffering negative equity in the 1990–91 recession often because of bankruptcy or unemployment. The problem for the Conservatives in the 1990s was that the neo-liberal doctrines to which the party had been wedded for the previous twenty years offered few positive ways of providing relief.

Self-Government and Public Service

An important feature of the pre-Thatcher Conservative Party was that its leaders saw themselves as the natural governing class, the voice of the Establishment, and therefore as the guardians of the old constitutional state and its institutions, and the guarantors of the special balance between order and liberty on which that state had been founded. It was closely identified with the British public realm, the key public institutions of the state and civil society, and defended the practices and privileges of the established groups within it. It strongly resisted constitutional reform.[70] This Establishment was a dense network of personal and family connections founded on the public schools, Oxford and Cambridge, and the leading professions. *The Times* newspaper was its journal of record.

It was this consolidation of the Establishment recruited on the basis of property ownership and educational privilege which also gave a particular flavour to the English class system. Big inequalities of income and wealth had to be reconciled to the status hierarchies of the English Establishment. English elites were not closed, but recruited from all classes and all parts of the UK as well as from wider parts of the Empire, but those who aspired to enter them had to ensure that either they or their children learnt its codes and its manners. The gulf between the ethos and culture of the English Establishment and that of the British working class and indeed of the British electorate as a whole was as a result extremely wide.[71] What the old constitutional state sought to inculcate was deference. In the age of democracy it offered the people a ruling class of skill, experience, knowledge and authority: a class that could be trusted and relied upon to provide disinterested public service. Its exemplar was the BBC, and the Monarchy.

The mystique of the English Establishment had been wearing thin for some time, but the Thatcher Government finally shattered it. This was despite the deep attachment of Margaret Thatcher and many of her Ministers to the outward forms of the old constitutional state. In constitutional matters they were at their most conservative, blocking any moves to electoral reform, devolution to Scotland and Wales, or a bill of rights. They sought to bolster the authority of the Westminster Parliament, and proclaimed the doctrine of unfettered parliamentary sovereignty. But this conservatism about formal constitutional arrangements was accompanied by the deliberate overriding of many of the conventions which had been established which softened the impact of executive absolutism which the doctrine of parliamentary sovereignty and the residual prerogative powers of the sovereign made possible.[72] The Thatcher Government made fuller use of its patronage powers in pursuit of its programme, excluding non-Conservatives from many of the quangos it established to implement government policy. It also reduced the amount of consultation with organized interests and professional bodies over proposed reforms.[73] The potential for elective dictatorship in British constitutional arrangements of which Lord Hailsham warned under the Callaghan Government was much more starkly visible under the Thatcher Government, a government in which he served as Lord Chancellor.

An unwillingness to be bound by precedent and convention was characteristic of the Thatcher Government. To this extent at least it can be considered a radical government, because on many occasions it showed itself not prepared to work within existing constraints where these were blocking the kind of reforms it wanted to enact. The most important constraints from the Thatcherite perspective which had to be removed in the pursuit of its programme were the special interests which infested all the institutions of the state. The culture of dependency and the collectivist consensus which legitimated government intervention and control had its roots in the kind of state and its Establishment which had grown up in the twentieth century.

To their great surprise the conservative institutions of the English state began to discover that they were one of the main targets of the Thatcherite revolution. The Thatcherites appeared to be conducting a long march through the institutions, attacking the professions as vested interests which needed to be subjected to market disciplines. In some cases, such as the Monarchy and the Church and the BBC, conflict erupted over ideological criticisms of the direction of government policy. In many others explicit restructuring of the institutions was sought in order to make them more pliant instruments in the achievement of the government's aims. In this way major reshaping of the civil service, the health service, the schools, the universities, as well as the Law, the Armed Forces, and the Police were launched. In some cases the government's plans encountered such resistance that they had to be modified or postponed, but in most a substantial reshaping had taken place by the end of the 1980s. The Thatcher Government was responsible for attempting the most far-reaching reform not only of the machinery but also of the ethos of government. The public sector was devalued and increasingly denied legitimacy, subjected instead to a utilitarian calculus, with market criteria being applied wherever possible to determine the usefulness of particular services. Nothing was any longer assumed to be of value just because it had existed for a long time and was sanctified by the Establishment. If it was sanctified by the Establishment, that for Thatcherites was a reason to be suspicious.[74]

A radical bourgeois modernization of the English state was something which critics of this last *ancien régime* and its antiquated institutional arrangements had long called for.[75] The Thatcherite changes hardly amounted to that. They were never linked to any wider programme for establishing a more egalitarian civil society, and did not make much use of the language of citizenship, although the Thatcherite media did engage intermittently in wide-ranging attacks on the Monarchy, on aristocrats, and more generally on 'grandees'. The tone of Thatcherism was often meritocratic in the American sense and rejected deference. But it also celebrated inequality. The really deserving individuals were those who were self-made, not those who were born to wealth.

This lack of deference both for established institutions and for established status and wealth was part of Thatcherism's popular appeal and was enthusiastically endorsed by most of the tabloids, particularly the Murdoch Press with its own Anglo-American agenda, but it also ensured that the Conservatives became thoroughly estranged from many of the Establishment elites which formerly had been natural allies of the Conservatives. A strong anti-Conservative mood developed throughout the public sector. The exceptions were those services, notably the Armed Services and the Emergency Services, which still received praise and support from the Thatcher Government. They were a part of the public service to which the nostrums of New Right ideology did not apparently apply. But elsewhere public sector professionals felt that they were under attack, and that the ethos of public service had been devalued, so relentless was the government in advancing the argument that the public sector was inefficient and self-serving. The Church and the Monarchy, both strong upholders of the ethos of public service, clashed publicly with the government. There were running battles with the broadcasters, particularly with the BBC.

The position was in part remedied by the appointment and promotion of individuals within the Establishment who shared the government's objectives, but there were limits to what could be done. By the end of the 1980s the isolation of the Conservative Party from the Establishment for whom it had once been the natural voice was marked. This did not deter Ministers. The principles of the new public management, imported mostly from America, were applied in sector after sector and resistance to the new dispensation was steadily overcome, but the cost for the government was the breakdown of trust and support among many of its natural supporters. By the end of the Thatcher period it was hard to identify many parts of the public sector which remained unquestionably Conservative in their loyalties. From being the voice of the Establishment the Conservatives by the end of the Thatcher period had become identified as the critic of the Establishment and more estranged from it than at any previous time in the twentieth century. Conservatism had once been synonymous with a certain kind of public service; by the 1990s that was no longer the case.

Welfare to Workfare

The transatlantic influence was also highly visible in welfare reform. The Thatcher Government set out to move Britain much closer to an American style of welfare. One of the ways in which the Conservatives reinvented themselves after 1945 was to claim that they were the party which had established the welfare state, and they cited a long list of measures that Conservative governments had passed.[76] They needed to prove to voters that they would not dismantle the new universal welfare programmes introduced by Labour when they returned to power. Many in the Labour Party thought that the Conservatives would prove to be incapable of adapting, and that opinion would swing back to Labour. But the Conservatives disappointed these hopes. They made no serious move to change the principles on which the post-war welfare state was founded.[77]

The Conservatives opposed further major expansions of the welfare system and argued for selective rather than universal benefits as the most cost-effective solution to welfare problems, but they accepted the general case for services such as the National Health Service as part of the new basic minimum which government was expected to provide. The protectionist instincts of the party combined with political realism – once the suffrage was extended, a large part of the party's support had to come from the working class. Issues of economic security and welfare provision for basic needs were bound to be important to a large part of the Conservative electorate, and it was essential that Conservative governments were trusted to provide them. Labour was often able to outbid the Conservatives on welfare, but they always lagged behind on economic competence, so that there was little trust among voters that Labour could actually deliver its promises of higher spending on the welfare state without precipitating an economic crisis and being forced into large public expenditure cuts. This had after all been the pattern of the three post-war Labour governments before 1997.

The hard-won trust of the electorate that the Conservatives would not undermine the public services was a key pillar of Conservative political hegemony. It was another casualty of the Thatcher era. By 1997 the Conservatives had come to be seen as 'wreckers'. A number of factors contributed to this. Privatization was never popular with the electorate. Public expenditure was not cut dramatically, but years of tight restraint took their toll. Over eighteen years the public services became seriously underfunded, and the state of chronic underinvestment in them gradually became apparent to everyone, until it emerged as the big political issue in British politics at the end of the 1990s. The problem for the Conservatives was less the actual cuts they made to the public services as the attitude towards the public services with which they became associated. From the start, one of the central messages of Thatcherism was, as the 1980 Treasury White Paper put it, 'Public expenditure is at the heart of our current difficulties'.[78] The New Right onslaught on the dependency culture, the priority given to control of inflation and reducing taxes, the attempts to reorganize every major public service in order to cut costs, the denigration of people who worked in the public sector – all this helped give the Thatcher Government its cutting edge, and its reputation for radicalism, but it came at a price. Much of the policy towards the public sector was rhetorical rather than substantive. The NHS was not abolished, vouchers for schools were abandoned, the social security budget kept increasing. At the same time the Conservatives came to be perceived as fundamentally hostile to the public services and to a public service ethos. By 1997 despite the less abrasive tone of the Major Government this had become deeply etched in voters' attitudes. The Conservatives were no longer trusted as guardians of the welfare state, and their mantras about tax cuts no longer worked. Once their reputation for economic competence had been lost as well the Conservatives found themselves deeply unpopular.

Conclusion

The spectacle which the Conservative Party presented at the beginning of the twenty-first century was a party whose ideological tradition had become (at least temporarily) exhausted and its long political hegemony broken. The initiative had passed to its political opponents. The great campaigns on which the party had been built – agricultural protection, tariff reform, anti-socialism, anti-communism and Empire, were all in the past. National protectionism had been abandoned in the new-found enthusiasm for the mantras of economic liberalism; the retreat from Empire was complete, and England had given up many of its pretensions to be a great power; the Communist bloc in Europe had collapsed, removing the major external security threat of the post-war years; while at home the Labour movement had been confronted and defeated, and was no longer a threatening power to which concessions had to be made. Thatcherism was an expression of these changes, and in part had also been a catalyst for them.

The Thatcher years were some of the most triumphant and successful years in the party's history, but they were also the years in which the old pillars of Conservative political hegemony crumbled away. Thatcherism was a dynamic force which destroyed much more than the enemies that it chose to confront. It also succeeded in destroying the old Conservative Party, and creating the conditions in which a different kind of centre-left politics could emerge, with a radical programme of constitutional reform, to which Thatcherism had no answers. But so weighty was its legacy for the Conservatives, that the party, always so adaptable in the past, noticeably failed both before 1997 and after it to change. The result was the two great defeats of 1997 and 2001.

The severity of these defeats led some to wonder whether the party would ever recover, or whether it might not continue to decline until it was replaced as the main party of opposition by the Liberal Democrats. After 2001 the Conservatives although they only slightly improved their position did not lose any further ground. A total of 33 per cent support still gave them a powerful base on which to challenge in the future, and their protean ideological inheritance suggested many ways in which they might reinvent themselves[79] once they had shrugged off the pall of Thatcherism. John Major had attempted to do so during his premiership, but his efforts were in the end overwhelmed. Despite his best endeavours he ultimately failed to return the party to its old One Nation tradition.[80] Many of the old landmarks were no longer there, and the party was no longer the disciplined, governing force that it was. It had become infected with ideology and factional disputes, and fragmented in an orgy of recriminations over Europe; at the same time it was engulfed by sleaze and the perception grew that the party had become self-serving, incompetent, and above all out of touch with what the voters wanted. Thatcherism in its heyday had appeared to be consolidating and extending Conservative political hegemony, marginalizing and burying its political opponents. But in a longer perspective it becomes clear that what Thatcherism did was to help to destroy the old pattern of British politics altogether. Old Labour was one of its targets, but old Toryism also perished in the flames.

9
Labour Old and New

Her Majesty's Government does not accept the view ... that we have ceased to be a great Power, or the contention that we have ceased to play that role. We regard ourselves as one of the Powers most vital to the peace of the world, and we still have a historic part to play. The very fact we have fought so hard for liberty, and paid such a price, warrants our retaining that position; and indeed it places a duty upon us to continue to retain it.

Ernest Bevin, 1946[1]

We are the ally of the US not because they are powerful, but because we share their values ... There is no greater error in international politics than to believe that strong in Europe means weaker with the US. The roles reinforce one another ... There can be no international consensus unless Europe and the US stand together ... We can help to be a bridge between the US and Europe ... Europe should partner the US not be its rival.

Tony Blair, 2003[2]

The dramatic collapse of the Conservative Party in the 1990s from a position of such strength gave Labour new hope and opportunity to forge a political hegemony of its own. Having suffered its own spectacular meltdown in support in the 1980s the Labour Party had to find a new programme and a new appeal. It was eventually to do this by presenting itself as *new* Labour. As new Labour the party achieved the kind of electoral success which had eluded it in the previous hundred years. But despite some speculation that the new century might become a progressive century, dominated by Labour as the twentieth century had been dominated by the Conservatives, there were many unresolved tensions and conflicts in the

189

Labour Party, which raised doubts as to whether new Labour would become a permanent governing force.

As with the Conservatives, Labour has had to come to terms with a post-imperial political landscape dominated by the complex and unresolved choice between Europe and America. In 1983 Labour experimented briefly with rejecting both Europe and America, committing itself to withdraw from the EEC and to unilateral nuclear disarmament. In remaking itself after 1987, the party returned to its strong post-war Atlanticism, while at the same time discovering a new enthusiasm for Europe. The great Tory schism over Europe became Labour's opportunity, just as Labour's own schism over Europe had aided Conservative ascendancy in the 1980s. Labour set out to reposition itself as the party of Europe, but it was also now firmly again the party of the Atlantic Alliance, proclaiming the idea of Britain as a bridge between Europe and America.

In recent times the main fault-line in the Conservative Party appeared over Europe, but in the Labour Party it has developed over America. Divisions over Europe persisted in the party, but hostility to Europe was now a minority view, and in government after 1997 Labour demonstrated a new positive pro-European policy, proclaiming its goal of putting Britain at the heart of Europe. What this did not mean, however, was that Labour now saw Europe as the exclusive frame within which it should work out common policies on economics, on security and on foreign policy and defence. It sought to combine its European commitment with a renewed Atlanticist commitment. The leadership of new Labour, remaining firmly committed to the Atlantic Alliance, was strongly attracted to American models in economic policy, in welfare reform, and in the conduct of politics itself.[3] From the start new Labour modelled itself on the new Democrats, and showed greater affinity with America than with Europe. The Third Way of Clinton and Blair became a defining ideological choice for new Labour, separating it from other European social democratic parties. A succession of global security issues from Kosovo to Iraq also found the Blair Government choosing Anglo-America and the strategic alliance with the United States rather than Europe.

The leadership pursued this course against a rising tide of anti-Americanism in the party, which reached new heights in the Iraq crisis in 2002–3. Anti-Americanism had always been strong in the party, but in a minority position and confined to the left. The Atlantic Alliance had been a bedrock of the Labour mainstream since the 1940s. During the Reagan–Bush years, however, hostility to the ideology of the American conservatism and to the foreign policy of the United States deepened. After a lull during the Clinton presidency, it surged again during the presidency of George W. Bush following his proclamation of the doctrines of American primacy and American unilateralism. Supporters of the Atlantic alliance with the United States were now in a minority in the party and increasingly, as the Iraq crisis was to show, in the country. New Labour's choice of America over Europe threatened to divide the party and isolate the leadership.

New Labour

The re-election of the Labour Party in June 2001 with another huge parliamentary majority was the first time in its history that Labour had secured two full terms of office. Labour had become at last a successful party of government, and its constitutional reforms, the most significant element of its first-term programme, although very incomplete and at times incoherent,[4] appeared secure. A second phase in the transformation of British politics which Thatcherism had begun was well under way, and its agent was a new model Labour Party.

In the twentieth century Labour was much less successful than the Conservatives in forming governments. It was not until 1945 that Labour was able to form its first majority government. Until 1997 the Labour Party had only had two spells in government, 1945–50 and 1966–70, when it had a substantial parliamentary majority. It was no stranger, however, to minority government (1924, 1929–31, 1974, 1977–79) and majorities in single figures (1950–51, 1964–66, 1974–77). In the sixty-nine years up to 1997 since a democratic franchise was achieved in 1918, Labour was in government for only twenty of those years, or twenty-five counting its participation in the coalition government in the Second World War.

The period that opened in 1997 was therefore unprecedented in the party's history. It had never tasted such electoral success. But some argue that this is because this was no longer the Labour Party. So ingrained is the ethos of opposition rather than the ethos of government in the Labour movement that success on this scale was immediately suspect. If Labour is successful it can no longer be Labour, and many in Labour's ranks agreed that Labour had become a new party and deserved a new name – new Labour. There has been much controversy over whether these claims are justified; whether new Labour is really new, and has broken away entirely from its past, and whether new Labour is any longer a social democratic party. Some claim it has become a European Christian Democratic party, others that it is now a second Conservative party, others that it is a new catch-all party of the centre like the American Democrats, others that it is evolving into a European social democratic party. What most contributors to the debate seem to agree however is that the party is no longer the old Labour Party, the perpetual loser in British politics.[5]

Despite, or perhaps because of this, comment on new Labour has been overwhelmingly critical and hostile. One of new Labour's achievements has been to unite virtually all sections of left of centre opinion against it. The more successful new Labour became, the more dissatisfied and disillusioned its intellectual supporters have declared themselves.[6] The collapse of turnout in the 2001 election to 58 per cent, the lowest turnout since 1918, was taken as a sign that new Labour was the cause of a profound disengagement of voters, particularly core Labour voters, from politics.[7]

The idea of new Labour was carefully constructed after Tony Blair became Leader in 1994, and ever since it has been furiously deconstructed by an army of critics. What new Labour signified above all was an attempt to draw a line between the Labour Party under Blair and old Labour. It was this category of old Labour which gave most offence, since it quickly came to be understood as a general term which referred indiscriminately to all wings of the party, to the policies of all previous Labour governments and Labour oppositions, and to the trade unions and Labour local authorities. There were times when it seemed there was nothing in Labour's past from which new Labour did not want to dissociate itself.

The proclamation that Labour was now new Labour was originally intended to underline the changes which the modernizers in the party leadership had achieved since 1987, and to tie them to Tony Blair's leadership. There was a great deal of exaggeration involved, since there was obviously much continuity between Blair and his immediate predecessors, John Smith and Neil Kinnock, as well as with the party of Wilson and Callaghan, Gaitskell and Bevan, and Attlee and Morrison. But the idea that new Labour really was *new*, a clean break with the past and that old Labour had ceased to be, was seized on by all the opponents of the leadership inside and outside the party. If Labour was new, this meant that it was no longer a socialist party, no longer a social democratic party, no longer even a party of Labour. It had turned its back on the working class, on the poor, on the trade unions and on its active membership, and was looking for new allies and new voters.

This view was always overblown, whether it came from the modernizers or their critics. In all sorts of ways, new Labour was still recognizably old Labour in many of its practices, attitudes, and even policies, but many still suspected that the intentions of its leaders were unmistakable – they wanted to root out all traces of old Labour from the party, and transform it into a quite different kind of party, both in the way in which it operated and the policies it pursued. Underneath the rhetoric of staying true to traditional socialist and social democratic values, the real agenda was seen to be the hollowing out of the party and the destruction of its internal democracy and all the policies with which it had in the past been associated.

Modernizers in the party, like Peter Mandelson, use old Labour in two senses, to refer to the party between 1979 and 1983, and to the party in the 1960s and 1970s.[8] In the first period the left of the party was in the ascendancy (although never dominant).[9] This was when the party split with the setting up of the Social Democratic Party (SDP) by four former Labour Cabinet Ministers (Roy Jenkins, David Owen, Shirley Williams, and William Rodgers), and when it became committed to a major extension of public ownership, redistribution of wealth, unilateral nuclear disarmament, and withdrawal from the European Community. It coincided with two major election defeats – in 1979 following the public-sector strikes against the Labour government in the Winter of Discontent, and the 1983 election when the party slumped to 28 per cent of the vote, its worst showing since the 1920s. One of the key arguments of the modernizers in the party after 1983 was that the party had to change if it was to avoid further electoral decline. Responsibility for the electoral collapse was pinned firmly on the left and on the trade unions. This interpretation of old Labour became absolutely central to the new Labour narrative. The left had caused the party to split, they had committed the party to electorally unpopular and politically impracticable policies, and they had attempted to subordinate the leadership of the party to the decisions of the rank and file in the constituency parties and the trade unions. The proclamation that Labour was new was intended first and foremost as a proclamation that the left in the party no longer had any significant influence.

The second sense of old Labour used by the modernizers was more wide-ranging; it targeted core aspects of the party as it had been in the 1960s and 1970s, particularly the strong link with the trade unions and the commitment to policies of high spending and high taxation. What the modernizers objected to in this version of old Labour was less the specific policies to which old Labour was committed, than the fact that these policies were associated with economic and electoral failure. The party had failed to prove itself a successful governing party because of the failures of the economic modernization programme of the Wilson Government between 1964 and 1970 and the travails of the Wilson/Callaghan Government between 1974 and 1979. The indelible association of Labour with trade unions and strikes, with corporatism (loosely defined as any involvement of the trade unions in the management of the economy), with high taxation, and with economic stagnation became the second identity of old Labour against which new Labour wanted to define itself.[10]

The most potent symbol that new Labour really was new was the decision shortly after Tony Blair became Leader to rewrite Clause IV of the party constitution. This had been drafted by Sidney Webb and adopted by the party in 1918, and ever since had been the guarantee for the socialist wing of the party that whatever the backslidings and equivocations of the party leadership in practice, in principle the party still remained committed to the ultimate goal of a socialist society, understood as a society in which all property was collectively owned. The wording of the clause was very specific on this.[11] Tony Blair was not however the first Labour leader to propose revising Clause IV. Hugh Gaitskell had tried and failed in 1960, after Labour had suffered a third successive election defeat. Tony Blair's call to revise it came after Labour had suffered four successive election defeats, and after almost all the industries taken into public ownership by the 1945 Labour government had been privatized. What Gaitskell and Blair shared was a desire to bring the party's rhetoric and its statement of ultimate aims in line with its actual policies.

It was a measure of the changed situation facing Labour that Blair succeeded relatively painlessly where Gaitskell failed. The change was trivial in itself, since it involved no change of policy, but its symbolic importance was immense. It signalled the final victory of the revisionists in the battle for the party, delayed for thirty-five years. Like so much with new Labour, however, the change could be represented as a sign that it really was new, marking a break with the party as it had existed before, or instead as showing how new Labour was in a direct line of descent with other modernizing and revisionist forces in the party, specifically the revisionists of the 1950s and 1960s.[12]

For those wanting to make the case for continuity there were other parallels too. Under Blair the parliamentary leadership achieved a level of dominance over both the parliamentary party and the party in the country which several previous leaders had sought, but none had achieved to the same degree. That familiar battle in the history of the Labour Party, the degree of autonomy exercised by the parliamentary leadership and its independence from the party organization, appeared to have reached a climax under Blair. But although the degree of control obtained was unprecedented, and some of the means were novel, the kind of centralized control which Blair established was also reminiscent of the methods used by the Labour right to control the party in the 1950s. At that time the right had been less successful, partly because it faced a much larger and more confident left.

In policy too there were some remarkable continuities. Too much attention tends to be given to domestic policy and the abandonment of the priorities of the post-war compromise. But even here there were strong continuities, particularly the importance new Labour gave to maintaining universal public services in education and health. Provision of such services has been so much at the heart of Labour's practice and its values that a repudiation of a commitment to the National Health Service, for example, or state education are still unthinkable. That really would mark Labour out as new. Even new Labour's attitude to redistribution, a word new Labour Ministers at first refused to utter, so redolent was it of old Labour, had strong links to earlier revisionist accounts of redistribution. Tony Crosland who made redistribution the centrepiece of his socialism always saw it as dependent upon the achievement of economic growth. Only if the economy was growing would Labour governments have the flexibility to divert a larger share of the growing wealth to those most disadvantaged. Crosland never held out much hope in a democratic polity of achieving redistribution through confiscation,[13] and his enthusiasm for measures to improve Britain's rate of growth was because this offered the surest way to make redistributive policies possible. Exactly the same logic underpinned the economic strategy undertaken by Gordon Brown after 1997. Financial stability and a growing economy were combined with modest tax increases to generate budget surpluses which were spent with clear redistributive objectives.[14]

The most obvious area for continuity however lay in foreign policy and the strong revival of Atlanticism under new Labour. It had been the Attlee Government which had played a key role in persuading the United States to assume global responsibilities both in security through NATO and in the reconstruction of the world economy through the Marshall Plan and the establishment of the new global institutions, such as the General Agreement on Trade and Tariffs (GATT) and the IMF and World Bank.[15] Old Labour was one of the key architects of the post-war order and of the cold war, and a strong Atlanticism was chararacteristic of every Labour leadership until the 1980s. This had already begun to change under Kinnock and Smith, but Blair's elevation to the leadership, and the rapport which he forged first with Clinton over the Third Way and over foreign policy intervention in Iraq and Kosovo, and then more improbably with George Bush and the war on terrorism after 9/11, re-established the connection and emphasized once again the importance of the Atlantic Alliance for Labour's politics.[16]

Social Democracy and Democratic Socialism

The evidence for continuity is at least superficially strong, but the argument for discontinuity believes there has been a deeper reconstruction of Labour, so that it is no longer a democratic socialist party or even a social democratic party, but a neo-liberal party, a party which has become an instrument of the neo-liberal or conservative consensus established in the 1980s and 1990s in both Britain and America. On this view the abandonment of Clause IV is an important symbol of the change, but still more significant is the repudiation of Keynesian social democracy, particularly the abandonment of commitments to full employment, demand management, employment protection, the defence of trade unions, equality and redistribution. Beyond all these and perhaps most important, is the acceptance of the market and capitalist social relations as a given, within which governments have to work.[17] The social democratic assumption that markets have to be controlled and regulated in the public interest is either diluted or abandoned altogether. New Labour appears as a pro-market, pro-business party in a way in which old Labour never was, and not because of the practical difficulty of being anything else, but out of conviction that this is the right way the economy should be organized.

This argument is a serious one, and needs careful consideration. One difficulty with it is that it suggests that one particular phase of Labour's development, the reconstruction of the party around a programme of Keynesianism, planning, and welfare following the 1931 defeat, contains the essence of what Labour both is and should be, and a standard by which the party before and since can be judged. Such a procedure naturally tends to elevate the Attlee Government of 1945–51 into the exemplary Labour government, 'Labour's finest hour', when the party dominated both in votes and in ideas, and laid the foundations for the post-war welfare state and managed economy.

Important though this period was in Labour's history, however, there is no reason to accord it sacred status, or imply that it set a standard against which all subsequent Labour governments have to be judged. There are other accounts, as we shall see, that are disinclined to treat the Attlee Government as sacred, and it is certainly not how it was viewed or experienced at the time. Disillusion and cynicism were never far away. Labour governments have never satisfied their supporters or met their expectations. It is difficult to estimate which Labour government has done worst in this regard, but measured against the Wilson Government re-elected in 1966 or the Wilson/Callaghan Government of 1974–79 or Ramsay Macdonald's minority Government in 1929 the Blair Government has not clearly done any worse. In certain respects it has done better, at least on domestic policy.

The party has constantly been remaking itself throughout its history, not once but many times. There have been at least six Labour parties, starting with the small parliamentary pressure group between 1906 and 1918, representing the Labour interest. The next was Ramsay Macdonald's party which, armed with its new socialist constitution adopted in 1918, and taking advantage of the enlarged franchise and the disarray of the Liberals, emerged with some Conservative connivance as the main party of opposition in the 1920s. This was the party that Liberals like Hugh Massingham who joined Labour feared was 'a mere wages and hours party with an irreconcilable Communist wing', and no sense of strategy or broader purpose.[18] What strategy it did possess came from Ramsay Macdonald who sought to create a progressive coalition to reach out beyond the organized Labour movement and become an accepted governing party.[19] It was this party which broke apart in 1931 because of the tension between the extreme financial orthodoxy of the Chancellor, Philip Snowden, insisting on cuts in the dole to help balance the budget in the face of the slump, and trade union determination to defend working-class living standards.[20]

The third Labour Party was the party since celebrated as Labour's finest, the democratic socialist party which took shape under the leadership of Attlee, Dalton and Morrison in the 1930s. There were few signs, however, that this party was on the brink of gaining office. An election held in 1940 as scheduled would almost certainly have returned another Conservative majority. What transformed the position for Labour was the major shift of opinion which took place during the war, and the retrospective discrediting of Conservatism and the policy of appeasement. The appointment of Churchill as Prime Minister and the entry of Labour into the government as a full partner was not only a major repudiation of the foreign policy but also of the domestic strategy the Conservatives had been pursuing for ten years. The pent-up demands for a major expansion of public services and national planning could not be denied in the context of the wartime emergency. The plans for post-war reconstruction expressed through the Beveridge Report on Social Security and Butler's Education Bill were an essential element in the way the war was fought, and it encouraged a huge desire, particularly in the armed forces, for much more when the war was over.[21]

Labour's sweeping victory in 1945 still took many politicians and journalists by surprise, since they had assumed that Churchill was bound to be returned, as he might have been in a presidential system. What was voted out however, in 1945, was the Conservative Party, and its record in the 1930s, a myth which loomed over the next two decades as strongly as the myth of the Winter of Discontent that overshadowed the 1980s and 1990s. Labour had a clear programme based on its pre-war thinking and on its experience of running a planned economy during wartime. But it was still remarkably short of any plans as to how to implement many of its major reforms, including nationalization and the National Health Service, and these had to be improvised. There was no socialist blueprint which was available to be applied, and the conditions in the immediate aftermath of the war were exceptional, and would in any case have overridden any detailed plans which Labour possessed.[22]

What the Attlee Government achieved was a major extension of public ownership, principally of public utilities, and a big expansion of universal public services, of which the social security reforms and the National Health Service (an early monument to public private partnerships) were the most notable. The economy was reconstructed using the instruments of physical planning inherited from the war. Keynesianism was not needed. There would have been full employment anyway, and the more serious problem was inflation which again was tackled through direct intervention to hold down prices and wages. What Keynesianism did contribute was the idea that it was legitimate for governments to accept responsibility for the level of employment and the rate of inflation and for economic growth.[23]

The career of this Mark III Labour Party in government was cut short in 1951, and was followed by a long period of internecine warfare between the social democratic wing, in alliance with many of the trade unions, and the socialist wing. The struggle became personified in Gaitskell and Aneurin Bevan, which ended in victory for Gaitskell and the inauguration of the next phase of the party, the revisionist party of Gaitskell and Wilson. Gaitskell and his allies, who included Tony Crosland and Roy Jenkins, were chiefly responsible for developing a new rationale which clearly distinguished their position from that of the Bevanites.[24] It rejected the importance of public ownership for achieving socialism, instead giving priority to equality and redistribution, and therefore to the public services. The creation of strong public services on the basis of an efficient and prosperous private sector was advocated as the best way of achieving socialist goals.

Gaitskell's early death robbed the Gaitskellites of their leader. The new leader, Harold Wilson, had been a Bevanite, and had resigned with Bevan from the government in 1951. He had also stood against Gaitskell for the leadership after Gaitskell had proposed to revise Clause IV. But Wilson was highly pragmatic and was forced to recognize that electoral success required that the party modernize itself. Once he became Leader, he not only inherited the revisionist programme, but also a younger generation of party leaders many of them strongly influenced by revisionism. The strategy of modernizing the British economy and British society in order to enable it to compete more effectively and deliver better public services was taken up enthusiastically by Wilson and used to great effect against the Conservatives in the slogan – 'thirteen wasted years'. Yet although the

Wilson Government achieved more than it was credited with at the time, its reputation was severely damaged by a succession of crises, culminating in the 1967 devaluation, and the inability of Wilson in particular to convey any clear idea of strategic direction and long-term goals.[25]

Unexpected defeat at the general election in 1970 plunged the party into introspection about its defeat and its direction at the very moment that the global order began to fall apart, with the collapse of the Bretton Woods system, the acceleration of inflation, falling profitability, an upsurge of industrial militancy, and the approach of the first major post-war recession. The revisionist project was severely discredited, but there was little new thinking. Instead the momentum passed to its critics on right and left. Within the Labour Party the perceived failure of the Wilson Government and the revisionist project it embodied, and the mounting international capitalist crisis prompted a strong revival of the left and the project of a democratic socialism, this time drawing on the energies of the New Left from the 1960s in all its different manifestations.[26] The result was a period of increasing left ascendancy in the party which set out both a different programme and a different form of organization, making the parliamentary leadership permanently subordinate to the rank and file, and encouraging a new grass-roots delegate democracy throughout the party and the economy. The period of left ascendancy was never total, since the left never gained control of either the Cabinet or Shadow Cabinet, but for a period of thirteen years there was a situation of dual power in the party, with the party organization and the party Conference controlled by the left and the government and parliamentary party controlled by the right.[27] The campaign for intra-party democracy was spearheaded by the Campaign for Labour Party Democracy, which succeeded in getting two of its reforms through the party Conference in 1980. Tony Benn then challenged Denis Healey for the Deputy Leadership under the new electoral college rules for electing the leader. Benn lost by the narrowest of margins, principally due to the abstention of a number of left MPs, including Neil Kinnock.

This defeat in retrospect came to be seen as the highwater mark of the left's advance. The 1983 election result and the election of Neil Kinnock as leader signalled a new sixth phase in the history of the party, the 'modern-ization' of the party and its organization which led ultimately to the complete marginalization of the left inside the party and the birth of new Labour. Kinnock's nine years as leader were vital in laying the foundations for this transformation, and in particular destroying the power base of the left, expelling entryist groups like Militant, and jettisoning most of the poli-cies to which the left had committed the party in 1983.[28] The contrast between the programme on which Labour fought the 1983 election and the

1997 election was stark indeed. These were two such divergent views of what the party should stand for and what its programme should be for government that they were not reconcilable within the same party.[29] The tension that had always existed between the three strands of labour – socialist, social democratic and labourist – had finally exploded. The Mark VI Labour Party which new Labour represented was different from its predecessors mainly because many of the internal fault lines appeared to have disappeared. There was no longer a strong socialist wing in the party. Tony Benn recognized as much when he declared that the Labour Party had been taken over by another party, and that it was now indistinguishable in its policies from the Conservative Party.[30]

One of the problems in assessing Labour's history and its role in British politics is ascertaining whether the reason Labour was relatively so unsuccessful in forming governments and holding on to government before 1997 was because the party was a social democratic party and therefore a threat to the dominant capitalist order which brought attempts to destabilize it or because it was so divided that it always lacked credibility as a governing party. One of Labour's severest handicaps in the twentieth century was that it found it hard to develop a reputation for economic competence, and instead received the blame whenever the pound had to be devalued (1931, 1949, 1967, 1976). Sterling crises became synonymous with Labour governments and it was this inability to manage the economy successfully that weakened Labour's electoral appeal and was ruthlessly exploited by its political opponents.

Old Labour was however unlucky in its timing and new Labour was excessively fortunate. Consider what would have happened, for example, if Labour had not lost office in 1951, either because it won the election (it did come out with two hundred thousand more votes than the Conservatives) or because it chose not to call the election (it still had an overall majority of eight at the time the election was called). In either case the Labour government might have survived until the much more benign economic conditions of the mid-1950s, when the long boom in the global economy was beginning to take effect, and which helped the Conservatives stay in government for thirteen years. Ever after, the strategic error of losing office at that particular moment was much lamented in the party.[31] A long spell of post-war Labour government would have had profound effects on the structure of power in the Labour Party, as well as on the structure of power in the British state. As it was the Conservatives were able to resume their role within the British state with only a brief interruption, while Labour was consigned once again to opposition, and to its familiar routine of moral clarity but political sterility. It found it difficult to escape the ethos of opposition, and indeed even under new Labour which enforced a new unity on the party and made it a potent governing instrument, the culture of the party and of the wider Labour movement remained much more comfortable with opposition than with government. For the Conservatives, until recent times, it used to be the exact opposite.

Two other accidents are worth noting. The first is to reflect on what might have transpired had James Callaghan done what everyone expected him to do and called a general election in October 1978, before the Winter of Discontent. The Labour government had been through a torrid period since the IMF crisis of 1976, losing a succession of seats at by-elections, only rescued from a forced election in 1977 by the conclusion of the Lib–Lab pact. Yet by the summer of 1978 the government's fortunes had begun to improve; the pay policy had brought some stability, and the economy and sterling were both recovering sharply, the latter in anticipation of North Sea Oil coming on stream. In September 1978 the opinion polls showed Labour four points ahead of the Conservatives. If Callaghan had held the election then, he would almost certainly have improved Labour's overall position, or at least been in a position to continue governing through an understanding with the Liberals. An outright Conservative election victory was most unlikely. The consequences would have been considerable. Labour would have benefited from the North Sea Oil bonanza rather than the Conservatives; there would have been no SDP breakaway; no Thatcher Government; and Labour not the Conservatives would have presided over the adjustment of the British economy and British society to a more interdependent global economy. A very different process would have unfolded; a period of Labour dominance, rather than the eighteen years of Conservative rule which in fact resulted. But if there had been no Thatcherite revolution, the departure from the post-war compromise might have been much more gradual, and would have taken a different path.

Labour paid heavily for these mistakes, which delayed a period of sustained Labour hegemony in British politics until 1997. But new Labour's victory owed a considerable amount to another accident which this time worked in Labour's favour. In 1992 the election was close and Labour was widely expected to win or at least do well enough to create a hung parliament, with no party having an overall majority. In the event John Major scored a decisive victory, eight percentage points ahead of Labour, even though this margin only delivered a majority of 29 seats. Had Labour won it would have been confronted, within a few months of taking office, with the sterling crisis which forced the UK out of the Exchange Rate Mechanism.[32] Black Wednesday destroyed the Conservatives' record for economic competence in a way which rebounded hugely to Labour's advantage. For ten years after 1992, Labour maintained a strong lead over the Conservatives as the party most trusted to run the economy. A Labour government forced to leave the ERM in the manner that the Conservatives were, would have been blamed (however unfairly) for the debacle, and like all its predecessors might never have recovered and would now be remembered as another single-term Labour government. Instead, the Conservatives, following Black Wednesday and their deep internal divisions over the European Union, suffered a meltdown in their support which by 2001 had still not recovered, and handed both political initiative and political hegemony to new Labour.

Class and Progress

Labour has been interpreted in many ways through its chequered history, but two narratives have been particularly dominant, class and progress, associated with the socialist and social democratic wings of the party. Narratives of Labour as a class party emphasize the permanent conflict between labour and capital. Labour is a class party because it represents labour while the Conservatives represent capital. Class is regarded as the key opposition in politics which shapes everything else, because it arises from the social relationship which determines who has economic and political power, the relationship between those who own property and those who do not.

Most narratives of Labour as a class party have, unsurprisingly, been highly critical of Labour's political achievements. The explanation lies in the ambiguity which was present from the beginning in the way in which the Labour Party was organized. Established to promote the labour interest in Parliament, (the trade unions joined with the socialist societies, the Fabians, the Social Democratic Federation, and the Independent Labour Party, to create a new party), the emphasis from the start was on interest rather than on doctrine. The socialist societies believed that once a party had been created they could provide its intellectual leadership and its policy direction, transforming it from a Labour to a socialist party, like European socialist parties. This hope has sustained the involvement of generations of socialists in the Labour Party, and has been regularly dashed, giving rise to the classic account of the repeated attempts and repeated failure to make the Labour party a vehicle for socialism, Ralph Miliband's *Parliamentary Socialism* which first appeared in 1962, after the containment of Bevanism and the defeat of unilateralism at the Party Conference in 1962.[33]

For Miliband, there was an irreconcilable conflict between the organization of the Labour Party as a parliamentary party which discouraged all extra-parliamentary activity and tried to behave as a legitimate constitutional party, and its socialist objectives. He showed how, whenever this conflict became too sharp, the party would sacrifice its socialist objectives in order to preserve its constitutional legality. As a result the party was generally defensive and always prepared to retreat, never challenging capitalist power. Capital for its part was not so constrained, and was always ready to use non-constitutional and illegal means to secure its interests. The weakness of Labour's leaders in the face of the established order meant that it often became an instrument for disciplining and controlling its supporters in the interest of capital.[34]

Some critics of Miliband argued that all that he was claiming was that the Labour Party was not led by socialists, or that it was insufficiently socialist, whereas the whole point about the Labour Party was that it had not been set up as a socialist party. It was therefore unreasonable to berate the party for being something which it had never set out to be. Miliband's argument however can be interpreted in another way. What he drew attention to was the fundamental ambiguity of purpose which was enshrined in the Labour Party from the outset, which created the Labour Party as a political space which drew a myriad of groups and interests, all seeking to remake the party in their own image. Socialism was part of Labour from the start, and was codified (however ambiguously) in the 1918 Constitution, but the alliance that came to be formed by a right-wing parliamentary leadership and conservative trade-union leaders limited the party's internal democracy, and meant that the party was a class party in a Labourist rather than a socialist sense.

The stress on Labourism became an important strand in the class narrative. The root of the difficulty in transforming Labour into a socialist party was seen to lie partly in the absence of an agreed framework of ideology and doctrine, and partly in the relative weakness of Marxism on the British left and in British intellectual culture, so that the ideas and doctrines which had gained influence were those of Fabians and new Liberals, which did not disturb too much the defensive and cautious instincts of Labour's leaders.[35] Labourism both as doctrine and as practice was seen as extremely conservative, its horizons bounded by the need to defend existing rights and privileges of workers. It was a class perspective, but one limited to wages and hours, and rarely capable of embracing a broader vision of reconstructing social and economic relations. What gave it such prominence in the United Kingdom was the sheer size of the working class, and the extent of its unionization, bolstered by the existence of distinct working-class communities and a strong working-class culture.[36] Labourism expressed a powerful corporate interest, one which had to be accommodated, but one which was also subordinate, and mostly resigned to being subordinate, to other centres of power in the United Kingdom.

A third variant of the class narrative has concentrated on the constraints within which Labour and other centre-left parties have operated. Some of this analysis has pointed out the strength of the forces arrayed against Labour, the ubiquity of capitalist influence through civil society and the media, as well as in the organization of the state. Labour is depicted as lacking the capacities, even if had the strategy, to present an effective challenge to the dominant system of power. The frequency with which Labour governments were rocked by financial crises demonstrated the power of the capital markets, and through them the general interest of capital, to rein in left-of-centre governments planning to spend or interfere too much.[37]

One of the enduring puzzles of Labour as a class party is why the party should not have been more successful at least in electoral terms, given its demographic advantages in Britain. In the 1950s, 70 per cent of the British electorate was classified as working class.[38] Many factors have been adduced to explain why Labour has not done better. Adam Przeworksi has argued that social democratic parties have always faced a conflict between adherence to their ultimate goal, the achievement of socialism, and winning electoral support. Only by diluting their socialist aims and transforming themselves into catch-all parties of the centre could social democratic parties attract those sections of the electorate who were not part of their core working-class support. At the same time, by seeking to attract and hold this wider electorate necessary to win electoral majorities, social democratic parties also inevitably failed to meet the expectation of their core supporters. The cycle of raised expectations, increased mobilization, and electoral victory, was inevitably followed by compromise, retreat, disappointment, disillusion and electoral defeat.[39]

Other narratives founded on a class view of politics are less fatalistic, arguing that the task for democratic socialist parties may be difficult but is not impossible, and that Labour in particular has always done best when it has been committed to the formation of a broad, inclusive progressive coalition.[40] Concentration on manual workers, or workers in heavy industry, or workers in trade unions would never on its own deliver Labour electoral victory. There were always more workers outside trade unions than in, and the fluctuating rhythms of capitalist development meant that the pattern of occupations was constantly changing. Labour had steadily advanced since 1918, increasing its share of the vote at every general election until 1955. Although it lost office in 1951, that election still represented its high water mark, and one it has yet to surpass. Labour's constant dilemma was how to maintain its core vote which gave it both identity and purpose, while attracting the additional votes it needed to form governments. A large part of the working class remained anti-Labour in its politics, sufficient to give the Conservatives half their support, and Labour was hampered in reaching out beyond its core vote, because so long as it was Labourist in its organization and ethos, it often appeared to be identified with particular sectional interests rather than the wider public interest.[41]

The alternative narrative of Labour sees the party as a party of progress, representing progressive opinion against the diehard opinions of the party of order, the Conservatives, rather than as a class party representing labour against capital. What progressive opinion consists in is quite fluid, and many progressive values are not distinct from class values: all subscribe to liberty, equality, and solidarity in one form or another. The differences are mainly about means and about the importance to be assigned to class, and a class understanding of power and the possibilities of political action in a capitalist society. The more pessimistic class narratives tend to be fatalistic in their estimation of the chances of challenging the rule of capital, because they regard the hegemony of capital as so far-reaching and invasive. The state and all potential instruments of the public interest have been seized and corrupted by capital and cannot be used by the labour movement.[42]

Narratives of progress are more optimistic about the chances of political action to make worthwhile reforms. Within the Labour Party different interests and ideas struggle for supremacy but progressives believe the party has the potential to become a vehicle for embodying progressive values and realizing a progressive agenda. It can become a party of reform, seeking to make society more equal, more free, more inclusive, more communitarian – to reduce human suffering and human misery, and to release human potential. The achievement of social rights in the welfare state was seen as the culmination of a long struggle to win full citizenship rights, and many believed that it would be irreversible, because democracies would not vote to bring back privilege and hierarchy once it had been abolished.[43] Similarly the remorseless growth of collective control of the economy and of society was also often treated as an example of progress, the victory of society over the individual and the rationality of planning over the irrationality of the market. Many progressives believed that steady incremental change would eventually deliver a fully collectivized society.[44]

Against such historicism, there were also radical notions of progress, which drew from the radical dissenting tradition, derived in England and Scotland from the militant Protestantism and the radical movements it spawned in the seventeenth century. Radical notions of progress have been important in the Labour Party through the New Left of the 1950s and the 1960s,[45] and the influence of pacifism, first in the 1930s and then again in the Campaign for Nuclear Disarmament and Peace Movement from the 1950s through to the 1980s, and more recently in the anti-globalization and stop-the-war movements.[46] Another strong strand has been environmentalism as well as many forms of direct community action and community involvement. The Labour Party has often been as great a disappointment to radical opinion as to socialist opinion, but this has not prevented the Labour Party periodically being the focus of its hopes and expectations.

David Marquand has analysed the perennial progressive dilemma as the question of whether progressives should commit themselves to work for the Labour Party.[47] The same has been true for socialists. The Labour Party being what it is, a party of Labour rather than a party committed either to a socialist doctrine or a radical doctrine, it will always appear a very imperfect instrument for the realization of socialist or radical purposes. This explains why so many narratives of the party are about betrayal and disillusion, and contain much agonizing about whether or not engagement with the Labour Party should continue or be broken off. It is not just the Militant Tendency in the 1980s who were entryists. Socialists and social democrats, reds and greens, pacifists and collectivists have all been entryists in the Labour Party, seeking to make the party their party, and generally being disappointed at the failure of the party to become what they want, and at its failure to become more successful and dominant in British politics.

Union and Empire

In the course of the various struggles to make it a party of class, a party of progress, or just a party of labour, the Labour Party has been shaped by and helped to shape the key historical relationships of British politics, the four circles which have defined its patterns of identity and political economy.

Labour was from the outset a Unionist party, a party of Britain not England, but it was divided over the question of devolution, and the political recognition of the separate identities of Scotland and Wales. As an anti-Establishment party, Labour, like the Liberals before it, strongly identified with the periphery against the centre. Wales and Scotland were to become Labour strongholds, and in certain periods, such as the 1980s, they contributed a disproportionate part of Labour's parliamentary representation. But whereas the Liberals, the original architects of Home Rule for Ireland, had no difficulty in supporting devolution for the whole United Kingdom and were attracted by ideas of a written constitution and a federal state,[48] Labour was split over the question of whether power should be centralized or devolved. The early anti-state tradition in Labour pointed to as much devolution as possible to give people in their localities power and responsibility, so that they could protect themselves from a central state whose policies were global and imperial and often at odds with the interests of particular regions and localities.

Against that, the collectivist tradition in Labour associated with the Webbs was highly centralist, believing that universal public services and effective planning had to be delivered centrally and uniformly. Otherwise there would be huge anomalies because some citizens were receiving services which others were not, and even where this was not so, there would be serious problems of coordination. Particularly in its democratic socialist phase after 1931, Labour became committed to an ideal of a national welfare state administered by a strong central state. Welfare and the Empire became the two main integrative devices for the British nation. With renewed pressure for devolution in the 1960s and 1970s Labour was very divided on the issue. Eventually the party did back devolution for Scotland and attempted to legislate in the 1970s, but it lacked a sufficient majority to get the measure through against the opposition of the Conservatives and a significant minority of its own backbenchers who were able to impose a series of wrecking amendments which ultimately led to the defeat of devolution.[49]

Ireland was always different. Labour sentiment was pro-Irish and anti-Unionist. From the start Labour opinion supported the Irish right to self-determination and the principle of a united Ireland. After partition the Unionist party in Northern Ireland became formally linked to the Conservative Party, allowed to operate its own devolved system until it had to be forcibly suspended in 1972. Northern Ireland was as a result never part of the working-class Britain which Labour regarded as its heartland. It was regarded by Labour as an illegitimate statelet set up to appease the Ulster Unionists.

Labour did not emerge as a major party in British politics until the Irish issue was virtually settled and independence and partition had been agreed. For the centre left in British politics this separation was a huge political setback. Had Ireland remained within the United Kingdom after universal suffrage was finally achieved in 1918 and 1928, the bulk of the Irish vote would have been an anti-Conservative vote, voting against parties identified with the Establishment and the centre. Whether the Irish MPs had become part of Labour's coalition, or formed an alliance with it, similar to the alliance between the 80 Irish Nationalists and the Liberals in the Parliaments before 1914, the party balance in the British Parliament would have been very different through the twentieth century. The Conservatives would have had a much harder task in maintaining their dominance, and left-of-centre governments would have been more likely.

In government, Labour's attitude to Northern Ireland has been pragmatic. It was a Labour government which committed troops in 1969 as communal violence escalated. It was Labour which imposed the Prevention of Terrorism Act in the wake of the Guildford and Birmingham bombings, and it was the Callaghan Government which pursued a tough security policy. But in opposition, Labour soon moved to oppose the annual renewal of the Prevention of Terrorism Act, and the pro-Irish sentiment in the party began to make itself felt. Many on the Labour left openly supported a United Ireland and the troops-out campaign, and called for negotiations with Sinn Fein. By the time Labour returned to government in 1997 the peace process had begun, and Labour was able to throw its weight behind solutions which involved full recognition of the Irish dimension of the problem, and the full involvement of the Republic of Ireland as a partner in negotiations, as well as the United States.[50] Labour reacted in the way it did to Ireland because so many in the party saw it as a colonial issue, and never felt that Northern Ireland was truly part of the United Kingdom. 'West Britain' had never been part of the United Kingdom for the majority of the people who lived there in the way that North Britain had been.

On the Empire more generally Labour's instincts were mostly hostile. It inherited from the Liberals the radical anti-colonial tradition of the party, to which were added new socialist arguments about the exploitation of the colonies by monopoly capital seeking cheap labour, cheap resources, and outlets for surplus capital. The Empire was overwhelmingly identified with the Conservatives and with the established order.[51] As a result Labour came to define itself against the British Empire and for socialism. Empire became one of the great dividing lines in British politics through the twentieth century. Although there were some in the Labour Party who advocated that the United Kingdom should be a trustee for the colonies and administer them on Fabian principles, the stronger instinct of the party was to support colonial freedom and anti-colonial movements. In all the great flashpoints of the British imperial withdrawal – India, Suez, Kenya, Cyprus, Aden, and Rhodesia – the Labour leadership may sometimes have equivocated, but there was never much doubt about attitudes in the party. Extra-parliamentary campaigns like the Anti-Apartheid movement were crucial in reinforcing these anti-imperial and anti-colonial sentiments. Labour governments sometimes adopted policies which reflected the priorities of particular sections of the British state, rather than party priorities. But even here the dominant drift of policy was to facilitate the winding down of the Empire and of imperial commitments. The decision to withdraw from military bases east of Suez became a major plank of Labour's defence review in the 1960s, and symbolized Labour's determination to leave the Empire behind.[52]

The problem for Labour in its attitudes towards Empire was that it was easy for its opponents to portray the party as anti-patriotic, so central had the Empire become to British identity. A constant stream of Conservative propaganda attacked Labour (and before them the Liberals) for their little Englandism and pacificism, their willingness to sacrifice British interests and endanger British lives.[53] Since the maintenance of the Empire required constant engagement of British troops, and there were so many kinship links of British families with those who had settled in the colonies, Labour's anti-imperial attitudes often aroused extreme hostility, not least from the Conservative papers like the *Daily Mail* and *Daily Express*.

The party attempted to counter this by emphasizing its support for transforming the British Empire into the British Commonwealth, changing the relationship between the United Kingdom and the territories that had been incorporated into the Empire. Labour became the strongest defender of the Commonwealth, even as Conservative support for it dwindled as it became more independent of the UK. The Attlee Government legislated for Indian Independence in 1947 and the Wilson Government imposed sanctions on Rhodesia. The ethical dimension to foreign policy which Labour promised in 1997 was not a departure from Labour tradition but deeply rooted in the party's anti-imperial and anti-colonial past. What it meant practically was that the party was much more disposed than the Conservatives to countenance liberal interventionism, whether increasing foreign aid or intervening to assist a legitimate government as in Sierra Leone in 1999, a former British colony, where no immediate British interest was at stake.[54] The party in government always, however, had a big problem over arms sales, particularly to regimes such as apartheid South Africa. Labour governments found it very difficult to resist the logic of such arms sales, which were so tied in to the structure of imperial defence and the arms industry which had arisen to service it, and on which so many jobs had come to depend.

Labour also had to face the challenge of immigration.[55] It was the Empire coming home, and it set up numerous conflicts and strains, not least in large sections of Labour's core white working-class support. Sections of the Conservative Party played the race card from the beginning, and many Labour MPs were uneasy, but Labour acquired a reputation of being more well-disposed to the rights and welfare of immigrants than the Conservatives, and this was reflected in the overwhelming electoral support which the immigrant communities gave to Labour.[56] The issues of multi-culturalism and anti-racism helped transform Labour in the 1980s and 1990s, significantly diluting the old Labourist image of the party as the preserve of the white, male unionized working class, and obliging the party to come to terms with very different conceptions of British identity and Britishness. The asylum issue, however, which erupted in the second half of the 1990s, as well as persistent racial conflict and attacks in particular cities, were seized on by particular sections of the media, and showed the potency of old notions of Empire in defining British identity in ways that were still fundamentally racist;[57] and put Labour continually on the defensive.

Anglo-America and Europe

As the Empire has receded and the Union has weakened, so the choice between Europe and America has become starker. In relation to Anglo-America, the Labour Party has always been ambivalent. At one level Labour is part of the internal ideological debate within Anglo-America which has raged since the seventeenth century.[58] In this debate Labour is part of the radical tradition, the tradition of the Levellers, the Diggers, Tom Paine and Thomas Jefferson, the tradition of radical dissenting Protestantism. This tradition was from the start against monarchy, against aristocracy and hereditary right, and for representation, freedom, and equality. The British Crown and British Establishment whom the American colonists defied were also the enemies of the radicals and democrats in England. When the British Establishment made clear its preferences for the Confederacy in the Civil War, the British Labour movement and radical opinion in England sided with the North regarding it as a just war to rid the United States of slavery. For many British democrats the American republic was a model, a country of liberty, free of the corruptions and oppressions of monarchy and aristocracy. In some respects it was regarded as a model society, a true new world, and this was one of the reasons why it remained so attractive to immigrants from Europe. It was a reservoir of social experimentation and social freedom, in which new forms of society and community could be tried out.

This attitude towards the new world republic did not survive. A number of developments, among them the rise of monopoly capitalism in America, the expropriation and destruction of native Americans, and above all the emergence of America as a global power, changed attitudes towards the United States and the nature of the arguments within Anglo-America. The labour movement and the radical liberals had sympathized most closely with the Republicans because they were Lincoln's party, while the Democrats were the party of the old South built on racial oppression and denial of civil rights to blacks. Following the reconstruction of the Democratic party in the 1930s under Franklin Roosevelt and the broadening of its coalition to take in organized labour and many of America's new ethnic minorities, it became the natural ally for Labour. The New Deal of the 1930s, the Great Society of the 1960s and the Third Way of the 1990s were all profoundly influential on British Labour in its own domestic policies. While there were important differences between the US Democrats and British Labour, there were some important similarities, and a regular exchange of ideas between the intellectuals and politicians on both sides. Both parties in practice were in favour of capitalism and markets, but both also believed in the role of active government in redressing the problems of capitalist market economies. Keynes became a key bridging figure between the two traditions, and the battle over Keynesianism both for and against was largely an internal dispute within Anglo-America.[59]

The other aspect of the narrative of Anglo-America which was so important through the twentieth century was the question of global hegemony, and the transfer of hegemony between England and America. Many British Conservatives were opposed to the ascendancy of the United States because they knew it must lead to the eclipse of the British Empire. Many in the Labour Party were opposed because their sympathies were with the new workers' state of the Soviet Union, and they distrusted the United States as the leading capitalist power. It fell to the Labour government elected in 1945 to shape British policy in the post-war world. Under Ernest Bevin at the Foreign Office it chose decisively to seek to continue the wartime alliance with the United States, and to persuade the United States government not to disengage but to assume the global responsibilities which its power and status warranted.[60]

Bevin's foreign policy was from the start designed to contain the threat of communism and keep the United States involved in Europe. Early optimism that left would speak to left soon faded. Despite the strong criticism many in the Labour Party had made of Churchill's intervention in the Greek civil war in support of the Greek monarchy, Bevin was equally resolute, and manoeuvred until he had persuaded the Americans to give security guarantees to both Greece and Turkey. Bevin was a crucial influence too in the negotiations which led to the setting up of NATO and the launch of the Marshall Plan. The Attlee Government is remembered for its domestic reforms, but at least as important for the future of British politics was the consolidation of the Atlantic Alliance as the linchpin of the United

Kingdom's post-war foreign and defence policy.[61] This remained the settled policy of all Labour governments, although it was frequently challenged, most notably over the nuclear strategy of the Alliance, and over particular wars in which the United States became involved, most notably Vietnam, and more generally the counter-revolutionary strategy against national liberation movements in the Third World which the United States waged relentlessly.

The pattern of America's global hegemony as it unfolded sharply divided opinion in the Labour Party, but the Labour leadership remained steadfast in their support of the United States, and the global institutions which were set up to manage the new world order. On some occasions of sharp internal disagreement, as over Indian independence and the Suez invasion, the Labour leadership was divided from the Conservatives, but in tune with the United States. Close personal ties between Labour leaders and their American counterparts became the norm, although there were always exceptions, such as the relationship between Lyndon Johnson and Harold Wilson. The Labour government gave public support to the United States war in Vietnam, but refused to send any British troops, a rare example where a Labour government did not accede to an American request.[62]

When it came to Europe, the Labour tradition was ambivalent. Communism and Fascism, the two world wars, the Spanish Civil War, European social democracy, the student movements of 1968, and the long slow process of post-war European integration have all had a powerful influence on Labour. But British political parties tend to be insular, and Labour has been so too. There is a strong anti-European, chauvinist streak in Labour, a belief in British superiority, a preference for Anglo-America or the Commonwealth, and a dislike for European regimes, a desire to stay clear of them and keep the UK from being entangled with them.

British labour and its traditions have always been distinct from those elsewhere in Europe – the size of the British working class and its weight in the British social structure and the British electorate has no close parallel in the other major European states. The degree of union organization was also exceptional in the UK, and so too was the adversarial nature of the employer/employee relationship and the reliance placed in the UK on free collective bargaining rather than legal frameworks for industrial relations conferring legally enforceable rights and obligations.[63] The trade unions were treated as a corporate interest outside the state, whose needs were accommodated by granting them legal privileges, exemptions from the ordinary operation of the law, so that they could not be sued for the damages they inflicted on employers by taking strike action. This special status made the Labour movement a power and presence in British politics through the twentieth century which no other European labour movement could rival. It was the foundation for the success of the Labour party, but it was also a deeply conservative force which inhibited thinking and strategic policy-making on both right and left, because the interests of organized labour as a corporate interest were paramount.

The reform of industrial relations in the 1980s and 1990s as a direct result of the defeats suffered in the Thatcher years had the effect of liberating trade unions and also liberating the Labour Party from some of its insularity, and enabled both to become more open to European influence and European models.[64] The adoption of a legal framework for trade unions and the modification of the links between the unions and the party, and the introduction of 'one member, one vote' were signs of this.

It still took the party a long time to overcome its instinctive suspicion of European integration and the European project. This stemmed from many sources. As a result of two world wars, there was a deep vein of hostility towards Germany in British Labour, which surfaced in the strong opposition in the party led by Nye Bevan to German rearmament in the 1950s. Similarly there was a more moderate but still highly sceptical view of the ability of the European nations actually to work well together, which made any kind of federal solution wholly impractical.[65] Belief in the uniqueness of British socialism remained strong, and in the ability to build socialism within the bounded territory of the British Isles. Other nations might do as they do.

Labour and the English Model

At the heart of Labour's sense of itself as a political party has been a conception of capitalism. The assumption of a conflict of interest between labour and capital was indeed the very origin of the notion of a *labour* party, a party serving a distinct interest, the labour interest. But there were always many different ways of analysing capitalism and drawing out the implications for policy. Central to the early debates in the party were attitudes to public ownership, and whether the party aimed at complete nationalization of all productive assets, or whether its purposes were more limited and pragmatic. In the 1930s, Labour became committed to a major programme of public ownership focused on the main utilities and this programme was carried through by the Attlee Government after 1945. Many of the nationalizations, especially coal and railways (both of which were unprofitable anyway) received only token opposition from the Conservatives; there was much fiercer opposition over iron and steel, and still more when proposals were tabled in 1950 for extending public owner-ship into profitable manufacturing industries – sugar, cement and chemi-cals. At this stage many in the Labour Party still envisaged the gradual extension of public ownership until all the main sectors of the economy were brought under public control. Memories of the slump and the poor performance of capitalism in the 1930s encouraged the belief that only a fully planned economy would guarantee full employment, investment and economic growth.[66]

The sea change in Labour attitudes began in the 1950s when the rapid and sustained recovery of global capitalism removed one of the strongest arguments for national planning, that capitalism could no longer deliver economic growth and high employment. The revisionists argued that socialists' main goal was to achieve equality and that public ownership was only one means to achieve that, and no longer the most relevant one. They looked to policies on welfare spending and taxation to create a more equal society. This difference was fundamental. As Nye Bevan expressed it, the difference was between those 'who want the mainsprings of economic power transferred to the community, and those who believe that private enterprise should still remain supreme but that its worst characteristics should be modified by liberal ideas of justice and equality'.[67] Elsewhere Bevan wrote that socialism had to mean the supplanting of private owner-ship by public ownership. But it became clear that very few in the party were prepared to support a rolling programme of incremental public owner-ship which such a principle required. In government even between 1945 and 1951 the party had to accept that private enterprise was indeed supreme, and that whatever goals the party wished to accomplish had to be achieved with the cooperation of private capital. That fundamental constraint on Labour governments was never challenged, and since there was no will to challenge it, sooner or later it became logical that the doctrines of the party be brought into line with its revisionist practice.

The problem throughout the Labour Party's history has been reconciling the necessity of managing capitalism when it is in government with a radi-cal rhetoric which looks forward to the replacement of capitalism by an alternative economic system. This has often prevented clear thinking about what it is Labour governments wish to achieve and the best means at hand for achieving them. In particular it has led on right and left of the party to an identification of capitalism with the market, so that any measures taken to suppress markets tended to be regarded as socialist and in the public interest. But this simple opposition between state and market was quite inadequate for understanding the complexities of a modern capitalist econ-omy and the possibilities for active intervention by governments, some of which had to involve markets. Instead the dominant Labour conception of capitalism proceeded to demonize markets by opposing them to the state and treating the state and the public sector as inherently good and the private sector as inherently bad. This way of posing the issue was a huge impediment to the effectiveness of the party in achieving its objectives in government since it was not able in practice to dispense with markets. This problem was as great for new Labour as for previous Labour governments, but it was not new.[68]

The emphasis on the labour interest meant that Labour identified itself above all as the party of manual labour, and in particular manual workers in manufacturing. The Labour interest became the preservation and extension of the public sector, the protection of manufacturing, and more generally the defence of workers' pay and conditions throughout the economy. Pay became a key problem for Labour governments, and led to frequent clashes, because of the desire of governments to impose effective controls on pay and to reduce the number of strikes. Until the 1980s however all serious reforms of the trade unions failed, and all pay policies eventually collapsed, partly because the way the unions were organized meant that whenever the leaders signed up to deals with government, they could not always command their members, or at least, only for short periods. This ungovernability of labour became a critical issue for the Labour Party in the 1960s and 1970s,[69] and was in marked contrast with the more successful corporatist regimes in many other European countries. It stemmed from the voluntarist and adversarial tradition in the Labour movement, which at root was anti-state, and embraced an ethos of permanent opposition to the established power of capital, in industry and in the state. Once Labour began to form governments this created serious conflicts, because the unions, despite the loyalty of many of their leaders to Labour governments and despite their desire to see them succeed, were ultimately unable to restrain their members. The logic of adversarialism was too strong. As a corporate interest the unions made impressive gains in the twentieth century, but their power was largely defensive, and the weakness of their position was that they could not agree either on supporting a socialist programme to replace capitalism (since that would have meant the subordination of the unions to central planning bodies) or to negotiate an effective system of corporate representation, giving up some of their privileges in exchange for influence.

In its attitudes towards the Constitution and to the Westminster model, Labour was from the start pitched against the traditional Establishment of Crown, Aristocracy, High Church, the Law, the Military, and Oxbridge. It was a movement from below, with few connections immediately to the elites and centres which governed England. The one institution of the state which it accepted was Parliament, because as the franchise widened this offered a means to obtain representation for the labour interest. Parliament and as a result the doctrine of parliamentary sovereignty, has played an enormous role in Labour's thinking. The existence of Parliament is the guarantee that the British state is a state of liberty, which can enact meaningful problems, can redress grievances, accommodate new interests, and recognize the justice of claims.

Central to Labour attitudes to Parliament, therefore, has been the extension of democracy, starting with the franchise itself. The struggle for the vote for all citizens, men and women, the lowering of the age of the vote, and ensuring that all votes were equal, became a great radical cause in the nineteenth and early twentieth centuries. It was one of the main meeting points of radical liberalism and socialism. If Parliament was to achieve its promise, and become truly responsive to the citizen body, then it had to be made fully representative. The struggle for basic political rights for all citizens became a key part of Labour's creed.

The achievement of mass democracy raised further questions, however, particularly concerning the form that representation should take. Initially simple considerations of fairness, as well as advantage as a third party, pushed Labour to advocate forms of proportional representation. The reformers however were not successful. There have been a few moments this century when change seemed possible, as in 1930 when a bill to introduce the Alternative Vote did pass the House of Commons with Labour and Liberal support, but it was rejected by the House of Lords and the government fell before it could be reintroduced. The more Labour became entrenched as the main party of opposition in the two-party system, the more its enthusiasm for changing the electoral system waned, and it discovered all kinds of special virtues in the first-past-the-post system, despite the growing evidence of the glaring mismatch between votes cast and seats won.

Apart from the granting of basic political rights, Labour governments proved more cautious than Liberal governments in tackling constitutional change. The Attlee Government further restricted the powers of the House of Lords, but the Wilson Government reform foundered, and it was not until the Blair Government that House of Lords Reform was eventually pushed through, and even then in a form which disappointed most reformers.[70] Similarly it was not until new Labour that devolution measures were enacted; before that, opposition within Labour's ranks had been too great. Critics of new Labour noted how unenthusiastic the government appeared about its own reforms, and how committed it remained to centralized government. Nevertheless the Blair Government was the first time a Labour government had returned to the unfinished pre-1914 Liberal agenda and had introduced changes, including the incorporation of the European Convention of Human Rights into British law, and the devolution legislation which in practice looked irreversible and had the force of entrenched constitutional provisions.[71]

The divisions over public and private ownership were not replicated in the field of welfare. This was because the consolidation of the welfare state became Labour's key objective in the twentieth century. The National Health Service was its proudest achievement, and the essence of Labour's conception of the public realm. The public realm became identified with the public sector, and the provision of universal public services free at the point of use became Labour's central purpose, particularly after nationalized industries were discredited. Education, social security, and health became the key part of Labour's message, and in electoral terms the party was strongly identified with these services and was perceived by voters as the party best able to defend and sustain them. Until the advent of new Labour this was in marked contrast to Labour's scores for other policies, particularly competence at managing the economy.

The principle of universalism and 'no charges' were regarded by many in the party as the touchstone of Labour's commitment to social justice. Nye Bevan, the architect of the NHS, resigned from the government in 1951 along with Richard Crossman and Harold Wilson when Hugh Gaitskell as Chancellor of the Exchequer imposed prescription charges. In opposition before the 1964 election, Labour was committed to abolishing all prescription charges. It carried out its promise only to reimpose them at the height of the economic crisis a few years later. This highlighted a perennial dilemma. The expectations of what the public services should provide and at what standard, always outpaced government resources. Prescription charges were a symbol for a much larger problem of public finance. By continually raising expectations of what public services government would fund, Labour could only deliver its promises by raising taxation. The balance between the level of taxes and the level of services became highly sensitive politically, because the electorate wanted both better public services and lower taxes, and the parties competed to deliver both. Any government becomes electorally vulnerable if it delivers worse public services and higher taxes, which Labour managed in the 1970s, and the Conservatives in the 1990s.

Labour made the achievement of universal public services the test of its claims to create a good society, but often failed to distinguish between the public service and the public sector. This had a rationale, since the public sector was highly unionized, and the public sector unions were extremely important inside the Labour Party, and became more so after the Thatcher years. But the question of whether there should be public services, and the question of how they could be best delivered were separate questions, although often confused in Labour Party debates.[72] For many in the Labour Party, the public sector was an island of purity and altruism in a sea of private interest and greed. It was the last guarantee that somehow despite all the evidence to the contrary Labour was still an anti-capitalist party.

10

The Future of British Politics

> Until recently, English historiography resembled the work of a
> landscape gardener at a stately home; vistas of Saxon lawn and
> Norman shrubbery led up past Tudor and Hanoverian
> flowerbeds to the terrace of the present, where the proprietor
> sat contentedly surveying his estate. Other countries are rest-
> less, grubbing up old interpretations in each generation.
>
> Neal Ascherson, 2002[1]

In the last twenty-five years the choice between Europe and America has
come to dominate the future of British politics. It has done so at a time
when many long-established features of the British political landscape have
been uprooted or refashioned. Many more are in process of renovation and
modernization, and the changes are far from complete. The British have
been busy grubbing up old interpretations of their past, and a new landscape is coming into view, but its shape owes more to accident than to rational design or political intention. In the recent past there have been projects
of both right and left to change British politics, and charismatic leaders,
Thatcher and Blair, but the outcomes have often been very different to the
ones their authors intended. Politics often proceeds through muddle, confusion, and accident, and recent British politics has been no exception. Yet
even if politicians rarely achieve what they hope, they can on occasion be
the unwitting agents of far-reaching change.

Since the referendum in 1975 which confirmed Britain's membership of
the emerging European Union, Empire has steadily receded as the main
frame of reference for British politics, and the debates on socialism and
decline, which dominated so much of the twentieth century in different
forms have run their course. Other questions have become more important
for the future of British politics. Overshadowing all of them are the changing roles which Europe and America have come to play in British politics,

and the ways in which Britain is now perceived as between Europe and America strategically, economically, politically, culturally, and ideologically. Europe and America have come to represent different models of social, economic and political organization. This question of Europe and America and whether Britain should choose between them, or whether there is any need for a choice, is not a new issue, but it is posed anew at this juncture of English and British history, because Europe and America loom much larger in the British political imagination. With Empire gone, the future of Britain as an independent nation now depends on the multilateral relationships it forges with the rest of the world, and to which of those it chooses to give priority. Europe and America in this sense offer different futures. The choice is not an exclusive one, because Europe and America are not monolithic, but highly complex and differentiated political spaces. There is not one Europe or one America but several, and the differences between liberal and conservative America, or between social democratic and conservative Europe are wide. Yet although Britain will always be part of both Europe and of Anglo-America, there remains a question of priority between the two which was posed ever more insistently by the circumstances leading up to the second Iraq War in 2003. During England's long career of expansion the circles of Empire and of Union were so decisive in shaping British identity. Now it is the circles of Europe and America which loom larger. How this choice is resolved will determine the future of the Union, the future of the British state, and the future of Britain itself.

After Empire

The decisive break with Empire in British domestic politics was one of the unintended consequences of Thatcherism. The policies of the Thatcher Government after 1979 did mark a watershed, ending the post-war compromise and reordering the British political economy and highlighting the choice between Europe and America, but the price was high, particularly for English Conservatism. The political reaction to Thatcherism generated the support for the constitutional changes which have begun to lay to rest a certain idea of England, which grew up during the long period of expansion, and based on the notions of Crown-in-Parliament, undivided and unlimited sovereignty, ever-expanding empire. English sovereignty in the future is likely to take federal or quasi-federal forms, whether in relation to the Union or to Europe, and England will never be an Empire again. Its identity and its political economy will be determined primarily by its relationship with Europe and with America.

The mould has been broken and cannot be reset. In relation to the Constitution in particular this seems to be true despite the timid and incoherent implementation of many of its own constitutional reforms by the Blair Government. It failed to develop either a consistent story or a consistent approach, and has been perversely reluctant to claim credit for the changes for which it is likely to be most remembered, and has frequently acted to slow down, and occasionally obstruct the pace of reform. After six years much remained undone, particularly the completion of the reform of the House of Lords, the extension of proportional representation to Westminster, substantive freedom of information, and constitutional rules to define the role of the Head of State and the powers of the Prime Minister in relation to Parliament. Yet although the reform programme is unlikely to be completed under the Blair Government, several key breaks with the old constitutional state were made. Of particular symbolic significance has been the legislation establishing a separate Scottish Parliament and a Welsh Assembly, and the first stage of House of Lords reform, removing all but 92 hereditary peers from the Chamber.

Although often devised in the least radical and most cautious manner possible, these reforms have nevertheless established a clear direction of change, and will lead to further changes as anomalies accumulate and pressure builds for the reforms to be extended.[2] Once the principle of the unitary and undivided nature of sovereignty has been abandoned it becomes necessary to explore the alternative of federal and quasi-federal forms of rule, in which political power necessarily becomes more decentralized, and more accountable.

No one supposes that the reforms so far introduced are the last word. The relationships will keep evolving, and further powers are bound to be devolved. Some form of Constitutional Court will be needed to adjudicate on disputes, as well as a new formula for allocating resources between the different parts of the Union. Regional government for England will also be available for any region which chooses it, and the demonstration effect is likely to prove powerful. Within a few years a much more decentralized system of government is likely to have been consolidated.

The real test of the Union will come when different parties are in office in Edinburgh and in London, particularly if it is the Scottish National Party that holds Edinburgh. The conflict that could result could then provide the momentum to full independence as many nationalists expect. But it could also lead to the kind of constitutional concessions that keep Scotland in the Union. A referendum on secession in a democracy is very hard to win. But it might accelerate the emergence of a true federal Union, of the kind Gladstone was seeking at the end of the nineteenth century with his proposal of Home Rule for Ireland. Without the Empire to resist Scottish demands by force as it once resisted Irish, the breakup of Britain is not certain. But it will be a very different Britain.

This process of change matters greatly for Scotland and Wales as they begin to define themselves as separate parts of the Union, rather than as appendages of England, but it matters hugely for England also, because England must contemplate a future after Empire, and a different relationship with the other nations of the Union and with the nations of Europe. All the nations of Britain must also come to terms with the multiethnic and multicultural character which Empire has left them, and also with the role of Britain in Anglo-America.

Empire for England always meant both territorial empire and cosmopolitan empire – the empire of colonies and the empire of trade - which although they overlapped, were also distinct. The cosmopolitan empire signalled the growth of interdependence and the rise of what became a two hundred year liberal hegemony, in which first Britain and then the United States took the leading role. In the era of American supremacy since the end of the Cold War, this Anglo-American hegemony is more dominant than it has ever been, and as events since 9/11 have demonstrated, the alliance on military and security matters between the United States and Britain remains strong. Faced with a choice between Europe and America in security and defence issues, British governments still choose America. The Blair Government like the Thatcher and Major Governments before it has been a close ally of the United States. Blair has increasingly articulated the need for Britain to play a role alongside the United States in promoting a doctrine of liberal interventionism, in defence of human rights and a liberal world order.[3]

The British political class remains wedded to the idea of a special relationship with the United States, but this special relationship is very different from how it was envisaged in the 1940s. At that time the British political class believed in a partnership between Britain and the United States. Although no longer the equal of the United States Britain considered itself an independent great power with a right to act on its own. That aspiration had to be abandoned after the United States compelled Britain to halt its military action with France at Suez in 1956, and the special relationship became a lot less special in the next two decades. It was revived in a new form after 1979 by Thatcher, Major and Blair. As American policy became more unilateralist and less hegemonic in response to the loss of American power, so the value of Britain to the United States once more increased. The role of chief ally in the construction and policing of a new world order was already evident under Thatcher and Major, but reached a new intensity under Blair, following 9/11, and the elaboration of the doctrine of American primacy, pre-emptive strikes, and a unipolar world.

At the same time, the Blair Government's foreign policy has exposed huge contradictions between Europe and America. Britain is part of Europe just as it is part of Anglo-America, and neither is about to disappear. The Blair Government has constantly proclaimed its belief in a partnership between Europe and America, with Britain providing the bridge between them, but this stance was placed under huge international and domestic strain by the Iraq crisis. The opposition of Germany and France in the Security Council to the use of force to disarm Iraq reflected a much wider popular hostility throughout Europe and the rest of the world to the increasing unilateralism of the Bush Administration. Even in those European countries whose governments supported the United States, including Britain, Italy and Spain, there was evidence from opinion polls of strong popular opposition. The isolation of the United States in world opinion was much greater than at any time in the previous fifty years, and it was the first time in the democratic era that a British government had committed troops to a war without popular endorsement. In the Iraq crisis of 2002/3 British public opinion was very similar to public opinion in all other European countries. A majority of the British political class and a majority of the British media supported the United States, but they failed to persuade the British electorate of the case for war. Only after the war had started did a majority come to support it.

While it remains true that the choice between Europe and America for Britain can never be an exclusive one, since both European and American influence on British politics is deep and lasting, there is a question of priority for the future, and whether if the United States continues its pursuit of American primacy, the long-established commitment by the British state to its strategic alliance with the United States will be sustainable. This policy appeared to reach breaking point at the time of the Iraq war, and it raised doubts as to whether any future British government would be able to support the United States in the way the Blair government managed to do. Even then it suffered the largest parliamentary revolt since the vote in 1846 against the repeal of the Corn Laws.

At the time of the Iraq war British public opinion showed itself to be much more European than American in its reaction to the crisis. Like Joschka Fischer, the German Foreign Minister, in his remarkable exchange with Donald Rumsfeld, the British public was 'not convinced'. The reasons why the government case was so unconvincing were stated concisely by Robin Cook in his resignation speech on March 17th, three days before war began.[4]

What many of the opponents of war criticized in the behaviour of the United States was its abandonment of multilateralist policies and institutions, and the open contempt of many of those around Bush for multilateralist solutions. Growing criticism of the policy of the United States highlighted the importance of Europe as an alternative pole to the United States in the world order. In a multipolar world the EU will have a central place, and it is for this reason that the EU continues to grow in importance in British politics, despite the long rearguard action by Euro-sceptics in all parties. The extreme wing of Atlanticist opinion may dream that Britain might disengage from further European involvement and might even leave the EU altogether, but the chances of this are slim.

The Blair Government is in any case wedded to the idea of Britain as a bridge between Europe and America, and Ministers have constantly asserted the importance of Britain being at the heart of Europe. Labour gave some practical support to that aim by reversing one of the UK's opt-outs from the Maastricht Treaty (the Social Chapter), by signing the Nice Treaty extending the use of qualified majority voting, and by pressing for enlargement. The key symbolic decision for the future of British politics, however, will be when and if the government holds a referendum on the euro and wins it. Polls in 2002 and early 2003 still indicated sizeable majorities against joining, but also that large majorities thought that eventual adoption was inevitable. City analysts do not expect immediate entry but tell their clients the UK will be inside by 2011.[5] Ireland is already part of the eurozone, Scotland if it became independent would join too. By the time the latest round of enlargement is complete there may soon be twenty-four EU countries in the eurozone and only one outside it.

Britain's recent macroeconomic success is frequently offered as the reason why Britain should not join the euro. Yet many other European countries with a better long-term record in combining growth and welfare than Britain have embraced the euro, believing that it offers them still better opportunities to combine high levels of both in the future. The establishment of the euro faces Britain with the choice of helping to shape European developments from within or remaining isolated on the outside. Exclusion from the eurozone will significantly reduce Britain's ability to influence the next phase of European integration and the big questions on the European agenda – consolidating the enlargement of the Union to the east; formulating a new constitutional framework for Europe; developing new regulatory capacities at the European level to counter global inequality and to limit enviornmental damage; and contributing to the development of a multipolar world.

The institutions of the emerging global economy and global polity increasingly shape domestic choices. Nation-states by themselves can exercise little effective sovereignty within this new world order. Their best hope of maintaining self-government is to pool sovereignty and establish new democratic and transnational forms of cooperation. The European Union is an example of what can be achieved. It has emerged as the major counterweight to the United States in the global economy; and it has developed much stronger regulatory powers than those found in other regional groupings or global bodies.

There is never one pre-ordained future. European integration is not a single process with a single destination, but a complex experiment which opens up very different possibilities and alternatives for Britain as for the other member states. But Britain is still ambivalent as to how far it wants to be involved. Hesitation over the euro expresses a deeper uncertainty about the future the British want for themselves.

After Decline

As consideration of the euro indicates, the choice between Europe and America is far from being only a choice about security and defence. It is also a choice about economic and social models. British politics has been transformed since 1979 firstly by the economic reforms which reshaped the post-war compromise between labour and capital, and secondly by the constitutional reforms which have begun to alter the nature of the British state. These have helped to mark the final passing of Empire, and of that particular conception of England which was inextricably connected with Empire. They also mark a move beyond decline and the debates and anxieties that preoccupied the political class during the contraction of British power. What has emerged is a new class compromise, a different party system, and different issues. But all of them are framed by the overarching choice between Europe and America.

The old class compromise had been the major domestic political achievement in the twentieth century. Worked out over several decades between Conservatism and the Labour movement, it helped preserve the British state and the British Empire, and inaugurated the welfare state, the main contribution of British socialism. The Conservatives on behalf of the British state conceded universal welfare programmes and accepted trade unions as an estate of the realm with their own special privileges as a reasonable price for domestic peace, and for the preservation of British interests and roles abroad.

In the political circumstances of the 1970s, however, this compromise no longer seemed necessary or desirable in the eyes of growing numbers of Conservatives. The Thatcher project took shape as an ambitious attempt to break the logjam of British politics, by launching a determined assault upon the power of organized labour in the workplace, in the public sector and in local government. The policies pursued after 1979 were opportunistic and pragmatic, but in the end highly effective. The shock of three million unemployed, plunging profits, and widespread bankruptcies forced a radical restructuring of British industry. High profile confrontations with the unions, backed up by tough new anti-union laws tore up the accommodation with organized labour which went back to the Trade Disputes Act of 1906. Deep cuts in public spending programmes helped restructure the welfare state, and taxation on upper incomes was sharply reduced, reversing post-war trends towards greater equality. A more liberal model of capitalism was back, although one which was more American than Gladstonian. With it returned the weapons of unemployment and bankruptcy to discipline workers, which the power of organized labour had blunted for a time.

Unwinding the coils of socialism which had fastened around England became a Thatcherite mantra, but to do it required more state powers not less, a strong state which could intervene to re-establish the rules of a market order and police them effectively. The strong state lay to hand in the undivided and unlimited sovereignty of Crown-in-Parliament. The Thatcher Government made full use of its powers, disregarding conventions when necessary. In retrospect it can be seen as a final fling of the old constitutional state, a last attempt to breathe life into the old certainties of Empire. The Falklands campaign was in this sense emblematic of Thatcherism. It was high risk but it was also an affirmation of the deepest things in which Conservatives believed and which they wished to see return.

In another sense, however, the Falklands war was also an impossible dream, because the Empire could never return. Thatcher knew this, and Thatcherism was never nostalgic. The Thatcher Government increasingly put forward a new future for Britain. The best way for 'England' to be preserved was through America. The attempt to revive a traditional notion of England, an England Strong and Free, was pursued through the strengthening of the partnership with the United States both in the battle against the evil empire of the Soviet Union, and in the attempt to restore a liberal model of capitalism. For many Thatcherites the battle against socialism abroad in the shape of communism and the battle against socialism at home were part of the same fight. Had not Hayek taught that all forms of socialism, even the mildest, were steps on the road to serfdom?[6]

This renewed commitment to a particular idea of Anglo-America as the means to sustain Britain's traditional role in the world and restore the English model, induced many Thatcherites, including Thatcher herself, to stress the need to defend national sovereignty, the traditional sovereignty of the British state, the sovereignty of England. This meant standing firm against proposals for domestic constitutional reform, whether of the electoral system, or for devolution of powers to Scotland and Wales. It also meant turning against further European integration, and questioning whether membership of the European Community was any longer in Britain's interest. The Thatcherites were the first to identify the crucial choice for the future of British politics as a choice between Europe and America, splitting their party, and their own ranks, and bringing down their leader as a result. One group wanted to maintain a balance between Europe and the United States, another rejected any links with either, while a third was for giving much higher priority to the United States and disengaging or even withdrawing altogether from the European Union. For this last group, which in the course of the 1990s was to capture the party, the EU became identified as yet another of the coils of socialism around England – bureaucratic, sclerotic, centralizing, and above all a threat to English self-government and self-reliance. An England rescued from decline through the vanquishing of socialism at home had no need to let socialism in through the back-door by subordinating its government to Brussels.

Thatcherism did vanquish 'socialism', if by that is understood the specific forms of socialism which had emerged in Britain during the twentieth century as part of the political compromise. The power bases of the Labour movement were weakened or destroyed, new anti-trade union laws were pushed through, the public sector was dismantled, and the tax burden successfully shifted from rich to poor. Inequality was widened and poverty was increased. Aided by the splits among its opponents, and emboldened by the opportunities created by the changes taking place in the global economy, the Thatcher Government pushed for deregulation and privatization whenever opportunities presented themselves. The post-war compromise between capital and labour was thrown away in these years; capital and business were in the ascendant, and although the Conservatives never won more than 43 per cent of the vote, the Conservatives triumphed in four successive general elections.

Thatcherism, however, was so successful that it self-destructed, and one of its chief victims was the Conservative Party. Thatcher governed with such Cromwellian intensity that she unleashed counter-forces that proved lethal to the Conservative political hegemony. Conservative statecraft had generally tried the tactics of concession and appeasement in the face of opposition, so as to preserve intact the institutions it valued most and its own ruling position. The Thatcher Government confronted those who opposed it and won some decisive victories, exploiting to the full its constitutional powers. The old Constitution was stretched to breaking point, and it snapped.

One of Thatcher's most enduring achievements was to transform the Labour Party, forcing the party to end the pretence that it was seriously committed to extending socialism through centralized state control. She showed that the electorate would not vote for it, and that the forces supporting it could be defeated, and branded as self-seeking vested interests. But in doing this she helped liberate the left from itself, forcing it into a fundamental rethinking of its strategy and its beliefs. In particular she reignited the campaign for a Scottish Parliament, and for constitutional reform across a broad front.

The new class compromise that Thatcherism inaugurated helped make the British economy one of the stronger performers among leading economies between 1992 and 2002. This was a novel experience, since for the previous four decades the British economy had been a weak economy. The low rate of inflation, the improving record on official unemployment, and the reduction in days lost through strikes were all signs that the British political economy had become much less prone to instability and crisis since the 1970s. But doubts remained about the number of jobless (as opposed to those claiming benefit) and the level of investment and productivity in British industry, which remained considerably below levels in other European countries. This was no miracle economy, but by 2000 steady growth had made it no longer ungovernable or under-performing in the way that it had been thirty years before. The Blair Government adopted the main reforms of its predecessors, particularly on taxation, unions, privatization and deregulation, as well as the addition of some new policies such as independence for the Bank of England's Monetary Policy Committee to set interest rates, tight fiscal rules, and the introduction of a minimum wage. Labour helped consolidate and embed the main reforms of the Thatcher Government and ensure that Labour gained the reputation for economic competence which the Conservatives had lost. What it did not indicate was that Labour had any strategy for escaping from the low wage, low skill, low productivity syndrome which had come to characterize so many sectors in the British economy.[7] Without such a breakout, critics doubted that Labour could raise productivity, skills, or living standards to European levels.[8]

Acceptance of the new class compromise had however been crucial in the survival of Labour as a leading political party, and in reshaping the terrain of party politics to its advantage. Optimists believed that Labour's policies created a solid foundation on which a different kind of left-of-centre politics could emerge, one that was no longer dogged by attempts to use national planning to construct a socialist economy, but which could focus once more on the best available means to achieve equal citizenship through steady increases in public spending targeted at alleviating poverty and at investment in public services. Pessimists thought that the foundations were extremely flimsy and would unravel once economic conditions became harsher.

Despite Labour's caution, its economic policy was by 2002 delivering a substantial and sustained increase in spending on public services, as well as modest redistribution. Within this programme there was much scope for debate and controversy on how far specific policies such as the Private Finance Initiative (PFI) and the New Deal were advancing social democratic objectives. The particular mix of policies chosen by the Blair Government did not exhaust the possibilities, but it did demonstrate that within the framework of neo-liberal consensus, there were significant choices that a government of the centre left could make, such as the introduction of a minimum wage and increases in taxation to fund higher NHS spending which were different from those of the right.

The Conservatives by contrast were hampered not just because of legacies from their eighteen years in office, but also because they found it hard either to combat the formula of economic competence and investment in public services adopted by Labour, or to find a strong position on constitutional change. The party of England, of Union and Empire, found that it had little support left except in England, and then only in certain parts of England. With the passing of the old constitutional state, the party which had been its support and articulator, also seemed in danger of passing away.

That was not inevitable. But what Conservatives needed to do after 1997, but found so difficult, under the leadership first of William Hague and then Iain Duncan Smith, was to acknowledge that if they were to have a future in British politics they had to accept rather than resist Labour's new constitutional and political settlement, and work to develop a Conservative view on the implications for the future role of England within the Union and Britain within Europe, and a Conservative view on how to improve public services. After 2001, the second did begin to emerge, but Europe remained a poison in the Conservative bloodstream, which, at times, it seemed would only be purged once a referendum on the euro were held and lost. Only then might the Conservatives end their great schism on Europe and recover their appetite for government.

After 1997 the future of British politics appeared for a time to lie with the parties of the centre left. The combined strength of Labour and the Liberal Democrats and the disarray of the Conservatives made the prospect of a Progressive Century following the Conservative Century seem within reach,[9] even if the ambition of Tony Blair and Paddy Ashdown before 1997 to reunite the centre left through a coalition in government and the introduction of proportional representation was not realized. Whether the new century will turn out to be a Progressive Century remains unclear. Labour has not yet demonstrated that it has transformed itself into a governing party in the manner of the Conservatives in the past, and it has failed to back the constitutional reforms, notably proportional representation for Westminster which might have made centre-left coalitions the normal expectation in British politics. It is also deeply divided over how to reform public services.

If Europe is the fault-line for the Conservatives, America has become the fault-line for Labour, as the Iraq war demonstrated. The continuing attachment of the Labour leadership to an Atlanticist view of security and Britain's national interest provoked the largest rebellion in the history of the Labour Party over Iraq in 2003, and came close to removing Tony Blair from office. The American political style and American policies of new Labour have also been deeply unpopular and controversial within the party, but they have become distinguishing hallmarks of the Labour leadership reflecting the fact that a significant part of it is more Atlanticist than it is European, as so often in the past. The most promising future governing strategy for Labour would be to embrace Europe as a model both for capitalism and for welfare and for democracy, to join the euro, and to participate fully in developing Britain's European identity and deepening the integration of Europe. But the proportion of the party that is strongly committed to Europe remains rather small. Atlanticism is still the preference of much of the leadership, which hopes for the return of liberal America and the Democrats, but will cooperate with Conservative America in the meantime. In the rest of the party there is a growing aversion to America, but also a scepticism towards Europe, and a hankering after national sovereignty and British socialism. If the party continues to reject America but refuses to commit itself to Europe it is unlikely to consolidate its position as the natural governing party. Internal splits will destroy it and at some stage, although probably not quickly, it will be swept away by a revived Conservative Party.

The other alternative is that the Liberal Democrats will replace the Conservatives as the main opposition party, and a more general realignment of British politics will take place, with an Atlanticist and neo-liberal Labour Party facing a European and social democratic Liberal Democratic

Party. Labour would shed its connections with the trade unions, and take over a large part of Conservative support, while much of Labour's existing base would transfer to the Liberal Democrats. Such a transformation is unlikely but not impossible, as the virtual disappearance of the Conservative Party from so many regions and large cities throughout Britain testifies. One of the strengths of the Liberal Democrats in contrast to the other two parties is their consistent position on Europe, but in other areas they lack the clear identity and purpose of the other two parties, which the afterglow of socialism and of Empire still lends them, and they have so far failed to make a decisive electoral breakthrough.

The Liberal Democrats suffer in this respect from a malaise that affects all the political parties. It is no longer clear what the public and public service mean in British politics. In the past both socialism and imperialism gave clear accounts of the public interest and the public good, and of the obligations of citizens. They provided their parties with an ethos as well as a programme, a deeply felt set of values and commitments, a wider frame and narrative which made sense of political activity and political involvement. One of the familiar complaints about contemporary politics is that it has become devoid of meaning and purpose, and the increasing disengagement of citizens from politics has spread alarm. The recovery of self-confidence about the public realm and public purposes is indispensable for any serious politics, whether right or left.

The future of British politics will be determined by the way in which the choice between Europe and America is finally resolved. Many of the tensions in British politics, and the travails of its political parties, are because Britain has been drawing ever closer to Europe, but this has been resisted by a significant part of the political class which prefers America, and also by a large part of the electorate, which is hostile to both Europe and America and would prefer to remain detached from both. This option is unlikely to be a British choice, but it might be an English choice, and has always had some political support, expressed in the past by Enoch Powell and Tony Benn. But it has only very briefly won the support of one of the main parties.

The more likely choice which will shape the future of British politics is between two kinds of European future. The first is Tony Blair's advocacy of Britain as a bridge between Europe and America, in which the main goal is maintaining a close partnership between America and Europe, and not cutting Britain off from either. This is a hard balancing act, as Tony Blair discovered in the Iraq crisis, and its thrust is ultimately more Atlanticist than European. The idea is to make Europe more like America than America like Europe, and the American model of capitalism and welfare is the one which is regarded as superior, and therefore should be exported to the rest of Europe. Britain is conceived as the carrier of the Anglo-American model to Europe, but to do this Britain has to be fully involved in Europe. It cannot stand outside it, as the bulk of the Conservative Party would rather do. What Blair has identified, reinforced by his security choices, and his alliances with conservative politicians such as Aznar and Berlusconi rather than mainstream social democratic politicians such as Jospin, is a rational conservative strategy which affirms the primacy of America for Britain while still being fully engaged and committed to Europe, including full membership of the eurozone.

The main alternative to this position is that Britain seeks to become a normal European country, aspiring to European standards of wealth and welfare, moving away from adversary towards consensus politics, and abandoning a role in the world which still relies heavily on any kind of unilateral military intervention, either alone or in alliance with the Americans. There is a great deal of evidence that this is where most of the British public would want to be, given a choice, but only the Liberal Democrats come close to offering it. Most of the rest of the political class, including the bulk of the media, remains attached to a world role for Britain, which inevitably means identifying the national interest and the patriotic interest with the strategic alliance with the United States. Behind this lies the old idea of England, and the Empire of England, which can now only exist by projecting that role on to the United States. Such a role is incompatible with full membership of a European Union in which the establishment of a common position between all the members takes priority over bilateral relations with outsiders. The British political class has accepted those obligations over many areas of policy, but not over defence and foreign policy, and not yet over monetary union. A European future seems inescapable, but what kind of European future it will be, will help determine whether there is also a future for Britain, or whether England will find itself alone again.

Notes and References

Chapter 1

1. Friedrich Engels, *The Condition of the Working Class in England*, in Karl Marx and Friedrich Engels, *Collected Works* 4 (London: Lawrence & Wishart, 1975) p. 320.
2. Selina Chen and Tony Wright (eds), *The English Question* (London: Fabian Society, 2000).
3. Edward Thompson, 'The Peculiarities of the English', *Socialist Register*, 1965, pp. 311–62; Philip Corrigan and Derek Sayer, *The Great Arch* (Oxford: Blackwell, 1985).
4. Tom Nairn, *After Britain* (London: Verso, 2000); John Curtice, David McCrone, Alison Park and Lindsay Paterson (eds), *New Scotland, New Society* (Edinburgh: Polygon, 2002); Alice Brown, David McCrone and Lindsay Paterson, *Politics and Society in Scotland* (London: Palgrave, 1998).
5. Anthony Giddens, *Beyond Left and Right: The Future of Radical Politics* (Cambridge: Polity, 1994); Noberto Bobbio, *Left and Right* (Cambridge: Polity, 1996).
6. Jonathan Freedland, *Bring Home the Revolution: The Case for a British Republic* (London: Fourth Estate, 1999).
7. David Marsh *et al.* (eds), *Postwar British Politics in Perspective* (Cambridge: Polity, 1999).
8. Richard Heffernan, *New Labour and Thatcherism: Political Change in Britain* (London: Palgrave, 2000); Peter Kerr, *Postwar British Politics: from conflict to consensus* (London: Routledge, 2001).
9. Gosta Esping-Andersen, *The Three Worlds of Welfare Capitalism* (Cambridge: Polity, 1990).
10. Stephen Driver and Luke Martell, *Blair's Britain* (Cambridge: Polity, 2002); Steve Ludlam and Martin Smith (eds), *New Labour in Government* (London: Palgrave, 2001).
11. Steve Ludlam, 'The Spectre Haunting Conservatism: Europe and Backbench Rebellion', in S. Ludlam and M.J. Smith (eds), *Contemporary British Conservatism* (London: Macmillan, 1996), pp. 98–120.
12. Robert Hazell, *Delivering Constitutional Reform: The Collected Briefings of the Constitution Unit* (London: Chartered Institute of Public Finance and Accountancy, 1997). See also issues of the Constitution Unit's *Monitor*.
13. Dennis Kavanagh, *The Reordering of British Politics: Politics after Thatcher* (Oxford: Oxford University Press, 1997); Mark Bevir and Rod Rhodes, *Understanding British Government* (London: Routledge, 2003); Joel Krieger, *British Politics in the Global Age* (Cambridge: Polity, 1999).

14.   Kevin Davey, *English Imaginaries: Six Studies in Anglo-British Modernity* (London: Lawrence & Wishart, 1999).

15.   Tom Nairn, *The Breakup of Britain* (London: Verso, 1977); and *After Britain*.

16.   Yasmin Alibhai-Brown, *Who Do We Think We Are? Imagining the New Britain* (London: Allen Lane, 2000).

17.   Bhikhu Parekh, *Rethinking Multiculturalism: Cultural Diversity and Political Theory* (London: Macmillan 2000); Bhikhu Parekh (ed.), *The Future of Multi-Ethnic Britain* (London: Profile Books, 2000).

18.   John Redwood, *Stars and Strife: The Coming Conflicts between the USA and the European Union* (London: Palgrave, 2001).

19.   Peter Mandelson, *The Blair Revolution Revisited* (London: Politico's, 2002).

20.   Will Hutton, *The World We're In* (London: Little, Brown, 2002).

21.   Dick Leonard and Mark Leonard (eds), *The Pro-European Reader* (London: Palgrave, 2002); Martin Holmes (ed.), *The Eurosceptical Reader 2* (London: Palgrave, 2002).

22.   Geoffrey Owen, *From Empire to Europe: the Decline and Revival of British Industry Since the Second World War* (London: Harper Collins, 2000).

23.   Colin Hay, *The Political Economy of New Labour: Labouring under False Pretences?* (Manchester: Manchester University Press, 1999).

24.   Friedrich Engels, *The Condition of the English Working Class*.

25.   Colin Leys, *Market Driven Politics: Neo-liberal Democracy and the Public Interest* (London: Verso, 2001).

26.   Tony Giddens, *The Third Way and its Critics* (Cambridge: Polity, 2000).

27.   Colin Crouch, *Post-Democracy* (London: Fabian Society, 2000).

Chapter 2

1.   William Shakespeare, *Richard II* (speech by John of Gaunt, Act 2, Scene 1).

2.   Karl Marx, *Capital*, Volume One (Harmondsworth: Penguin, 1976) p. 90.

3.   John Seeley, *The Expansion of England* (London: Macmillan, 1902).

4.   Seeley, *The Expansion of England*.

5.   Hugh Kearney, *The British Isles: A History of Four Nations* (Cambridge: Cambridge University Press, 1989); J.G.A. Pocock, *The Limits and Divisions of British History* (Glasgow: Centre for the Study of Public Policy, 1979).

6.   David Armitage, *The Ideological Origins of the British Empire* (Cambridge: Cambridge University Press, 2000).

7.   There is no longer an accepted term for what used to be known as the British Isles, following the rejection of the majority of the Irish of a British identity. Attempts to provide an alternative, such as East Atlantic Archipelago, have

proved too cumbersome to be widely adoped. See Norman Davies, *The Isles: A History* (London: Macmillan, 1999).

8. Recent additions include Richard Weight, *Patriots: National Identity in Britain* (London: Macmillan, 2002); Robert Colls, *Identity of England* (Oxford: Oxford University Press, 2002).

9. Jeremy Paxman, *The English: A Portrait of a People* (London: Michael Joseph, 1998).

10. Roger Scruton, *England: An Elegy* (London: Pimlico, 2001).

11. Christopher Harvie, *Scotland and Nationalism: Scottish Society and Politics 1707–present* (London: Routledge, 1998).

12. Tom Nairn, *After Britain: New Labour and the Return of Scotland* (London: Granta, 1999).

13. Bernard Semmel, *Imperialism and Social Reform* (London: Allen & Unwin, 1960).

14. John Gray, *Is Conservatism Dead?* (London: Profile Books, 1997).

15. Mark Evans, *Charter 88: A Successful Challenge to the British Political Tradition?* (Aldershot: Dartmouth, 1995); IPPR, *The Constitution of the United Kingdom* (London: IPPR, 1991); Richard Holme and Michael Elliott (eds), *1688–1988: Time for a New Constitution* (London: Macmillan, 1988).

16. Philip Corrigan and Derek Sayer, *The Great Arch* (Oxford: Blackwell, 1985); Nevil Johnson, 'The Constitution', in Ian Holliday *et al.* (eds), *Fundamentals in British Politics* (London: Macmillan, 1999), pp. 45–70.

17. Jonathan Freedland, *Bring Home the Revolution: The Case for a British Republic* (London: Fourth Estate, 1999); Anthony Barnett, *This Time: Our Constitutional Revolution* (London: Vintage, 1997).

18. Peter Mandelson and Roger Liddle, *The Blair Revolution: Can New Labour Deliver?* (London: Faber, 1996).

19. Tony Benn and Andrew Hood, *Common Sense: A New Constitution for Britain* (London: Hutchinson, 1993); Tony Benn, *Arguments for Democracy* (London: Cape, 1981).

20. David Willetts, *Modern Conservatism* (London: Penguin, 1992).

21. Nevil Johnson, 'The Constitution'.

22. Roger Scruton, *England: An Elegy* (London: Pimlico, 2001).

23. Simon Heffer, *Nor Shall My Sword: The Reinvention of England* (London: Phoenix, 2000).

24. Jim Buller, *National Statecraft and European Integration: The Conservative Government and the European Union 1979–1997* (London: Pinter, 2000).

25. Richard English and Michael Kenny (eds), *Rethinking British Decline* (London: Macmillan, 1999).

26. Anthony Barnett, *Iron Britannia* (London: Allison & Busby, 1982).

27. Clive Ponting, *1940: Myth and Reality* (London: Hamilton, 1990).

28. Corelli Barnett, *The Collapse of British Power* (London: Eyre Methuen, 1972).

29. David Coates, *The Question of UK Decline* (London: Harvester Wheatsheaf, 1994).
30. Andrew Gamble, *Britain in Decline* (London: Macmillan, 1994).
31. Peter Hitchens, *The Abolition of Britain* (London: Quartet, 1999); Simon Heffer, *Nor Shall My Sword: The Re-Invention of England*; Roger Scruton, *England: An Elegy*; John Redwood, *The Death of Britain?* (London: Palgrave, 1999); Tom Nairn, *After Britain*; Robert Colls, *Identity of England*.
32. Peter Hitchens, *The Abolition of Britain*, p. 349.
33. Nick Crafts, *Britain's Relative Economic Performance, 1870–1999* (London: IEA, 2002).
34. Peter Hitchens, *The Abolition of Britain*.
35. Similar themes are developed by Daily Mail columnists including Melanie Phillips and Chris Woodhead.
36. Enoch Powell, *Freedom and Reality* (London: Batsford, 1969).
37. Enoch Powell, *Reflections of a Statesman: The Writings and Speeches of Enoch Powell*, selected by Rex Collings (London: Bellew Publishing, 1991); Simon Heffer, *Like the Roman: The Life of Enoch Powell* (London: Weidenfeld, 1998).
38. Tony Benn, *Free At Last: Diaries 1990–2001* (London: Hutchinson, 2002).
39. Paul Allender, *What's Wrong with Labour? A Critical History of the Labour Party in the Twentieth Century* (London: Merlin, 2001); Hitchens, *The Abolition of Britain*.
40. Norman Davies, *The Isles*; Hugh Kearney, *The British Isles: A History of Four Nations*.
41. Philip Corrigan and Derek Sayer, *The Great Arch*.
42. Linda Colley, *Britons: Forging the Nation 1707–1837* (New Haven, CT: Yale University Press, 1992).
43. James Mitchell, *Conservatives and the Union: A Study of Conservative Party Attitudes to Scotland* (Edinburgh: Edinburgh University Press, 1990).
44. Jim Bulpitt, *Territory and Power in the United Kingdom* (Manchester: Manchester University Press, 1983).
45. Norman Davies, *The Isles*.
46. Shakespeare, *Richard II*.
47. Jeremy Paxman, *The English*; George Orwell, *The Lion and the Unicorn: Socialism and the English Genius* (Harmondsworth: Penguin, 1982).
48. Christopher Harvie, *Scotland and Nationalism: Scottish Society and Politics 1707–1994* (London: Routledge, 1977).
49. Philip Corrigan and Derek Sayer, *The Great Arch*.
50. Roger Scruton, *England: An Elegy*.
51. Stuart Hall and Bill Schwarz, 'State and Society, 1880–1930', in M. Langan and B. Schwarz (eds), *Crises in the British State* (London: Hutchinson, 1985).

Chapter 3

1. Neal Ascherson, *Games With Shadows* (London: Radius, 1988), p. 6.
2. Seymour Martin Lipset, *American Exceptionalism: A Double-Edged Sword* (New York: Norton, 1996).
3. Philip Corrigan and Derek Sayer, *The Great Arch: English State Formation as Cultural Revolution* (Oxford: Blackwell, 1985).
4. Ernest Gellner, *Nations and Nationalism* (Oxford: Blackwell, 1983).
5. Eric Hobsbawm, *Nations and Nationalism since 1780: Programme, Myth, Reality* (Cambridge: Cambridge Uuniversity Press, 1992).
6. Norman Davies, *The Isles: A History* (London: Macmillan, 1999).
7. Hugh Kearney, *The British Isles: A History of Four Nations.* (Cambridge: Cambridge University Press, 1989).
8. Tom Nairn, *After Britain* (London: Granta, 1999).
9. Davies, *The Isles.*
10. Bernard Crick, 'The English and the British', in B. Crick (ed.), *National Identities: The Constitution of the United Kingdom* (Oxford: Blackwell, 1991).
11. Crick, 'The English and the British', p. 90.
12. Jonathan Clark (ed.), *Ideas and Politics in Modern Britain* (London: Macmillan, 1990).
13. Liam de Paor, *Divided Ulster* (Harmondsworth: Penguin, 1971); John Whyte, *Interpreting Northern Ireland* (Oxford: Clarendon, 1990); John McGarry and Brendan O'Leary, *Explaining Northern Ireland* (Oxford: Blackwell, 1995).
14. Linda Colley, *Britons: Forging the Nation 1707–1837* (New Haven, CT: Yale University Press, 1992).
15. J.G.A. Pocock, 'The Limits and Divisions of British History' (Glasgow: Centre for the Study of Public Policy, 1979).
16. David Cannadine, 'British History as a new subject', in A. Grant and K. Stringer, *Writing the Kingdom* (London: Routledge, 1995).
17. Hugh Kearney, 'The Importance of Being British', *The Political Quarterly* 71(1), 2000, pp. 15–25.
18. Norman Davies, *The Isles.*
19. Linda Colley, *Britons.*
20. Kenneth Dyson, *The State Tradition in Western Europe* (Oxford: Martin Robertson, 1980).
21. W.L. Guttsman, *The British Political Elite* (London: MacGibbon & Kee, 1965).
22. Hugh Thomas, *The Establishment* (London: Blond, 1959); Anthony Sampson, *Anatomy of Britain* (London: Hodder & Stoughton, 1962).
23. David Marquand, *The Unprincipled Society: New Demands and Old Politics* (London: Cape, 1988).
24. Jim Bulpitt, *Territory and Power in the United Kingdom* (Manchester: Manchester University Press, 1983); Peter Madgwick and Richard Rose (eds),

The Territorial Dimension in United Kingdom Politics (London: Macmillan, 1982).

25. Corrigan and Sayer, *The Great Arch.*
26. Susan Kingsley Kent, *Gender and Power in Britain, 1640–1990* (London: Routledge, 1999).
27. Liam de Paor, *Divided Ulster.*
28. Ron Johnston and Charles Pattie, 'Devolution and Equality of Representation in the United Kingdom: A Constitutional Mess?', *The Political Quarterly*, 73(2), 2002, pp. 58–71.
29. Colley, *Britons.*
30. W.D. Rubinstein, *Capitalism, Culture and Decline in Britain* (London: Routledge, 1993).
31. David Marquand, *The New Reckoning: Capitalism, States, and Citizens* (Cambridge: Polity, 1997).
32. Jim Bulpitt, *Territory and Power in the United Kingdom.*
33. Christopher Harvie, *Scotland and Nationalism: Scottish Society and Politics 1707–Present* (London: Routledge, 1998).
34. Colley, *Britons.*
35. Clifford Longley, *Chosen People: The Big Idea that Shapes England and America* (London: Hodder & Stoughton, 2002).
36. Longley, *Chosen People.*
37. Colley, *Britons.*
38. Alexander Grant and Keith Stringer (eds), *Uniting the Kingdom? The Making of British History* (London: Routledge, 1995).
39. Paul Addison, *The Road to 1945: British Politics and the Second World War* (London: Pimlico, 1994); Anthony Barnett, *Iron Britannia* (London: Allison & Busby, 1982); Tom Nairn, *After Britain.*
40. Bernard Semmell, *Imperialism and Social Reform* (London: Allen & Unwin, 1960).
41. Gary Herrigel, *Industrial Constructions: The Sources of German Industrial Power* (New York: Cambridge University Press, 1996).
42. T.H. Marshall, *Citizenship and Social Class, and Other Essays* (Cambridge: Cambridge University Press, 1950).
43. Paul Pierson, *Dismantling the Welfare State? Reagan, Thatcher and the Politics of Retrenchment* (Cambridge: Cambridge University Press, 1994); Rodney Lowe, *The Welfare State in Britain since 1945* (London: Palgrave, 1999).
44. Gosta Esping Andersen, *The Three Worlds of Welfare Capitalism* (Cambridge: Polity, 1990); Christopher Pierson, *Beyond the Welfare State: The New Political Economy of Welfare* (Cambridge: Polity, 1991).
45. Robert Hazell, *The State and the Nations; The First Year of Devolution in the United Kingdom* (London: Academic, 2000).
46. J.H. Grainger, *Character and Style in English Politics* (Cambridge: Cambridge University Press, 1969).

47. Whyte, *Interpreting Northern Ireland.*
48. Leo Amery, quoted in J.H. Grainger, *Patriotisms: Britain 1900–1936* (London: Routledge, 1986), p. 244.
49. A.T.Q. Stewart, *The Ulster Crisis* (London: Faber, 1967).
50. A.J.P. Taylor, *English History1914–1945* (Oxford: Clarendon, 1965).
51. Whyte, *Interpreting Northern Ireland*; Grainger, *Patriotisms.*
52. Charles Moore, *How to Be British* (London: Centre for Policy Studies, 1995).
53. T.E. Utley, *Enoch Powell: The Man and his Thinking* (London: Kimber, 1968).
54. Paul Bew, *The British State and the Ulster Crisis* (London: Verso, 1985); Liam de Paor, *Divided Ulster.*
55. Whyte, *Interpreting Northern Ireland.*
56. Simon Heffer, *Nor Shall My Sword: The Reinvention of England* (London: Phoenix, 2000).
57. Paul Dixon, *Northern Ireland: The Politics of War and Peace* (London: Palgrave, 2001).
58. Christopher Harvie, *Scotland and Nationalism: Scottish Society and Politics 1707–present* (London: Routledge, 1998).
59. Vernon Bogdanor, *Devolution in the United Kingdom* (Oxford: Oxford University Press, 1999).
60. Archie Brown, 'Asymmetrical Devolution: The Scottish Case', *The Political Quarterly* 69(3), 1998, pp. 215–23.
61. Jim Bulpitt, *Territory and Power in the United Kingdom.*
62. Robert McCreadie, 'Scottish Identity and the Constitution', in B. Crick (ed.), *National Identities* (Oxford: Blackwell, 1991), 38–56.
63. Paddy Ashdown, *The Ashdown Diaries 1988–97 & 1997–99* (London: Penguin, 2001).
64. Mark Evans, *Charter 88: A Successful Challenge to the British Political Tradition?* (Aldershot: Dartmouth, 1995); IPPR, *The Constitution of the United Kingdom* (London: IPPR, 1991).
65. Will Hutton, *The State We're In* (London: Cape, 1995); Anthony Barnett, *This Time: Our Constitutional Revolution* (London: Vintage, 1997).
66. Ian McLean, Alice Brown, David McCrone, and Lindsay Paterson, *Politics and Society in Scotland* (London: Macmillan, 1998).
67. John Curtice, David McCrone, Alison Park and Lindsay Paterson, *New Scotland, New Society?* (Edinburgh: Polygon, 2002).

Chapter 4

1. Halford Mackinder, *Britain and the British Seas* (London: Heinemann, 1902), p. 343.
2. Hugh Kearney, 'Four Nations or One?', in B. Crick (ed.), *National Identities* (Oxford: Blackwell, 1991), p. 2.

3.   P.J. Cain and A.G. Hopkins, *British Imperialism: Innovation and Expansion 1688– 1914* (London: Longman, 1993).

4.   John Darwin, *Britain and Decolonisation: The Retreat from Empire in the Post-War World* (London: Macmillan, 1988); P.J. Cain and A.G. Hopkins, *British Imperialism: Crisis and Deconstruction 1914–1990* (London: Longman, 1993).

5.   Eric Hobsbawm, *Industry and Empire* (London: Weidenfeld & Nicolson, 1968).

6.   Hugh Thomas, *The Slave Trade: The Story of the Atlantic Slave Trade, 1440–1870* (New York: Simon & Schuster, 1997); Robin Blackburn, *The Making of New World Slavery: From the Baroque to the Modern 1492–1800* (London: Verso, 1997).

7.   A.P. Thornton, *The Imperial Idea and its Enemies: a study in British power* (London: Macmillan, 1985).

8.   J.A. Hobson, *Imperialism* (London: Unwin Hyman, 1902; Third Edition, 1988) p. 114.

9.   Hobson, *Imperialism. Ibid.*

10. Thornton, *The Imperial Idea and its Enemies.*

11. Zig Layton-Henry, *The Politics of Race in Britain* (London: Allen & Unwin, 1984); John Solomos, *Race and Racism in Britain* (London: Palgrave, 2003).

12. Colin Holmes, *John Bull's Other Island: Immigration and British Society 1871–1971* (London: Macmillan, 1988).

13. Linda Colley, *Britons: Forging the Nation 1707–1837* (New Haven, CT: Yale University Press, 1992).

14. Arthur Marwick, *British Society since 1945* (London: Penguin, 1990).

15. Layton-Henry, *The Politics of Race in Britain.*

16. *Ibid.*

17. Paul Foot, *Immigration and Race in British Politics* (Harmondsworth: Penguin, 1965).

18. Layton-Henry, *The Politics of Race in Britain.*

19. Simon Heffer, *Like the Roman: The Life of Enoch Powell* (London: Weidenfeld, 1998); T.E. Utley, *Enoch Powell: The Man and his Thinking* (London: Kimber, 1968); Douglas Schoen, *Enoch Powell and the Powellites* (London: Macmillan, 1977).

20. Enoch Powell, *Freedom and Reality* (Kingswood: Elliot Right Way Books, 1969), p. 283.

21. Powell, *Freedom and Reality*, p. 282.

22. Powell, *Freedom and Reality*, p. 289.

23. Powell, *Freedom and Reality*, p. 313.

24. Brian Barry, *Culture and Equality: An Egalitarian Critique of Multiculturalism* (Cambridge: Polity, 2000); Bhikhu Parekh, *The Future of Multi-Ethnic Britain* (London: Profile Books, 2000).

25. Bhikhu Parekh, *Rethinking Multiculturalism: Cultural Diversity and Political Theory* (London: Palgrave, 2000); Solomos, *Race and Racism in Britain.*

26. John Seeley, *The Expansion of England* (London: Macmillan, 1902).
27. Norman Davies, *The Isles: A History* (London: Macmillan, 1999).
28. Davies, *The Isles*, p. 276–7.
29. Hugh Kearney, *The British Isles: A History of Four Nations* (Cambridge: Cambridge University Press, 1989).
30. Paul Kennedy, *The Rise and Fall of British Naval Mastery* (London: Fontana, 1991).
31. Norman Davies, *The Isles*.
32. Colley, *Britons*.
33. Eric Hobsbawm, *Industry and Empire*.
34. W.L. Guttsman, *The British Political Elite* (London: MacGibbon & Kee, 1965).
35. A.P. Thornton, *The Imperial Idea and its Enemies*.
36. Bernard Semmel, *Imperialism and Social Reform* (London: Allen & Unwin, 1960); G.R. Searle, *The Quest for National Efficiency: A Study in British Politics and Political Thought 1889–1914* (Oxford: Blackwell, 1971).
37. Geoff Mulgan, *Politics in an Anti-Political Age* (Cambridge: Polity, 1994).
38. Paul Kennedy, *The Rise and Fall of the Great Powers: Economic Change and Military Conflict from 1500 to 2000* (London: Fontana, 1989).
39. Robert Blake, *The Decline of Power 1915–1964* (London: Granada, 1985).
40. Niall Ferguson, *The Pity of War* (London: Penguin, 1999).
41. Blake, *The Decline of Power*; Max Beloff, *Imperial Sunset: Vol 2 Dream of Commonwealth 1921–1942* (London: Macmillan, 1989); Correlli Barnett, *The Collapse of British Power* (London: Eyre Methuen, 1972).
42. Winston Churchill, *The Second World War: Volume 2 Their Finest Hour* (London: Cassell, 1949); Clive Ponting, *1940: Myth and Reality* (London: Hamilton, 1990).
43. Winston Churchill, Speech in the House of Commons, June 18 1940.
44. Benjamin Disraeli, Letter to Lord Malmesbury, August 13 1852.
45. Robert McKenzie and Allan Silver, *Angels in Marble: Working Class Conservatives in Urban England* (London: Heinemann, 1968).
46. J.A. Hobson, *Imperialism* (London: Unwin Hyman, 1902); Richard Cobden, *The Political Writings of Richard Cobden* (London: Ridgway, 2 vols, 1867).
47. A.P. Thornton, *The Imperial Idea and its Enemies*.
48. Bernard Semmel, *Imperialism and Social Reform*.
49. Leo Amery, *My Political Life, Vols 1–3* (London: Hutchinson, 1953–5).
50. W.H. Mallock, *A Critical Examination of Socialism* (London: John Murray, 1908).
51. Hobson, *Imperialism*, p. 151.
52. Hobson, *Imperialism*, p. 160.
53. Jim Bulpitt, *Territory and Power in the United Kingdom* (Manchester: Manchester University Press, 1983).
54. Philip Corrigan and Derek Sayer, *The Great Arch* (Oxford: Blackwell, 1985); Stuart Hall and Bill Schwarz, 'State and Society, 1880–1930', in M. Langan and B. Schwarz (eds), *Crises in the British State* (London: Hutchinson, 1985).

55. David Edgerton, *England and the Aeroplane: An Essay on a Militant and Technological Nation* (London: Macmillan, 1991).
56. Correlli Barnett, *The Collapse of British Power*; Correlli Barnett, *Britain and her army 1500–1970* (London: Allen Lane, 1970).
57. Frank Prochaska, *Royal Bounty: The Making of a Welfare Monarchy* (New Haven, CT: Yale University Press, 1995).
58. Mulgan, *Politics in an Anti-Political Age*, ch. 8.
59. Kennedy, *The Rise and Fall of the Great Powers*.
60. Stephen Blank, 'The Politics of Foreign Economic Policy', *International Organisation* 31(4), 1977, pp. 673–722.
61. Hobson, *Imperialism*; Thornton, *The Imperial Idea and Its Enemies*.
62. Cain and Hopkins, *British Imperialism: Innovation and Expansion*.
63. Martin Wiener, *English Culture and the Decline of the Industrial Spirit 1850–1980* (London: Penguin, 1985).
64. Correlli Barnett, *The Audit of War: The Illusion and Reality of Britain as a Great Nation* (London: Macmillan, 1986).
65. Julian Amery, *Joseph Chamberlain and the Tariff Reform Campaign 1903–1968* (London: Macmillan, 1969).
66. Susan Strange, *Sterling and British Policy* (London: Oxford University Press, 1971).
67. David Kynaston, *The City of London: Volume 1: A World of its Own, 1815–1890* (London: Chatto & Windus, 1994).
68. Semmel, *Imperialism and Social Reform*.
69. John Peterson, *Europe and America: The Prospects for Partnership* (London: Routledge, 1996); Dick Leonard and Mark Leonard (eds), *The Pro-European Reader* (London: Palgrave, 2002); Martin Holmes (ed.), *The Eurosceptical Reader 2* (London: Palgrave, 2002).

Chapter 5

1. Joseph Chamberlain, quoted by J.A. Hobson, *Imperialism* (London: Unwin Hyman, 1988), p. 160.
2. Winston Churchill, *War Speeches 1940–45* (London: Cassell, 1966), p. 35.
3. Jonathan Freedland, *Bring Home the Revolution: The Case for a British Republic* (London: Fourth Estate, 1999); Peter Hitchens, *The Abolition of Britain* (London: Quartet, 1999).
4. P.J. Cain and A.G. Hopkins, *Innovation and Expansion 1688–1914* (London: Longman, 1993); P.J. Cain and A.G. Hopkins, *Crisis and Deconstruction 1914–1990* (London: Longman, 1993).
5. Bernard Semmel, *Imperialism and Social Reform* (London: Allen & Unwin, 1960).
6. Paul Kennedy, *The Rise and Fall of the Great Powers: Economic Change and Military Conflict from 1500 to 2000* (London: Fontana, 1989); John Darwin,

Britain and Decolonisation: The Retreat from Empire in the Post-War World (London: Macmillan, 1988).

7. Roger Louis and Hedley Bull (eds), *The Special Relationship: Anglo-American Relations since 1945* (Oxford: OUP, 1986); Donald Cameron Watt, *Succeeding John Bull: America in Britain's Place 1900–1975* (Cambridge: CUP, 1984); John Dumbrell, *A Special Relationship: Anglo-American Relations in the Cold War and After* (London: Palgrave, 2001); David Sanders, *Losing an Empire, Finding a Role* (London: Macmillan, 1990).

8. Kenneth Hoover and Raymond Plant, *Conservative Capitalism in Britain and the United States* (London: Routledge, 1988).

9. Benedict Anderson, *Imagined Communities: Reflections on the Origin and Spread of Nationalism* (London: Verso, 1991).

10. Christopher Hitchens, *Blood, Class and Nostalgia: Anglo-American Ironies* (London: Chatto & Windus, 1990); Charles Dilke, *Problems of Greater Britain* (London: Macmillan, 1980).

11. David Held, *Democracy and the Global Order: From the Modern State to Cosmopolitan Governance* (Cambridge: Polity, 1995); Jan Aart Scholte, *Globalisation* (London: Macmillan, 2000); Mark Rupert, *Ideologies of Globalisation: Contending Visions of a New World Order* (London: Routledge, 2000).

12. John Redwood, *Stars and Strife: The Coming Conflicts between the USA and the European Union* (London: Palgrave, 2001).

13. Hitchens, *Blood, Class and Nostalgia*.

14. Aaron Friedberg, *The Weary Titan: Britain and the Experience of Relative Decline 1895–1905* (Princeton: Princeton University Press, 1988); Watt, *Succeeding John Bull*.

15. Michael Hardt and Antonio Negri, *Empire* (Cambridge: Harvard University Press, 2000); Naomi Klein, *No Logo* (New York: Picador, 1999).

16. David Held, Anthony McGrew, David Goldblatt and Jonathan Perraton, *Global Transformations: Politics, Economics, and Culture* (Cambridge: Polity, 1999).

17. Immanuel Wallerstein, *The Modern World System* (New York: Academic Press, 1974).

18. Kennedy, *The Rise and Fall of the Great Powers*.

19. Paul Hirst and Grahame Thompson, *Globalisation in Question: The International Economy and the Possibilities of Governance* (Cambridge: Polity, 1999).

20. C.P. Kindleberger, *The World in Depression 1929–1939* (Harmondsworth: Penguin, 1987).

21. Robert Gilpin, *The Political Economy of International Relations* (Princeton: Princeton University Press, 1987).

22. A.H. Imlah, *Economic Elements in the Pax Britannica: Studies in British Foreign Trade in the Nineteenth Century* (London: Oxford University Press, 1958).

23. Geoffrey Ingham, *Capitalism Divided? The City and Industry in British Social Development* (London: Macmillan, 1984).
24. Semmel, *Imperialism and Social Reform.*
25. David Kynaston, *The City of London: Volume 1: A World of its Own, 1815–1890* (London: Chatto & Windus, 1994).
26. Eric Hobsbawm, *Industry and Empire* (London: Penguin, 1968).
27. Rhiannon Vickers, *Manipulating Hegemony: State Power, Labour and the Marshall Plan in Britain* (London: Macmillan, 2000); Peter Burnham, *The Political Economy of PostWar Reconstruction* (London: Macmillan, 1989).
28. Paul Kennedy, *The Rise and Fall of British Naval Mastery* (London: Fontana, 1991).
29. Friedrich List, *The National System of Political Economy* (New York: Kelley, 1966).
30. Halford Mackinder, *Britain and the British Seas* (London: Heinemann, 1902); *Democratic Ideals and Reality: A Study in the Politics of Reconstruction* (New York: Holt, 1942).
31. Semmel, *Imperialism and Social Reform.*
32. Richard Gardner, *Sterling–Dollar Diplomacy in Current Perspective: The Origins and Prospects of our International Economic Order* (New York: Columbia University Press, 1980).
33. Lord Milner, *The Nation and the Empire* (London: Constable, 1913).
34. Paul Kennedy, *Strategy and Diplomacy 1870–1945* (London: Fontana, 1983) p. 27.
35. R. Heindel, *The American Impact on Great Britain, 1898–1914* (New York: Octagon, 1968).
36. Leon Trotsky, *Where is Britain Going?* (London: New Park Publications, 1970).
37. Watt, *Succeeding John Bull.*
38. Maurice Cowling, *The Impact of Hitler: British Politics and British Policy 1933–1940* (London: Cambridge University Press, 1975).
39. Gardner, *Sterling–Dollar Diplomacy.*
40. Kees van der Pijl, *The Making of an Atlantic Ruling Class* (London: Verso, 1984).
41. Lord Keynes, quoted by Gardner, *Sterling–Doller Diplomacy*, p. 125.
42. Peter Burnham, *Remaking the Postwar World Economy* (London: Palgrave, 2003).
43. Andrew Shonfield, *Modern Capitalism: The Changing Balance of Public and Private Power* (London: OUP, 1965); Michel Albert, *Capitalism against Capitalism* (London: Whurr, 1993); David Coates, *Models of Capitalism* (Cambridge: Polity, 2000).
44. Simon Clarke, *Keynesianism, Monetarism and the Crisis of the State* (Aldershot: Edward Elgar, 1987).
45. Stephen Gill, 'European Governance and New Constitutionalism: Economic and Monetary Union and Alternatives to Disciplinary Neoliberalism in Europe', *New Political Economy* (1996) 3(1), pp. 5–26.

46. Francis Fukuyama, *The End of History and the Last Man* (London: Hamish Hamilton, 1992); Andrew Gamble, *Politics and Fate* (Cambridge: Polity, 2000).
47. Coates, *Models of Capitalism*.
48. Gosta Esping-Andersen, *The Three Worlds of Welfare Capitalism* (Cambridge: Polity, 1990).
49. John Parkinson, Andrew Gamble and Gavin Kelly (eds), *The Political Economy of the Company* (London: Hart, 2000).
50. Shonfield, *Modern Capitalism*.
51. Kennedy, *The Rise and Fall of the Great Powers*.

Chapter 6

1. John Maynard Keynes, *The Economic Consequences of the Peace* (London: Macmillan, 1919), p. 2.
2. Norman Davies, *The Isles: A History* (London: Macmillan, 1999).
3. Winston Churchill, *A History of the English Speaking Peoples* (London: Cassell, 1949).
4. Clive Ponting, *1940: Myth and Reality* (London: Hamilton, 1990).
5. Margaret Thatcher, *Statecraft* (London: HarperCollins, 2002).
6. G.K. Chesterton, *A Short History of England* (London: Chatto & Windus, 1917).
7. Mark Greengrass, *Samuel Hartlib and Universal Reformation* (Cambridge: CUP, 1994).
8. Norman Davies, *Europe: A History* (London: Pimlico, 1997).
9. Kenneth Dyson, *European States and the Euro* (Oxford: OUP, 2001).
10. Perry Anderson, 'The Europe to Come', in Peter Gowan and Perry Anderson, *The Question of Europe* (London: Verso, 1997).
11. Steve Ludlam, 'The Spectre Haunting Conservatism: Europe and Backbench Rebellion', in S. Ludlam and M.J. Smith (eds), *Contemporary British Conservatism* (London: Macmillan, 1996), pp. 98–120.
12. David Baker, Andrew Gamble and Steve Ludlam, '1846 . . . 1906 . . . 1996? Conservative Splits and European Integration', *The Political Quarterly*, 64(4) (1993), pp. 420–34.
13. Anthony Eden, *Full Circle* (London: Cassell, 1960).
14. Alan Milward and G. Brennan, *Britain's Place in the World: A Historical Enquiry into Import Controls 1945–1960* (London: Routledge, 1996).
15. Alfred Grosser, *The Western Alliance: European-American Relations since 1945* (London: Macmillan, 1978); Robert Blake, *The Decline of Power 1915–1964* (London: Granada, 1985).
16. Alan Milward, *Widening, Deepening and Accelerating: The European Economic Community 1957–1963* (Baden-Baden: Nomos, 1999).
17. Representative is Michael Shanks, *The Stagnant Society* (London: Penguin, 1961).

18. Andrew Gamble, *The Conservative Nation* (London: Routledge, 1974).
19. Edward Heath, 'A Historic Decision', in Dick Leonard and Mark Leonard (eds), *The Pro-European Reader* (London: Palgrave, 2002), pp. 57–64.
20. Martin Holmes (ed.), *The Eurosceptic Reader* (London: Macmillan, 1996); Enoch Powell, *The Common Market: The Case Against* (Kingswood: Elliott, 1971).
21. Holmes, *The Eurosceptic Reader*.
22. Tom Nairn, *The Left Against Europe* (Harmondsworth: Penguin, 1970).
23. Nora Beloff, *The General Says No: Britain's Exclusion from Europe* (Harmondsworth: Penguin, 1963).
24. John Campbell, *Edward Heath* (London: Cape, 1993).
25. Kenneth Morgan, *Britain since 1945: The People's Peace* (Oxford: Oxford University Press, 2001).
26. Stephen George, *An Awkward Partner: Britain in the European Union* (Oxford: OUP, 1998).
27. Denis Healey, *The Time of My Life* (London: Michael Joseph, 1989).
28. Patrick Seyd, *The Rise and Fall of the Labour Left* (London: Macmillan, 1987).
29. Sam Aaronovitch, *The Road from Thatcherism: The Alternative Economic Strategy* (London: Lawrence & Wishart, 1981).
30. CSE, *The Alternative Economic Strategy* (London: CSE, 1981).
31. Ian Gilmour, *Dancing With Dogma: Britain under Thatcherism* (London: Simon & Schuster, 1992).
32. Jim Buller, *National Statecraft and European Integration: The Conservative Government and the European Union 1979–1997* (London: Pinter, 2000).
33. George, *An Awkward Partner*, p. 205.
34. Hugo Young, *This Blessed Plot: Britain and Europe from Churchill to Blair* (London: Macmillan, 1998).
35. Buller, *National Statecraft and European Integration*.
36. Holmes, *The Eurosceptic Reader*.
37. Will Hutton, *The World We're In* (London: Little, Brown, 2002).
38. *Thatcher*, Statecraft.
39. David Baker, Imogen Fountain, Andrew Gamble and Steve Ludlam, 'The Blue Map of Europe: Conservative Parliamentarians and European Integration', in C.Rallings *et al.* (eds), *British Elections and Parties Yearbook 1995* (London: Cass, 1996).
40. John Ruggie, 'Territoriality and Beyond: Problematising Modernity in International Relations', *International Organisation*, 47(1), 1993, pp. 139–74.
41. Larry Siedentop, *Democracy in Europe* (London: Allen Lane, 2000).
42. Andrew Gamble and Anthony Payne (eds), *Regionalism and World Order* (London: Macmillan, 1996).
43. Alan Milward 'Approaching Reality: Euromoney and the Left', *New Left Review*, 216 (1996), pp. 55–65.
44. Andrew Gamble, 'Economic Recession and Political Disenchantment', *West European Politics*, 18(3) (1995), pp. 158–74.

45. Michael Spicer, *A Treaty Too Far: A New Policy for Europe* (London: Fourth Estate, 1992); Holmes, *The Eurosceptical Reader*.

Chapter 7

1. Henry Hallam, *A View of the State of Europe During the Middle Ages*, quoted by Ferdinand Mount in *The British Constitution Now* (London: Heinemann, 1992), pp. 8–9.
2. Will Hutton, *The World We're In* (London: Little, Brown, 2002).
3. T.H. Marshall, *Citizenship and Social Class and other Essays* (Cambridge: Cambridge University Press, 1950).
4. G.C. Allen, *The British Disease* (London: IEA, 1979).
5. Richard English and Michael Kenny (eds), *Rethinking British Decline* (London: Macmillan, 1999).
6. Alan Sked, *Britain's Decline: Problems and Perspectives* (Oxford: Blackwell, 1987).
7. David Coates and John Hillard, *The Economic Decline of Modern Britain: The Debate between Left and Right* (Brighton: Wheatsheaf, 1986).
8. Samuel Beer, *Britain Against Itself: The Political Contradictions of Collectivism* (London: Faber, 1982).
9. Hugh Thomas, *The Slave Trade: The Story of the Atlantic Slave Trade, 1440–1870* (New York: Simon & Schuster, 1997); Robin Blackburn, *The Making of New World Slavery: From the Baroque to the Modern 1492–1800* (London: Verso, 1997).
10. Paul Kennedy, *The Rise and Fall of British Naval Mastery* (London: Fontana, 1991).
11. Alan Macfarlane, *The Origins of English Individualism: The Family, Property and Social Transition* (Oxford: Blackwell, 1978).
12. Susan Kingsley Kent, *Gender and Power in Britain 1640–1990* (London: Routledge, 1999).
13. Eric Hobsbawm, *Industry and Empire* (London: Weidenfeld & Nicolson, 1968); Harold Perkin, *The Origins of Modern English Society 1780–1880* (London: Routledge, 1969).
14. Lionel Robbins, *The Theory of Economic Policy in English Classical Economy* (London: Macmillan, 1978).
15. Raymond Williams, *Culture and Society* (London: Hogarth, 1987).
16. Elie Halevy, *The Growth of Philosophical Radicalism* (London: Benn, 1928).
17. Adam Smith, *An Inquiry into the Nature and Causes of the Wealth of Nations* (London: Methuen, 1950).
18. Karl Polanyi, *The Great Transformation: The Political and Economic Origins of our Time* (Boston: Beacon Press, 1957).
19. Joseph Schumpeter, *Capitalism, Socialism and Democracy* (London: Allen and Unwin, 1949).

20. Robbins, *The Theory of Economic Policy in English Classical Political Economy*.
21. Bishop Carleton Hunt, *The Development of the Business Corporation in England 1800–1867* (Cambridge, MA: Harvard University Press, 1936).
22. Gregory Jackson, 'Comparative Corporate Governance', in J. Parkinson, A. Gamble and G. Kelly (eds), *The Political Economy of the Company* (London: Hart, 2000).
23. Hobsbawm, *Industry and Empire*.
24. Friedrich List, *The National System of Political Economy* (New York: Kelley, 1966).
25. Karl Marx and Friedrich Engels, *The Communist Manifesto* (London: Verso, 1998); Richard Cobden, *The Political Writings of Richard Cobden* (London: W. Ridgway, 1867).
26. Susan Strange, *Sterling and British Policy* (London: Oxford University Press, 1971).
27. A.J.P. Taylor, *English History 1914–1945* (Oxford: Clarendon, 1965).
28. Philip Corrigan and Derek Sayer, *The Great Arch* (Oxford: Blackwell, 1985).
29. Linda Colley, *Britons: Forging the Nation 1707–1837* (New Haven, CA: Yale University Press, 1992).
30. Raphael Samuel, 'The Workshop of the World', *History Workshop*, 3 (1977), pp. 6–72.
31. Alfred Chandler, *The Visible Hand: The Managerial Revolution in American Business* (Cambridge, Mass: Harvard University Press, 1977).
32. Sidney Pollard, *Britain's Prime and Britain's Decline: The British Economy 1870–1914* (London: Edward Arnold, 1989).
33. Bernard Elbaum and William Lazonick (eds), *The Decline of the British Economy* (Oxford: Clarendon, 1986).
34. Elbaum and Lazonick, *The Decline of the British Economy*.
35. Edward Lorenz, *Economic Decline in Britain: The Shipbuilding Industry 1890–1970* (Oxford: Clarendon, 1991).
36. Martin Wiener, *English Culture and the Decline of the Industrial Spirit 1850–1980* (London: Penguin, 1985), Correlli Barnett, *The Audit of War: The Illusion and Reality of Britain as a Great Nation* (London: Macmillan, 1986).
37. P.J. Cain and A.G. Hopkins, *British Imperialism: Innovation and Expansion 1688–1914* (London: Longman, 1993); P.J. Cain and A.G. Hopkins, *British Imperialism: Crisis and Deconstruction 1914–1990* (London: Longman, 1993).
38. Wiener, *English Culture and the Decline of the Industrial Spirit*.
39. Cain and Hopkins, *British Imperialism*.
40. Geoffrey Ingham, *Capitalism Divided? The City and Industry in British Social Development* (London: Macmillan, 1984).
41. David Kynaston, *The City of London: Volume 1: A World of its Own, 1815–1890* (London: Chatto & Windus, 1994).
42. Bryan Gould, John Mills and Shaun Stewart, *Monetarism or Prosperity?* (London: Macmillan, 1981).

43. Frank Longstreth, 'The City, Industry and the State', in C. Crouch (ed.), *State and Economy in Contemporary Capitalism* (London: Croom Helm, 1979).

44. Shonfield, *Modern Capitalism: The Changing Balance of Public and Private Power* (London: OUP, 1965).

45. Will Hutton, *The World We're In*.

46. Peter Hall, *Governing the Economy: The Politics of State Intervention in Britain and France* (Cambridge: Polity, 1986).

47. Geoffrey Owen, *From Empire to Europe: The Decline and Revival of British Industry since the Second World War* (London: HarperCollins, 1999).

48. Nick Gardner, *Decade of Discontent: The Changing British Economy since 1973* (Oxford: Blackwell, 1987).

49. Barnett, *Audit of War*; Stuart Holland, *The Socialist Challenge* (London: Quartet Books, 1975).

50. Mark Wickham-Jones, *Economic Strategy and the Labour Party: Politics and Policy-Making 1970–83* (London: Macmillan, 1996).

51. Noel Thompson, *Political Economy and the Labour Party: The Economics of Democratic Socialism 1884–1995* (London: UCL Press, 1996).

52. Barbara Wootton, *Freedom Under Planning* (London: Allen & Unwin, 1945).

53. Richard Cockett, *Thinking the Unthinkable* (London: Fontana, 1994).

54. Martin Jacques and Stuart Hall (eds), *The Politics of Thatcherism* (London: Lawrence & Wishart, 1983).

55. Andrew Denham and Mark Garnett, *Keith Joseph* (Chesham: Acumen, 2001).

56. Kenneth Hoover and Raymond Plant, *Conservative Capitalism in Britain and the United States* (London: Routledge, 1988).

57. David Marquand, *The Unprincipled Society: New Demands and Old Politics* (London: Cape, 1988); Hutton, *The State We're In* (London: Cape, 1995).

58. Martin Rhodes, 'Restructuring the British Welfare State: Between Domestic Constraints and Global Imperatives', in Fritz Scharpf and Vivien Schmidt, *Welfare and Work in the Open Economy: Diverse Responses to Common Challenges* (Oxford: OUP, 2000), pp. 19–68.

59. Robert Reich, *The Work of Nations: Preparing Ourselves for Twenty First Century Capitalism* (New York: Vintage Books, 1992); Anthony Giddens, *The Third Way* (Cambridge: Polity, 1997).

60. E.P. Thompson, *The Making of the English Working Class* (Harmondsworth: Penguin, 1968).

61. E.P. Thompson, 'The Peculiarities of the English', *Socialist Register*, 1965, pp. 311–62.

62. Thompson, *The Making of the English Working Class*.

63. Corrigan and Sayer, *The Great Arch*.

64. Nevil Johnson, 'The Constitution', in Ian Holliday *et al.* (eds), *Fundamentals in British Politics* (London: Macmillan, 1999), pp. 45–70.

65. A.H. Birch, *Representative and Responsible Government: An Essay on the British Constitution* (London: Allen & Unwin, 1964).

66. Corrigan and Sayer, *The Great Arch*.

67. Stuart Hall and Bill Schwarz, 'State and Society, 1880–1930', in M. Langan and B. Schwarz (eds), *Crises in the British State* (London: Hutchinson, 1985).
68. Alan Macfarlane, *The Origins of English Individualism*.
69. Corrigan and Sayer, *The Great Arch*.
70. Vernon Bogdanor, *The Monarchy and the Constitution* (Oxford: OUP, 1995).
71. Walter Bagehot, *The English Constitution* (London: Collins, 1963).
72. Norman Davies, *The Isles* (London: Macmillan, 1999) p. 619.
73. Leo Amery, *Thoughts on the Constitution* (London: OUP, 1964).
74. S.E. Finer (ed.), *Adversary Politics and Electoral Reform* (London: Wigram, 1975); Nevil Johnson, *In Search of the Constitution: Reflections on State and Society in Britain* (Oxford: OUP, 1997); Ferdinand Mount, *The British Constitution Now: Recovery or Decline?* (London: Heinemann, 1992); Anthony Barnett, Charles Ellis, and Paul Hirst (eds), *Debating the Constitution* (Cambridge: Polity, 1993).
75. Ferdinand Mount, *The British Constitution Now: Recovery or Decline?* (London: Heinemann, 1992).
76. Johnson, *In Search of the Constitution*.
77. Lord Hailsham, *Elective Dictatorship* (London: BBC, 1976); David Judge, *The Parliamentary State* (London: Sage, 1993).
78. Finer, *Adversary Politics and Electoral Reform*.
79. Mark Evans, *Charter 88: A Successful Challenge to the British Political Tradition?* (Aldershot: Dartmouth, 1995); *The Constitution of the United Kingdom* (London: IPPR, 1991); Richard Holme and Michael Elliott (eds), *1688–1988: Time for a New Constitution* (London: Macmillan, 1988).
80. Jim Bulpitt, *Territory and Power in the United Kingdom* (Manchester: Manchester University Press, 1983).
81. Jonathan Freedland, *Bring Home The Revolution: The Case for a British Republic* (London: Fourth Estate, 1999).
82. Arend Lijphart, *Patterns of Democracy* (New Haven, CT: Yale University Press, 1999).
83. Henry Pelling, *A Short History of the Labour Party* (London: Macmillan, 1995).
84. W.H. Greenleaf, *The British Political Tradition, Vol. 1: The Rise of Collectivism* (London: Methuen, 1983).
85. T.H. Marshall, *Citizenship and Social Class*; Ivor Jennings, *The British Constitution* (Cambridge: CUP, 1961).
86. John Strachey, *Contemporary Capitalism* (London: Gollancz, 1956).
87. Stephen Fielding, *Labour: Decline and Renewal* (Manchester: Baseline Books, 1995).
88. Michael Barratt Brown, *From Labourism to Socialism: the political economy of Labour in the 1970s* (Nottingham: Spokesman Books, 1972); Anthony Crosland, *The Future of Socialism* (London: Cape, 1956).
89. David Howell, *British Social Democracy: A Study in Development and Decay* (London: Croom Helm, 1976).

90. Keith Middlemas, *Politics in Industrial Society: the experience of the British system since 1911* (London: Andre Deutsch, 1979).

91. Ian Gough, *The Political Economy of the Welfare State* (London: Macmillan, 1979).

92. Susan Kingsley Kent, *Gender and Power in Britain 1640–1990* (London: Routledge, 1999).

93. Ruth Levitas (ed.), *The Ideology of the New Right* (Cambridge: Polity, 1986).

94. Shirley Robin Letwin, *The Anatomy of Thatcherism* (London: Fontana, 1992).

95. Kent, *Gender and Power in Britain*.

96. Conservative Party, *General Election Manifesto 1979*.

97. Letwin, *The Anatomy of Thatcherism*.

98. Paul Pierson, *Dismantling the Welfare State? Reagan, Thatcher and the Politics of Retrenchment* (Cambridge: Cambridge University Press, 1994)

99. Christopher Pierson, *Beyond the Welfare State: The New Political Economy of Welfare* (Cambridge: Polity, 1991).

100. Hutton, *The World We're In*.

101. David Seawright, *An Important Matter of Principle: The Decline of the Scottish Conservative and Unionist Party* (Aldershot: Ashgate, 1999).

Chapter 8

1. Benjamin Disraeli, Speech at the Mansion House, London, 10 November 1879.

2. Antony Seldon and Stuart Ball (eds), *Conservative Century: The Conservative Party Since 1900* (Oxford: Oxford University Press, 1994).

3. Helen Margetts and Gareth Smyth (eds), *Turning Japanese? Britain with a Permanent Party of Government* (London: Lawrence & Wishart, 1994).

4. Robert Eccleshall, 'The Doing of Conservatism', *Journal of Political Ideologies*, 5(3) (2000), pp. 275–88.

5. John Gray, *Endgames* (Cambridge: Polity, 1997).

6. David Willetts, *Modern Conservatism* (Harmondsworth: Penguin, 1992).

7. Ian Gilmour, *Dancing With Dogma: Britain under Thatcherism* (London: Simon & Schuster, 1992).

8. R.T. McKenzie and A. Silver, *Angels in Marble: Working Class Conservatives in Urban England* (London: Heinemann, 1968).

9. After the Conservatives split in 1846, the party did not form a stable administration again until 1874, although there were shortlived Conservative administrations in 1857 and 1867.

10. Tom Nairn, 'The Twilight of the British State', in *The Breakup of Britain* (London: Verso, 1981); Perry Anderson, 'The Figures of Descent', in *English Questions* (London: Verso, 1992).

11.   Stuart Hall & Bill Schwarz, 'State and Society, 1880–1930', in M. Langan and B. Schwarz (eds), *Crises in the British State* (London: Hutchinson, 1985).
12.   A.T.Q. Stewart, *The Ulster Crisis* (London: Faber, 1967).
13.   Maurice Cowling, *The Impact of Labour: The Beginnings of Modern British Politics* (Cambridge: CUP, 1971).
14.   Robert Blake, *The Conservative Party from Peel to Thatcher* (London: Methuen, 1985).
15.   Jim Bulpitt, 'The Discipline of the New Democracy: Mrs Thatcher's Domestic Statecraft', *Political Studies*, 34(1) (1985), p. 21.
16.   Benjamin Disraeli, Speech at the Crystal Palace, 1872.
17.   Blake, *The Conservative Party from Peel to Thatcher*.
18.   P.G. Cain and A.G. Hopkins, *British Imperialism: Innovation and Expansion 1688–1914* (London: Longman, 1993).
19.   Bernard Semmel, *Imperialism and Social Reform* (London: Allen & Unwin, 1960).
20.   Leo Amery, *Thoughts on the Constitution* (Oxford: OUP, 1947).
21.   Cowling, *The Impact of Labour*.
22.   Nigel Harris, *Competition and the Corporate Society: British Conservatives, the State and Industry 1945–1964* (London: Methuen, 1972).
23.   Semmell, *Imperialism and Social Reform*.
24.   McKenzie and Silver, *Angels in Marble*.
25.   Blake, *The Conservative Party From Peel to Thatcher*.
26.   David Willetts, *Modern Conservatism* (Harmondsworth: Penguin, 1992).
27.   F.A. Hayek, *The Constitution of Liberty* (London: Routledge, 1960), p. 398.
28.   Keith Joseph, *Stranded on the Middle Ground* (London: Centre for Policy Studies, 1976).
29.   Harold Macmillan, *The Middle Way* (London: Macmillan, 1938); Leo Amery, *My Political Life* (London: Hutchinson, 1953–5).
30.   Robert Behrens, *The Conservative Party from Heath to Thatcher:policies and politics 1974–1979* (Farnborough: Saxon House, 1980).
31.   Patrick Cosgrave, *Margaret Thatcher: A Tory and her Party* (London: Hutchinson, 1978).
32   Ian Gilmour, *Dancing With Dogma: Britain under Thatcherism* (London: Simon & Schuster, 1992).
33.   Dennis Kavanagh and Anthony Seldon (eds), *The Major Effect* (London: Macmillan, 1994).
34.   Gilmour, *Dancing With Dogma*; Shirley Robin Letwin, *The Anatomy of Thatcherism* (London: Fontana, 1992); Andrew Gamble, 'The entrails of Thatcherism', *New Left Review*, 198, (1993), pp. 117–128.
35.   John Gray, *The Undoing of Conservatism* (London: Social Market Foundation, 1994).
36.   Peter Hitchens, *The Abolition of Britain* (London: Quartet, 1999).
37.   Jim Bulpitt, *Territory and Power in the United Kingdom* (Manchester: Manchester University Press, 1983).

38. Stewart, *Ulster Crisis*; Blake, *The Conservative Party from Peel to Thatcher*.
39. Bulpitt, *Territory and Power*.
40. Arthur Midwinter, Michael Keating and James Mitchell, *Politics and Public Policy in Scotland* (London: Macmillan, 1991).
41. An immediate consequence was that the Conservatives, although polling more votes than any other party, had fewer parliamentary seats than Labour. If they had still been able to count on the Ulster Unionists they would have been the single largest party and Heath might have been able to continue at the head of a minority administration.
42. Paul Dixon, *Northern Ireland: The Politics of War and Peace* (London: Palgrave, 2001).
43. Andrew Marr, *The Battle for Scotland* (Harmondsworth: Penguin, 1992).
44. James Cooper, 'The Scottish Problem: English Conservatism and the Union with Scotland', in J. Lovenduski and J. Stanyer (eds), *Contemporary Political Studies 1995* (Political Studies Association, 1995), pp. 1384–93.
45. Semmel, *Imperialism and Social Reform*.
46. Amery, *My Political Life*.
47. Maurice Cowling, *The Impact of Hitler: British Politics and British Policy 1933–1940* (Cambridge: Cambridge University Press, 1975); John Charmley, *Chamberlain and the Lost Peace* (London: Hodder & Stoughton, 1989).
48. Peter Walker, *Staying Power: An Autobiography* (London: Bloomsbury, 1991).
49. Hugo Young, *One of Us* (London: Macmillan, 1992).
50. Kenneth Dyson and Kevin Featherstone, *The Road to Maastricht: Negotiating Economic and Monetary Union* (London: Oxford University Press, 1999).
51. David Baker, Andrew Gamble and Steve Ludlam, 'The Parliamentary Siege of Maastricht 1993: Conservative Divisions and British Ratification', *Parliamentary Affairs*, 47(1) (1994), pp. 37–60.
52. David Baker, Imogen Fountain, Andrew Gamble and Steve Ludlam, 'The Blue Map of Europe: Conservative Parliamentarians and European Integration Survey Results', in D. Denver (ed.), *British Elections and Parties Yearbook 1995* (London: Frank Cass, 1995).
53. Margaret Thatcher, *Statecraft* (London: HarperCollins, 2002).
54. David Baker and David Seawright, *Britain For and Against Europe: British Politics and the Question of European Integration* (Oxford: Oxford University Press, 1998).
55. Margaret Thatcher, *The Path to Power* (London, Harper Collins, 1995), ch. 13; Bernard Connolly, *The Rotten Heart of Europe: The Dirty War for Europe's Money* (London: Faber, 1995).
56. Michael Heseltine, *The Challenge of Europe* (London: Heinemann, 1989).
57. Harris, *Competition and the Corporate Society*.
58. K. Middlemas, *Politics in Industrial Society* (London: Andre Deutsch, 1979).
59. Macmillan, *The Middle Way*.

60. Martin Holmes, *Political Pressure and Economic Policy: British Government 1970–74* (London: Butterfield, 1982).

61. David Marsh, *The New Politics of British Trade Unionism: Union Power and the Thatcher Legacy* (London: Macmillan, 1992).

62. Conservative Party Manifesto, 1987; Geoffrey Maynard, *The Economy under Mrs Thatcher* (Oxford: Blackwell, 1988); Alan Walters, *Britain's Economic Renaissance* (Oxford: Oxford University Press, 1986).

63. Thatcher, *The Path to Power*, ch. 16; Nick Crafts, 'Reversing Relative Economic Decline? The 1980s in Historical Perspective', *Oxford Review of Economic Policy*, 7(3) (1991); Ken Coutts and Wyn Godley, 'The British Economy under Mrs Thatcher', *Political Quarterly*, 60(2) (1989), pp. 137–51; Jonathan Michie (ed.), *The Economic Legacy 1979–1992* (London: Academic Press, 1992); Nigel Healey (ed.), *Britain's Economic Miracle: Myth or Reality?* (London: Routledge, 1993); Francis Green (ed.), *The Restructuring of the UK Economy* (Brighton: Wheatsheaf, 1989).

64. Norman Barry, *The New Right* (London: Croom Helm, 1987).

65. Walker, *Staying Power*.

66. Nick Crafts, *Britain's Relative Economic Performance, 1870–1999* (London: IEA, 2002).

67. Martin Smith and Joanna Spear (eds), *The Changing Labour Party* (London: Routledge, 1992).

68. Edmund Dell, *A Strange Eventful History: Democratic Socialism in Britain* (London: HarperCollins, 2000).

69. Anthony Heath, Roger Jowell and John Curtice, *How Britain Votes* (Oxford: Pergamon, 1985).

70. Nairn, 'The Twilight of the British State'; Mount, *The British Constitution Now*; J.H. Grainger, 'Mrs Thatcher's Last Stand', *Quadrant*, 4 (1980).

71. David Cannadine, *Class in Britain* (London: Penguin, 2000).

72. Peter Hennessy, *The Prime Minister: The Office and its Holders since 1945* (London: Allen Lane, 2000); Richard Rose, *The Prime Minister in a Shrinking World* (Cambridge: Polity, 2001).

73. Rod Rhodes and Dave Marsh (eds), *Implementing Thatcherism* (London: Open University Press, 1992).

74. Norman Tebbit, *Upwardly Mobile* (London: Weidenfeld & Nicolson, 1988).

75. Anthony Sampson, *Anatomy of Britain* (London: Hodder & Stoughton, 1962); Tom Nairn, *The Breakup of Britain* (London: Verso, 1977).

76. Conservative Political Centre, *The New Conservatism* (London: CPC, 1955).

77. Blake, *The Conservative Party from Peel to Thatcher*.

78. HM Treasury, White Paper on Public Expenditure, November 1979.

79. Robert Eccleshall, 'The Doing of Conservatism', *Journal of Political Ideologies*.

80. Kavanagh and Seldon, *The Major Effect*.

Chapter 9

1. Speech by Ernest Bevin in the House of Commons, May 16 1947. Quoted in Rhiannon Vickers, *The Labour Party and the World* (London: Palgrave, 2003).
2. Speech by Tony Blair at the Foreign and Commonwealth Office leadership conference, London, January 7 2003.
3. Stephen Driver and Luke Martell, *New Labour: Politics after Thatcherism* (Cambridge: Polity, 1998).
4. Mark Evans, *Constitution-Making and the Labour Party* (London: Palgrave, 2003).
5. Stephen Driver and Luke Martell, *Blair's Britain* (Cambridge: Polity, 2002); Stephen Fielding, *Labour: Decline and Renewal* (Manchester: Baseline Books, 1999); Colin Hay, *The Political Economy of New Labour: Labouring under False Pretences?* (Manchester: Manchester University Press, 1999); Michael Kenny and Martin Smith, '(Mis)understanding Blair', *The Political Quarterly*, 68(3) (1997), pp. 220–30; John Callaghan, *The Retreat of Social Democracy* (Manchester: Manchester University Press, 2000).
6. *Marxism Today*, Special Issue, Nov–Dec 1998.
7. Tom Nairn, *Pariah: Misfortunes of the British Kingdom* (London: Verso, 2002).
8. Peter Mandelson and Roger Liddle, *The Blair Revolution* (London: Faber, 1996). Roger Liddle had been a special adviser in the Callaghan Government, and had then joined the SDP. After 1997 he became a special adviser again, in the Downing Street Policy Unit. Peter Mandelson, the grandson of Herbert Morrison, had been appointed to run the Shadow Communications Agency by Neil Kinnock, and had become a key Labour Party strategist, and a key confidant of first Neil Kinnock and then Tony Blair. He then became a key minister in the Blair government, but was forced to resign twice.
9. The Labour left never secured the leader of their choice (Tony Benn), failing narrowly to have him elected Deputy Leader in 1981. They never had a majority in the Shadow Cabinet. Their main power base remained the National Executive Committee of the Party. See Eric Shaw, *The Labour Party Since 1945* (Oxford: Blackwell, 1996); Patrick Seyd, *The Rise and Fall of the Labour Left* (London: Macmillan, 1987).
10. Samuel Beer, *Modern British Politics: Parties and Pressure Groups in the Collectivist Age* (London: Faber, 1969).
11. The wording of the old Clause IV was as follows: 'To secure for the workers by hand or by brain the full fruits of their industry and the most equitable distribution thereof that may be possible upon the basis of the common ownership of the means of production, distribution and exchange, and the best obtainable system of popular administration and control of each industry or service.' The new clause is: 'To work for a dynamic economy, serving the public interest, in which the enterprise of the market and the rigour of competition are joined

with the forces of partnership and co-operation . . . with a thriving private sector and high quality public services.'

12. Kenny and Smith, '(Mis)Understanding Blair'.
13. Anthony Crosland, *The Future of Socialism* (London: Cape, 1956); *The Conservative Enemy* (London: Cape, 1962); David Marquand, 'Anthony Crosland', in *The Progressive Dilemma* (London: Heinemann, 1991).
14. Driver and Martell, *Blair's Britain*.
15. Rhiannon Vickers, *Manipulating Hegemony: State Power, Labour and the Marshall Plan in Britain* (London: Palgrave, 2000).
16. Caroline Kennedy-Pipe and Rhiannon Vickers, 'Foreign Policy', in Patrick Dunleavy *et al.*, *Developments in British Politics 7* (London: Palgrave, 2003); Rhiannon Vickers, *The Labour Party and the World* (London: Palgrave, 2003).
17. Richard Heffernan, *New Labour and Thatcherism: Political Change in Britain* (London: Palgrave, 1999).
18. Hugh Massingham, quoted by Peter Clarke, *Liberals and Social Democrats* (Cambridge: Cambridge University Press, 1978), p. 238.
19. David Marquand, *Ramsay Macdonald* (London: Cape, 1977).
20. A.J.P. Taylor, *English History 1914–1945* (Oxford: Clarendon, 1965); Reginald Bassett, *1931: Political Crisis* (London: Macmillan, 1958).
21. Paul Addison, *The Road to 1945: British Politics and the Second World War* (London: Pimlico's, 1994).
22. Kenneth Morgan, *Labour in Power 1945–1951* (Oxford: Clarendon, 1984).
23. Donald Winch, *Economics and Policy* (London: Hodder & Stoughton, 1969); Alex Cairncross, *Years of Recovery: British Economic Policy 1945–51* (London: Methuen, 1985).
24. Stephen Haseler, *The Gaitskellites: Revisionism in the British Labour Party 1951–1964* (London: Macmillan, 1969).
25. Kenneth Morgan, *The People's Peace: British History 1945–1989* (Oxford: Oxford University Press, 1990).
26. Hilary Wainwright, *Labour: A Tale of Two Parties* (London: Hogarth, 1987); Shaw, *The Labour Party Since 1945*.
27. Seyd, *The Rise and Fall of the Labour Left*; Lewis Minkin, *The Labour Party Conference: A Study in the Politics of Intraparty Democracy* (Manchester: Manchester University Press, 1980); David Kogan and Maurice Kogan, *The Battle for the Labour Party* (London: Fontana, 1982).
28. Shaw, *The Labour Party Since 1945*.
29. Wainwright, *Labour: A Tale of Two Parties*.
30. Tony Benn, *Free At Last: Diaries 1990–2001* (London: Hutchinson, 2002).
31. Richard Crossman, 'The Lessons of 1945', in Perry Anderson and Robin Blackburn (eds), *Towards Socialism* (London: Fontana, 1965).
32. Philip Stephens, *Politics and the Pound: The Conservatives' Struggle with Sterling* (London: Macmillan, 1996).
33. Ralph Miliband, *Parliamentary Socialism: A Study in the Politics of Labour* (London: Allen & Unwin, 1961).

34. *Ibid.*
35. Anderson (ed.), *Towards Socialism.*
36. Eric Hobsbawm *et al., The Forward March of Labour Halted?* (London: NLB, 1981).
37. David Coates, *Labour in Power? A Study of the Labour Government 1974–79* (London: Longman, 1980).
38. David Butler and Donald Stokes, *Political Change in Britain: The Evolution of Electoral Choice* (London: Macmillan, 1974).
39. Adam Przeworski, *Capitalism and Social Democracy* (Cambridge: CUP, 1985).
40. Eric Hobsbawm, *Politics for a Rational Left* (London: Verso, 1999).
41. Mancur Olson, *The Rise and Decline of Nations: Economic Growth, Stagflaton and Social Rigidities* (New Haven, CT: Yale University Press, 1982).
42. Michael Hardt and Antonio Negri, *Empire* (Cambridge, MA: Harvard University Press, 2000).
43. T.H. Marshall, *Citizenship and Social Class and Other Essays* (Cambridge: Cambridge University Press, 1950).
44. W.H. Greenleaf, *The British Political Tradition. Volume 1: The Rise of Collectivism* (London: Methuen, 1983).
45. Michael Kenny, *The First New Left: British Intellectuals after Stalin* (London: Lawrence & Wishart, 1995).
46. Alex Callinicos, *An Anti-Capitalist Manifesto* (Cambridge: Polity, 2003).
47. David Marquand, *The Progressive Dilemma: From Lloyd George to Blair* (London: Phoenix, 1999).
48. Vernon Bogdanor (ed.), *Liberal Party Politics* (Oxford: Oxford University Press, 1983).
49. Vernon Bogdanor, *Devolution in the United Kingdom* (Oxford: OUP, 1999).
50. Paul Dixon, *Northern Ireland: The Politics of War and Peace* (London: Palgrave, 2001).
51. A.P. Thornton, *The Imperial Idea and its Enemies* (London: Macmillan, 1985).
52. Denis Healey, *The Time of my Life* (London: Penguin, 1990).
53. R.T. McKenzie and Allan Silver, *Angels in Marble* (London: Heinemann, 1968).
54. The Conservative Defence spokesperson, Iain Duncan Smith, criticized the intervention.
55. Zig Layton-Henry, *The Politics of Race in Britain* (London: Allen & Unwin, 1984).
56. *Ibid.*
57. Bhikhu Parekh, *Rethinking Multiculturalism: Cultural Diversity and Political Theory* (London: Palgrave, 2000).
58. Henry Pelling, *America and the British Left from Bright to Bevan* (London: Adam & Charles Black, 1956).

59. Robert Lekachman, *The Age of Keynes* (New York: McGraw-Hill, 1975).
60. Vickers, *Manipulating Hegemony*.
61. Alan Bullock, *Ernest Bevin* (Oxford: OUP, 1985).
62. Donald Cameron Watt, *Succeeding John Bull: America in Britain's Place 1900–1975* (Cambridge: CUP, 1984).
63. Fritz Scharpf and Vivien Schmidt (eds), *Welfare and Work in the Open Economy: From Vulnerability to Competitiveness* (Oxford: OUP, 2000).
64. Hugo Young, *This Blessed Plot: Britain and Europe from Churchill to Blair* (London: Macmillan, 1998).
65. Healey, *The Time of My Life*.
66. G.D.H. Cole, *The Post-War Condition of Britain* (London: Routledge, 1956).
67. W.H. Greenleaf, *The British Political Tradition: The Ideological Heritage* (London: Methuen, 1983), p. 470.
68. Anthony Crosland, *The Future of Socialism* (London: Cape, 1956).
69. Coates, *Labour in Power?*; Peter Jenkins, *Anatomy of Decline* (London: Indigo, 1995).
70. Evans, *Constitution-Making and the Labour Party*.
71. *Ibid.*
72. IPPR, *Building Better Partnerships* (London: IPPR, 2001); Colin Leys, *Market-Driven Politics: Neo-Liberal Democracy and the Public Interest* (London: Verso, 2001).

Chapter 10

1. Neal Ascherson, *Stone Voices: The Search for Scotland* (London: Granta, 2002), p. vii.
2. Mark Evans, *Constitution-Making and the Labour Party* (London: Palgrave, 2003).
3. Lawrence Freedman (ed.), *Superterrorism: Policy Responses* (Oxford: Blackwell, 2002); Peter Clarke, *A Question of Leadership: From Gladstone to Blair* (London: Penguin, 1999).
4. Robin Cook, Resignation Statement, House of Commons, March 17 2003.
5. L. Talani, 'Who Wins and Who Loses in the City of London from the Establishment of European Monetary Union?', in Colin Crouch (ed.), *After the Euro* (Oxford: OUP, 2000).
6. F.A. Hayek, *The Road to Serfdom* (London: Routledge, 1944).
7. Philip Arestis and Malcolm Sawyer, 'The Economic Analysis Underpinning the "Third Way" ', *New Political Economy*, 6(2) (2001), pp. 255–78.
8. Will Hutton, *The World We're In* (London: Little, Brown, 2002).
9. Neal Lawson and Neil Sherlock (eds), *The Progressive Century: The Future of the Centre-Left in Britain* (London: Palgrave, 2001).

Index